The Tyrannies of Virtue

The Tyrannies of Virtue

The Cultural Criticism of
John P. Sisk

edited and introduced by
Chris Anderson

University of Oklahoma Press : Norman and London

Library of Congress Cataloging-in-Publication Data

Sisk, John P., 1914–
 The tyrannies of virtue : the cultural criticism of John
Sisk / edited by Chris Anderson. — 1st ed.
  p.   cm.
 Includes bibliographical references.
 ISBN 0-8061-2267-6 (alk. paper)
 I. Anderson, Chris, 1955– . II. Title.
PS3569.I74T9   1990
814'.54—dc20   89-48726
                                                        CIP

The paper in this book meets the guidelines for perma-
nence and durability of the Committee on Production
Guidelines for Book Longevity of the Council on Library
Resources, Inc. ∞

For Gwen

Contents

Editor's Note and Acknowledgments

My purpose in assembling this book has been to make John Sisk's essays more accessible and better known. As a cultural critic Sisk is widely published, but because his work appears in the form of short essays scattered over time and throughout dozens of journals, it has not received the kind of attention it deserves. My role as editor of this collection has been to select and arrange the most representative of these essays—simply to bring them together in one place—as a way of demonstrating Sisk's achievement as a writer and thinker.

At Sisk's own request I have kept explanatory notes and documentation to a minimum. His writing is dense with allusions, and the elaborate apparatus that would be necessary to cite all the references would be inconsistent with his intentions as an essayist. As I argue in my introduction, these are "essays" not "articles," addressed to the broadly educated reader. Their purpose is not to document or prove but to stimulate reflection. This is why Sisk never uses footnotes or bibliography himself if he can help it, and why the editors of journals like *The American Scholar, Commentary,* and *The Georgia Review* originally published these pieces without scholarly apparatus. I have followed suit, adding an occasional note only when the allusion needs clarification, and including selected bibliography at the end of the book listing the major secondary works mentioned in the essays. Sisk cites what he thinks he needs to cite anyway, giving author and title in the text itself so that references are usually clear in context.

The original publication place and date are listed under the title of each of the fifteen essays included in the book. I want to thank *Commentary, The American Scholar, Harper's, The Hudson Review, The Southern Review, The Stanford Literature Review, Salmagundi, Philosophy and Literature, The Georgia Review,* and *The Antioch Review* for giving us permission to reprint these essays. A select bibliography of Sisk's other work is also appended.

The essays can be read separately, of course, but I have arranged them in a loosely chronological order to represent Sisk's critique of the sixties and seventies first and then his application of that critique to the eighties. Within that historical framework the scheme is thematic: fanaticism as the central theme, and then within each of the two large parts various angles or variations on that theme. Part I, for example, "Culture and Counterculture," begins with three shorter *Commentary* pieces, then concludes with two longer pieces from *The American Scholar.* The first two essays explore varieties of belief in the sixties and seventies, the second two varieties of skepticism. The last piece in this section, "Honesty as a Policy," is one of the clearest statements in Sisk's work of the idea of "character formation," and so lays out nicely the alternative to the kinds of fanaticism explored in the first four essays. Part II, "Deconstruction and Reconstruction," includes more variations on the theme of fanaticism, seen now from the perspective of the eighties: essays about the back-to-nature movement, technological innovations, television, ideas of heroism, political theory, tabloids and advertising, and deconstruction as a political and literary idea. The two pieces that make up the last section, "Chaos and Character: The Ironies of Belief," both with questions for titles, are meant to serve as summaries or reiterations of the ideas present in each of the previous essays.

In my introduction I provide a guide for first-time readers of Sisk, reviewing his life and education, summarizing the major themes that emerge from his writing, and briefly analyzing his style as an essayist. I want to thank Tom Radko of the University of Oklahoma Press for his support and latitude. I also want to thank Lois Gangle and Anne Wilson of the English Department staff at Oregon State University, who worked long and hard retyping the manuscript; Gini Lockhart, my student worker, who helped put together the selected bibliography; and Roberta Sobotka, my sister-in-law, who did the final proofreading. My colleagues Lex Runciman and Mike Oriard of Oregon State, Glen Love of the University of Oregon, and my father-in-law Franz Schneider of Gonzaga University were generous and shrewd in their readings of drafts of the introduction.

Finally, I want to thank John Sisk himself for his patience and good humor through all this. He has been too busy writing essays all these years to stop and put together a collection. It has been a privilege for me to have the chance to do that myself.

CHRIS ANDERSON

Corvallis, Oregon

Introduction

John P. Sisk As Critic and Essayist

By Chris Anderson

Corruption never ceases to be a problem, but it is a special
kind of problem in an age convinced that corruption is a
special characteristic of institutions, and that if it can be
eliminated from institutions (or eliminated with institutions) virtue will at last have a chance. Hence we make the
institution a scapegoat for our own corruption and the corruption of the institution our justification for those all-or-
nothing crusades in which virtue itself becomes a tyranny
even more constricting than the institution it sets out to
correct or remove. And tyrannous virtue, by staking all on
a passionately limited point of view, fails as charity and
fails as communication theory.

John P. Sisk, *Person and Institution*

When I was a student of John Sisk at Gonzaga University in the early seventies, another undergraduate in his
Shakespeare seminars, I was only vaguely aware that he
had published some sort of essays in some magazines
back East. I had been born and raised in Spokane,
Washington—like Sisk himself, it turned out. I was a
Westerner, I wasn't familiar with recent literary history
or the New York intellectual establishment, and if I
could not have said for sure what an "essay" was, I did
not have a clue about "cultural criticism." All I knew
was this man sitting in front of me, sixty-ish, in a cor-
duroy jacket and turtleneck sweater, his glasses over his
nose, leaning back in a chair with a steno pad on his

lap and making all these odd connections, it seemed to me then—linking Falstaff and the drug culture, comparing Iago to Lenny Bruce—teaching essayistically, I realize now, encouraging us to see past our own "passionately limited points of view" to the dangers of fanaticism in American culture and the need for a little Christian irony all around.

It was not until ten years later, when I was a college English teacher myself, that I came across some of the more than two hundred essays Sisk has turned out for publications like *Commonweal, Commentary, The American Scholar, Atlantic,* and *Harper's* and was able to appreciate his achievement as an essayist and cultural critic. Writing in the tradition of liberal humanism, very much influenced by Lionel Trilling, Philip Rieff, and others we now think of as neoconservatives, Sisk has argued over the years against the tyrannous oversimplifications and fanatical abstractions that threaten American culture and in favor of messiness, of the complex and the concrete. But he has participated in this conservative critique in a special way: a way that is both fundamentally Western and fundamentally Catholic—a way that is essayistic and literary, in keeping with the playfulness and subtlety of the poststructuralist cultural critics he nonetheless defines himself against. What Sisk offers is both an interesting style for cultural criticism—a charitable, ironic style—and a philosophical position based on charity and irony, a philosophy that is able to see beyond the illusions of culture without losing faith.

The Life and Times of John Sisk

Sisk's essays are sophisticated and urbane, written in the voice, it seems at first, of a worldly city-dweller. Yet I would argue that one of the most important influences on Sisk as a cultural critic, perhaps even the key, is that he grew up a cowboy. He was born in Spokane in 1914, the son of a postal clerk, and attended Spokane Catholic schools and eventually Gonzaga University, a small Jesuit college in town; but from the age of ten he spent his summers working as a general ranch hand in the Palouse country south of Spokane. At times he lived the stereotypical cowboy life of Western movies, "escorting cattle in and out of the arid summer pastures of the Snake River canyons," as he recalls in his autobiographical essay "Cowboy," living much the life of his grandfather, who came West to help build railroads after serving under General Sherman in the Civil War. From being a cowboy Sisk learned to distrust what he later called "pastoral oversimplifications," since most of what he and other cowboys did day to day were "domestic chores" like building and repairing fences, cleaning stables, slopping pigs, milking cows, even feeding chickens and working in the vegetable garden, "things that had no place in even the most pedestrian Western movie," which must by the conventions of the genre portray the hero as heroic and the challenges as epic. To grow up in the West for Sisk was to experience firsthand the "discrepancy between the legend and the reality" and so to become skeptical about all "the stereotypical distortions that city and country took to be the truth about one another."

Sisk also grew up Catholic, raised in a tradition of belief, ritual, and commitment to community. If he learned to "go it alone" as a cowboy, in the church he experienced what Rieff calls the therapeutic power of an institution like Catholicism to organize individual motives for the larger purposes of community, as well as the tendency of all institutions to repress dissent in the interest of harmony. If life on the range instilled in Sisk a certain skepticism, life in the Church instilled a capacity for belief, and a belief in the need for belief, in the humanizing effect of a faith. Trained by the Jesuits in high school and college, he developed a facility for close analysis, but for him analysis should always "return us to awe." Intellectual effort should lead "not to a vision that denies the given sensible universe," he says in "The Curious Analyzer," but to a vision that shows this universe "in a new and richer dimension." As Sisk told me in a recent interview, he is somehow Catholic in perspective even though his religious belief is rarely "spelled out specifically." The "structuring values" are always there: "respect for transcendent experience, a familiarity with a certain hierarchical structure of thinking."

Another important influence on Sisk was the broad liberal arts education he received in high school and college. He remembers the essayists as particularly important models of "wide-ranging" intellect and learning. "In Jesuit schools there is always a love affair with Addison and Steele," he said in our interview, perhaps because the intellectual breadth and urbanity of their *Tatler* and *Spectator* essays embodies something of the Jesuit liberal arts ideal. As an English major at the university, Sisk took as many courses in philosophy and history as in literature, so that in contemporary terms the B.A. he received in 1936 was as much a liberal arts degree as a degree in English. When he went on for his master's at Gonzaga, he continued in the same broadly based program, and when he joined the English faculty at Gonzaga he found himself teaching everything from Chaucer to Melville to composition. "There were no specialists then," he remembers, but having to teach almost every course in the English curriculum was an advantage. Sisk uses "specialist" as a term of criticism— in the sense of narrow, obsessive specialization—and generalist as a term of praise. As teachers the Jesuits were never specialists.

The depression and the war also kept Sisk from becoming a specialized scholar in the way that most academics are today. Jobs of any kind were hard to come by in the thirties, and Sisk did not expect to make teaching his profession. After teaching a freshman composition course for a half-dozen women in the music school

at Gonzaga, he thought his academic career was fin-
ished and went back to the ranch for the summer. When
the harvest was over he got an unexpected call from
Gonzaga and in a few days began his career as an English professor, ad hoc, filling in and making do term to
term from 1938 to 1942. During the war he enlisted in
the Air Force as a private and eventually served in British Guiana as a troop commander for the Air Transport
Command. He had assumed that the war would be the
end, at least, of his teaching. But he survived, and in the
fall of 1946 started back in the English Department. He
has been there ever since, teaching a five-course load in
the beginning, teaching every day in the week and also
weekends at a special Saturday school for nuns and at
the seminary outside of town, not to mention advising
students, serving on committees, eventually taking his
turn as department chair—too busy with students and
the day-to-day demands of an English Department in a
small liberal arts college to become a specialist.

For a summer after the war Sisk attended graduate
school at the University of Washington in Seattle with
the idea of going on for a Ph.D. But he soon discovered
that he was "wasting his time." He was thirty-seven
years old, married, and planning a family. He was already a teacher who had taught many of these courses
himself. He was also an established writer of essays, and
he realized that if he stayed in graduate school for the
Ph.D. he was "going to end up doing the kind of writing
I wasn't interested in." The summer in Seattle was "interesting," but it also "turned him off," and he never
went on for the doctorate.

Sisk eventually published several scholarly articles
on Shakespeare ("If you do that, you're authentic," he
said, chuckling), but from the beginning he thought of
himself more as "a writer," as an essayist, than as a
scholar. He wrote poetry and fiction from an early age.
While he was teaching at Gonzaga before the war he
began writing for the *Inland Catholic*, the regional dioc-
esan newspaper, where he had a "free hand" to experi-

ment with the possibilities of nonfiction prose. He recalls it as "a great time." In his monthly column he was able to write about the religious and cultural issues that interested him most and to develop a flexible, compact style. It was his apprenticeship in cultural criticism, leading him after the war to publish similar kinds of essays in *Commonweal*, beginning his career as a nationally known essayist and cultural critic.

Between 1948 and 1978 Sisk was one of *Commonweal*'s most frequent contributors, meanwhile publishing essays in *Thought, Prairie Schooner*, and other major periodicals and continuing to write fiction and poetry. It was at *Commonweal* that he developed his connections between literature, politics, and sociology, and where he perfected the art of condensing these very different perspectives into the short space of a magazine article. In the sixties he started branching out to periodicals like *Atlantic, Harper's, The American Scholar*, and especially *Commentary*, where again he became a frequent contributor. His development in the sixties, like that of Michael Novak and Richard Neuhaus, was from *Commonweal* to *Commentary*, from moderate liberalism to moderate conservatism. But ultimately Sisk made his move away from *Commonweal* not so much because of any real dissatisfaction with the magazine as from a desire to move up from his two-thousand-word limit there to the seven- or eight-thousand-word range. What he wanted was more room to develop the implications of his ideas and images. And he had ambitions as a writer. "If you can't make it in *Atlantic* or *Harper's*, you haven't made it."

In the sixties Sisk did "make it" as an essayist, and also as a fiction writer. In 1961 he won the Carl Foreman Award for *Trial of Strength*, a novel about the academic life. As he puts it, "things just caught on after a while." Now Arnold Professor of Humanities Emeritus—and recently a Senior Fellow of the National Endowment for the Humanities, an Associate at the National Humanities Faculty, and a panelist at the Aspen Institute on

Communications and Society—he continues to write essays from what he calls his "oasis" in the West, and he continues to teach the Shakespeare seminars he has taught for over thirty years. Here in the West, he says, teaching at a little Catholic liberal arts college, it is still possible "to stand off and be detached."

Sisk As Cultural Critic: The Major Themes

The pleasure and the challenge of Sisk's essays is that he rarely comes out and says what he means but proceeds instead through implication, irony, and progressive complication. His demand on us as readers is that we make connections and draw inferences ourselves. In the next section I want to suggest that this style has a thematic force: that it mirrors Sisk's belief in the complexity of ideas and experience. Here I want simply to summarize the major themes implicit in Sisk's work as a guide for first-time readers.

In *The Culture of Criticism and the Criticism of Culture* Giles Gunn uses the literary critic Alfred Kazin and the philosopher Richard Rorty as representative figures for describing the great shift in cultural criticism in this century. On the one hand there is Kazin's definition of cultural criticism as a kind of moral history "that sums up the spirit of the age and asks us to transcend it," a criticism that passionately declares "the true nature of man and what his proper destiny must be." This is the tradition of Emerson and Thoreau, and in this century of Reinhold Niebuhr, Philip Rieff, Christopher Lasch, and Lionel Trilling, the tradition of what Kazin calls "the great American lay philosophy." On the other hand there is the recent poststructuralist cultural criticism represented by Rorty, "the discourse of a culture," as Gunn puts it, "that must not only seek its reason for being within itself but has now lost faith in all those disciplines of the mind by which, traditionally, such reasons could be authoritatively established." This is the tradition of Derrida, De Man and Foucault, of the "her-

meneutics of suspicion," as well as the point of departure for Marxist, feminist, and other ideological critics,
for a criticism skeptical about the "mystifications" of
bourgeois culture and "committed" to a new political
order. The key to Sisk as a cultural critic, however subtle
and indirect he might be at times, is that he always belongs in the first tradition. He is on the other side of the
great divide, and argues for the values on that other
side, although he has been influenced by the poststructuralists and increasingly has tried to engage them on
their own terms. From the perspective of deconstruction his position is realist and pragmatic, a Johnsonian
kicking of stones. From the perspective of the contemporary Marxists and feminists who now claim the title
of cultural critics, his insistence on pluralism and the
values of individual consciousness is apolitical if not unconsciously reinforcing of the existing political order.
From his own perspective, Sisk's effort has been to
join—and then to carry on—the critique of American
culture begun by the liberal humanists of the thirties
and forties.

His earliest important statement came in 1952 in an
essay for *Thought*, "American Pastoral," where he identifies the pastoral urge for simplicity, for a pure life in
"Nature," as a politically dangerous desire to avoid the
hardship and complexity of day-to-day experience. "The
essential thing in pastoral," he says, alluding to the
work of Wolfe, Steinbeck, and Hemingway, "can be seen
as a certain critical vision of simplicity." The pastoral
in this sense is central to American history, where there
has always been the wilderness, the prairie, the frontier
imagined in some opposition to a European civilization
assumed to be artificial and decaying, something to escape from. In this sense, too, the pastoral urge goes
much deeper than simply the desire to "return to nature." For Sisk it is the purest expression of the longing
for utopia in any form, for all varieties of the wish to

transcend the "eternal un-ease of man in a complex world."

What makes these utopian longings dangerous, both culturally and psychologically, is that they delude us into thinking we can avoid the tough challenges at hand. They are unrealistic. "The point is that modern American pastoral is largely an escape from complexity," Sisk concludes, in tones both more explicit and more moralistic than he later allows himself to be:

It is dangerous to turn despairingly away from complexity to seek temporary comfort in naive and sentimental fantasies of simplicity. Complexity must be faced and contended with: simplicity must be earned in it. It is dangerous to pretend wistfully that the complexity is all an illusion, that it can be conquered by turning one's back on it, or that by sheer force of will simplicity can be rammed down its throat.

This is the central theme of all of Sisk's writing, from the forties through the eighties: the dangers and attractions of the pastoral fantasy, in all its "protean" forms— in the orgasmic fantasies of the liberation movements of the sixties, in the narcissism of the seventies, in the negative pastoral of the deconstructionists of the eighties.

It is a theme, of course, that develops in part from his experience as a ranch hand in the Palouse. It also owes much to Trilling, the critic Sisk acknowledges as his most important model. As Trilling argued in 1950 in the preface to *The Liberal Imagination*, the job of the critic is to resist the "simplifying" and "organizational impulses" of American culture by calling our attention back to the "practical, workaday world," to the "welter of ordinary undistinguished things and people," to "the tangible, quirky, unrefined elements of life"—elements which literature, above all, is capable of representing. "American Pastoral" is a restatement of Trilling's thesis from a Western perspective. It links Trilling's argument to the intellectual history of the frontier, which for Sisk, the "cowboy Emeritus," *is* the intellectual history of America.

Sisk's concern for the relationship of the individual and society is also evident in another seminal work, *Person and Institution*, originally a series of four essays published in *The National Catholic Reporter* and then published as a book in 1970 by Fides Press at the University of Notre Dame. Its immediate subject is the institutional dynamics of the post–Vatican II Church, although its implications extend to a larger critique of institutions in general. What Sisk sees as representative in the church of this time, at one extreme, is its desire to establish itself as a "metaphor of harmony." All institutions tend to be like poems, sometimes "cliché-ridden poems," organizing and subordinating their constituent parts into something ideally resembling the aesthetic wholeness of a lyric or ode. But because real life is not ordered like a poem, because it is in fact too messy and eccentric, attempts to set up organizations according to these "sweet dreams of harmony" inevitably lead to tyrannies to which the legitimate claims of the individual are unfairly sacrificed.

At the other extreme, "the sweet dreams of liberation" held by some Church reformers seem to assume that some kind of "deinstitutionalized" life is possible, and that, too, is a pastoral fantasy out of touch with the complexities of living. Without the checks and balances of institutional practice, the desires of individuals intensify until they become their own tyrannies. Successful living depends on an ongoing "dialectical engagement" between persons and institutions. Institutions "structure and conserve achieved or revealed values," while individual intellects "examine these values in the light of fresh information and unexpected perspectives."

Much of Sisk's argument here echoes Rieff in *The Triumph of the Therapeutic*, published in 1966. He explained in a recent letter: "both Rieff and Trilling have been important to me, as reinforcements or refinements of directions I was already taking." In fact, Sisk has always been drawn to the theorizing of sociologists like Rieff, Riesman, Nisbet, and others, and even says, "perhaps in other circumstances I would have become a sociologist or an historian." Earlier in the sixties Sisk contributed along with Lasch and others to a series on "Moral Choices in Contemporary Society" that Rieff edited for the National Endowment for the Humanities. From Rieff, Sisk says in "How Fast Should We Go?," we have learned that "the irreducible function of culture is to prevent the expression and experience of everything and thus to conserve the value of what we do experience."

In his essays of the sixties and early seventies, Sisk comes at these basic issues again and again, working subtly, with irony and dense allusion. The essays of the sixties are the first of Sisk's mature, fully developed work, both stylistically and conceptually. The countercultural movements of Reich, Marcuse, Brown and others, so obviously pastoral and utopian in impulse, seemed to galvanize the ideas and strategies he already had in place. In "On Intoxication," for example, Sisk compares Reich and others to "Falstaff, the Lord of Holiday," intoxicated literally and figuratively—by drugs, sex, utopian ideas—seeking always "fabulous states of mind," some higher, apparently transcendent value. Intoxication is "an expression of the urge to merge." What the counterculture forgets is that hangovers inevitably follow "alcoholic false consciousness," a consciousness not earned through hard work and discipline and thus not sustainable. To confound Holiday with Everyday is to lose the world, the young King tells Falstaff before banishing him from the kingdom.

Often the metaphor is explicitly religious. In "Salvation Unlimited" Sisk describes the various consciousness-raising movements of the sixties and seventies as a kind of Gnosticism or Puritanism attempting to achieve some "Third Realm"—"not a realm among realms but an end of realms, an establishment so intoxicatingly closed that it has cancelled out the possibility of finding a critical viewpoint anywhere outside of it." He makes the same point here with the metaphor of speed. Like Faustus, Americans have always wanted to gain salvation through landscape, culture, hard work, new beginnings. This has been historically true, from the Mayflower Compact and the Great Awakening to Transcendentalism and the Evangelical movement of the nineteenth century. But these movements always involved "slow-paced, self-denying discipline"; they have been "earned." In contemporary culture we want our salvation instantaneously, without earning it, without self-denial, as in EST, Assertiveness Training, Transcendental Meditation, or in the philosophies of Jerry Rubin in "The Yippie Manifesto," Ken Kesey in *The Electric Kool-Aid Acid Test*, even of Charles Manson. What we lack is an understanding of "evil," a recognition of limits and the need for distinction, hierarchy. Without a knowledge of evil there are no limits; without limits there is no sacrifice and no delaying; without delaying there is no real fulfillment.

In the seventies and eighties Sisk sees the same gnostic longings in America's love affair with technological innovation, in its naïve faith in wilderness, in its problem with drugs. In "The Politics of Transfiguration" he calls the "yuppie junior executive" the new "hyperathletic Puritan, to whom bourgeois creature comforts are obstacles to self-transcendence," and argues that the workaholic desire to succeed professionally is just as intoxicating, as speed-inducing, as the Reichian drive for orgasm. His most important argument in the eighties has been a direct response to the deconstructionists, a reiteration of his early argument—see, for example, "The Curious Analyzer" and "The Promise of Dirty Words"— that cynical or nihilistic nay-saying is just as absolutist, just as arbitrary, as the conventions it seeks to expose. As Hawthorne's Young Goodman Brown discovers in his encounter with the Devil, even if there is no truth, we can be absolutely dogmatic about the lack of truth, organizing ourselves with that certainty. "Only the Devil is beyond mere perspective," Sisk concludes in "The Devil and American Epic." The Devil is totalitarian because he posits an utterly simple and all-encompassing view of the world as venal. Shakespeare's Iago, too, is "the prince of deconstructionists," Sisk argues in "The Perils of Poetry," because he "knows in his bones that all faith positions are epistemological nonsense, mere points of view." He knows this with such conviction, ironically, that he is blind to the fact of his own deconstructible point of view. He is absolutist about his anti-absolutism. Thus deconstruction can be seen as "a continuation of the countercultural impulses of the sixties," a fanatic rejection of all structure; and it is subject to the same critique: that life isn't that simple (i.e., things are not that bad), and that however potentially illusory the beliefs of a culture might be, they are necessary for getting by in "the life of the quotidian world."

The implicit model in all these claims, borrowed in part from information theory, is that culture is a kind of "cybernetic" or closed economic system in which various energies must be controlled, vented, balanced. Sisk's assumption is that "information overload" is the central fact of contemporary life. Our challenge is complexity, the availability of perspectives, facts, possibilities. In our efforts to handle this challenge, Sisk is saying, we often resort to any number of dangerous oversimplifications, fanaticisms, reductions, taking one "virtue" among the many positive elements we need to balance to stay alive—like "reason" or "feeling"—and then isolating and exaggerating it, making it rule the complexity. "When information overload threatens the coherence of the structure of attention, the severe rationing of information in the interest of survival appears to be the only alternative to a demoralizing anomie," and this leads, almost inevitably, to various kinds of fanaticism, since fanaticism radically clarifies experience.[1] It leads to various "tyrannies of virtue."

The alternative is to be less virtuous in the sense of

being more charitable and realistic about the messiness, the unaestheticness, of daily existence. The alternative is to recognize that we *need* certain kinds of reductions, need kinds of organization, ceremony, and
illusion in order to handle information overload. This is
finally the implicit or explicit point of Sisk's argument
in all of his essays. We need to make choices, and repressions. But ideally these repressions come in the form not
of fanaticism but of what Sisk in "Honesty As a Policy,"
one of his most important essays from the sixties, calls
"character": "the principled organization of energies
and dispositions aimed at securing the subject's and society's best interests." Character defined in this way—
perhaps best represented by Rosalind in *As You Like
It*—"involves the conviction that the naked energies are
naturally unruly, that attitudes ruled by passion are impermanent, and that the necessities for humane living
are available only through disciplined effort." Unlike fanaticism, character is self-aware, ironic, acknowledging
limits and alternatives, acknowledging history, ambiguity, complexity, not trying to escape from history or
exclude or tyrannize other positions, not sacrificing the
particular for the general. As in Shakespeare's "admirable" women, "character is sufficiently flexible and
adaptable that we can honor our commitments without
ceasing to be our own persons."

Institutions have character in this sense, when they
are successful, managing to maintain "dialogue" rather
than lapsing into "monologue." The literary symbol
also has the structure of character, since it organizes information and experience in usable forms without losing a sense of recalcitrant concreteness, containing lay-
ers of meaning simultaneously. Theologically, Christ
has character, as does the incarnation itself. The incarnation is mystery made available to history and
its messiness. "Christ as past-in-our-present is Christ
as burden, as muddler of messages, as scrambler of
the clarities we have desperately censored our way to.
Christ the boundary crosser comes to us scandalously

mired in history, demanding too much."[2] This final
Christian possibility—always implicit in Sisk's work
but rarely articulated—is connected to the notion of belief as opposed to empiricism on the one hand and fanatical mysticism on the other, both of which claim
absolute knowledge. Belief is the alternative to fanaticism for Sisk because it accepts mystery and therefore
acknowledges gaps.

Sisk As Essayist: Style and Form

None of this is to suggest that Sisk is a didactic critic or
a Jeremiah. The philosophy I have summarized must be
extracted and assembled from his writing because it is
nowhere explicit. As I have suggested, Sisk's method is
rather to unravel the implications of an idea or position,
to break down and reverse the central terms, to complicate, elaborate, expand on the possibilities.

As Sisk described it to me, his habit as he composes is
to sit down with some representative anecdote from literature in view and then "brainstorm," "just jot down
everything that comes to mind." It is a process which
often leads to "messy things." Ideas keep "popping up."
The literary image or "occasion"—often drawn from
Shakespeare—"contains dramatically" what he wants
to do, and he simply goes from there, generating as
many different possibilities or levels as he can and then
structuring his essay to reflect that process of brain-
storming itself.

The result is a "metaphorical structure." Sisk thinks
of his essays as

> constantly bringing together the widely separated, the
> startling revelation, as metaphor does, the A of it and the Z
> of it. When the common expectation is that there is no con-
> nection, you bring things together and show the connec-
> tion. You keep doing that, jumping from one discipline to
> another, one time to another, one culture to another. The
> aim is to keep showing connection.

When the essayist succeeds in making these startling comparisons, bringing together the "far-fetched," he generates intellectual "excitement." The essay is an "entertainment" in its best form, "the entertainment coming from the excitement of bringing together elements that are thought of as widely separated."

To take one example, in "The Politics of Transfiguration," a recent essay published in *The Stanford Literature Review*, Sisk begins with the image of T.S. Eliot standing in the checkout line at the supermarket "snoopreading the tabloids." "Where might the poet have found better evidence of the human appetite for the fabulous as an escape from the unbearably boring, frightening, or anomic in the human condition than in *The Enquirer, The Examiner, The Star, The Globe,* or *The Weekly World News?*" The strategy is to juxtapose the famous line from Eliot's "Burnt Norton" that "human kind / Cannot bear very much reality" with tabloid headlines like "Woman gives birth to 69 babies in 30 years" or "Two-headed boy found in jungle," and that leads, in turn, to a series of parallel connections: Wordsworth's complaint in the Preface to the *Lyrical Ballads* about "the degrading thirst after outrageous stimulation"; Whitman's worries about the "nuisance and revolt" of a corrupted popular taste; Thoreau's conviction that he has "never read any memorable news in a newspaper"—and all these compared at intervals to the latest tabloid features about soap-opera queen Joan Collins and pop-rock star Michael Jackson.

The repetition of the metaphorical possibilities, the continued making of connections, Sisk compares to a jazz "riff." "I've fallen in love with riffs," he says, which he defines as "a sequence of parallel statements that has a cumulative effect," somewhat like the refrain in a ballad. First the unexpected metaphor, then the riff-like "incremental repetition" of the theme of the metaphor with further examples—this is the characteristic strategy for Sisk, with the effect not of diatribe or moralizing but of serious playfulness. Eliot leads to tabloids leads to Wordsworth leads to Whitman leads to Thoreau leads to rock stars Boy George and Madonna. Sisk's tone is ironic, often satirical, but "without malevolence," he hopes. He wants to "bring off a light piece that nevertheless cuts deep," and preferably without coming out and stating his own thesis. The goal is the making of riffs in the hope of demonstrating the levels of the issue, which is itself a way of demonstrating the theme that behind the apparent givens of our cultural life is an infinite regression of intellectual tensions.

Later in "The Politics of Transfiguration" Sisk takes these metaphors and riffs further. His developing thesis seems to be that human beings instinctively desire a transfiguration of their ordinary lives and that there is some danger in that desire. The connections then go like this: the erotic adventures of Zeus and Apollo—brought to mind because Sisk has recently vacationed in Greece—are not unlike the adventures of movie stars in the tabloids; Zeus's hyperbolic and transfigured world would have been congenial to the Shiite terrorists who at about this time hijacked TWA flight 847, since the Shiites, in their fanatic devotion to a higher cause, also wish to transfigure the ordinary world; the Shiites are in this sense not unlike the stereotypical yuppie overachiever of the eighties who strives to transfigure the mundane through self-denial and discipline. That is, tabloids and terrorism both share an unhappiness with the way things are, longing for some more fabulous reality, and on this extended line of thinking we can also chart not only the pleasure-seeking gods of Olympus but also the death-denying executives of corporate America:

The terrorists will continue to menace us (and preoccupy the fascinated media) because of their refusal to live in an untransfigured and anomic reality. Something in all of us responds to a willingness to put all in hazard in the service of a self-transcending cause, whether we see it in the Bassanio of Shakespeare's *The Merchant of Venice*, in Hassan's Assassins, about whom medieval Europe had such

mixed feelings, or in the yuppie junior executive who neither smokes nor drinks and daily runs five miles before
breakfast.

The structure of the riff is present even on the sentence
level in Sisk's dense subordinating of examples and allusions, which is in part why his essays often become
diffuse and hard to follow. As Sisk sets up and reverses
terms, repeating himself at a higher level of abstraction,
teasing out implications, it is easy to get lost, even
though in the end—and this is especially evident when
you read a number of his essays in succession—each essay resolves itself into the central theme of pastoral, its
temptations and impossibility. Part of the intellectual
excitement of reading over a series of the essays is seeing how many different approaches Sisk can take to the
same theme and how much he can complicate and delay, encase it, in any given passage.

In the collapsing and expanding of perspectives, the
inversions, the "intertextuality," as well as in his delight
in mixing high and popular culture, Sisk has much in
common with the poststructuralists. For him everything is "text," related to and commenting on itself. "I
was doing that years ago," he says of the poststructuralist habit of reading culture as poem, though his assumptions and ends are very different. Like the deconstructionists, too, Sisk does not rail against the excesses
of other positions, does not preach a moral cause, but
instead follows the implications of any given set of
terms to their logical extreme, and thus to their contradictions, their point of reversal.

But it would be wrong to think of Sisk's style or tone
as finally postmodern, however much he has learned
from postmodernism. The more important tradition for
him is the older tradition of the "essay" as a literary
form—the essay, that is, as opposed to the "article";
the reflective, exploratory, open-ended writing of Mon-
taigne, Johnson, Hazlitt, Emerson, Orwell, White, or

Woolf as opposed to the stolid, syllogistic writing of most contemporary academic prose. In the "article," according to William Gass in "Emerson and the Essay" (in his *Habitation of the Word*), we need to "pretend that everything is clear, that our arguments are unassailable, that there are no soggy patches, no illicit inferences, no illegitimate connections." The essay, on the other hand, embodies "activity," Gass says, "the process, the working, the wondering." It does not pretend that everything is clear and worked out. It "turns round and round upon its topic, exposing this aspect and then that; proposing possibilities, reciting opinions, disposing of prejudice and even of the simple truth itself as too undeveloped, not yet of an interesting age."

While Sisk continues to write fiction today, he discovered early on as a student reading the classic essayists and writing essays in reply that the form of the literary essay could be as expressive as other kinds of "creative" writing, and as satisfying as writing poetry. As a young teacher and intellectual he found in the essay form a freer rein to express his growing moral convictions. What he had admired in Addison and Steele he found in Huxley and Woolf; all became his early models of the power of the essayist to meld thought and experience, idea and image.

Sisk has been frequently approached by publishers about developing one of his essays into a book, but "I've never been tempted." His commitment is to the formal and technical power of the short essay, much as John Cheever's main commitment was to the form of the short story rather than to the novel. "The idea of the essays," as Sisk saw it, "was to take a subject that might very well become a book and compress it into seven thousand or so words and then get on to the next essay-adventure. The alternative would have been to stop doing what I liked to do most." What compels Sisk about the literary dimension of the essay is its capacity for compression—and thus intellectual excitement—as well as the freedom it gives him to move from piece to piece, approaching his subjects from a wide variety of perspectives.

But Sisk's affinities for the essay form run deeper than his literary instincts. In its embodiment of the mind thinking, in its capacity to "turn round and round upon its topic," in its freedom from narrow, systematic demonstration, the essay corresponds to Sisk's belief that the world is a complex place and that problems cannot be solved by reason or passion alone. The complexity of the form reflects the complexity of ideas and experience, their messiness. In the connections it allows Sisk to make, in the digressions it gives him permission to follow, the essay mirrors the interconnectedness of things as he understands them, rejecting obsessive specialization. For him the article would be a tyrannical form, forcing him to censor nuance and contradiction in the interests of harmonizing the argument. The essay is the ideal form for working against the pastoral, because it affects neither the aesthetic unity of a poem or novel nor the syllogistic closedness of argument and proof. It has a unity, but it is rather the unity and wholeness of the mind in the act of thinking, the mind struggling through problems that do not admit resolution. The essay can include bulky fact and contradictory positions and lyrical moments all at once. It is a form that openly reflects belief because it does not insist on argument, on the effort to prove.

In the end, the essay is the ideal form for embodying the "irony" of "character" as Sisk defines both those words. As he says in *Person and Institution*, "we know in part and we theorize in part, and if there is not a protective element of irony in our theorizing we are imprisoned in our theories as securely as we ever were in our institutions." A protective element of irony is everywhere present in the essays that follow. However consistent he is in analyzing the fanaticisms of the sixties, seventies, and eighties, Sisk is never fanatic himself. He never seems to take himself or anyone else too literally.

Yet the following essays should also make clear that for Sisk irony is connected in profound ways to "charity," a much tamed and misunderstood Christian virtue. If Sisk is Western in his skepticism, he is also Catholic in his values. Somehow these two dimensions of his personality are deeply related, as he articulates in *Person and Institution*:

> Charity in action, as Saint Paul defines it, is ironic; it is the Christian's intellectual and spiritual toughness in the face of the cross-purposes, internal contradictions, multiple perspectives and unanticipated consequences that result as much from the time-bound mysteriousness of man's environment as from his perversity and short-sightedness. (*Person and Institution*)

Both irony and charity are able to accept human limitation and see beyond it. Both are comic. Both are playful. Both carry on in the absence of utopia. "Without charity," Sisk says, "men make themselves mad attempting to drive life into a corner where it can be caught in one grand terminal formula that in effect stops time." What is charitable about Sisk's criticism is that he does not decry, prophesy, try to drive anyone into a corner. He wants to include us all in the forever unresolvable but essentially livable business of getting by, and he wants to celebrate that business, see it as both a test and a joy. It is what I remember most about sitting in his classrooms: his inclusiveness, his readiness to absorb all of our positions into his own, his openness to the papers we wrote for him, his effort to make connections that encompassed high and low culture, the past and the present.

Which is to say, finally, that what Sisk is most skeptical about is skepticism. In his view a truly charitable and ironic position cannot absolutely exclude the possibility of the absolute, both because transcendence is something that human beings actually experience at times and because to exclude transcendence—however it is defined—is to set up a tyrannous and contradictory harmony. This is why the essays gathered here are unique and important. They do not make the standard assumption of contemporary thought, that because belief has been (rightly) rendered problematic, it is no longer recoverable in any form. They try to rebel against such either/or tyrannizing. In light of poststructuralism, trying to take it all into account, they argue instead for at least the possibility of faith—faith, as Sisk puts it, always "reinforced by irony," which is, of course, what faith always is.

Part One

Culture and Counterculture Fanaticism in the Sixties and Seventies

Chapter 1
On Intoxication

Perhaps the best way to approach the subject of intoxication is to note that the word "whiskey" in its Gaelic derivation (*uisgebeatha*) meant exactly what whiskey ads have always implied: "water of life." It is not hard to find support in literature for the widespread conviction that this is the proper etymology for alcoholic beverages of all kinds. In fact, if one were to compile a toper's anthology of great alcoholic moments in literature, it would be no great problem to find prestigious entries. Such a collection might begin rather modestly with Saint Paul's prescription of a little wine for Timothy's stomach and end grandly with the Holy Bottle's oracular "Drink" at the end of Rabelais's *Pantagruel* and Bacbuc's explication thereof: "by wine we become divine . . . for 'tis in its power to fill the soul with all truth, learning, and philosophy." Somewhere in between room would have to be found for Falstaff's great speech in *Henry IV*, Part II, in which addiction to sack is called "the first humane principle." Since the anthology would have to be put together with one eye cocked on the abstemious opposition, I suggest as a disarming epigraph Iago's response in *Othello* to Casio's identification of wine with the devil: "Come, come; good wine is a good

"On Intoxication" first appeared in *Commentary* (February 1972): 56–61. Reprinted with permission.

familiar creature if it is well used; exclaim no more against it."

Such a publishing enterprise would of course have to be highly selective and not too respectful of context. The water of life flows abundantly in literature but the writer-class as a whole seems to be aware that the humane conviviality of Hogarth's Beer Street is more than offset by the degeneracy of his Gin Lane. Gin-saturated Krook's death by spontaneous combustion in Dickens's *Bleak House* is at least as likely to stick in the memory as Falstaff's apostrophe to sack. Indeed, writers tend if anything to be hard on heavy drinkers, possibly out of a need to punish themselves for overindulgence.

The plain fact is that in literature as in life people are most of the time driven to drink: they drink not so much out of a lust for life, as might appear to be the case with Falstaff and Pantagruel, but in order to make life more endurable. As Nietzsche says, we are "delicate children of life" and badly need the illusions of science, art, philosophy, and religion. But when the illusions fail—that is, when they appear to us as mere illusions— there is always intoxication to assuage the pain. Thus John K. Galbraith remembers Albert Speer's 1945 observation about the high Nazis who had to live with the prospect of the imminent collapse of the Third Reich. "In the last six months," said Speer, "one had always to deal with drunken men." Even Falstaff, Shakespeare scholar Tucker Brooke once argued, is given too much credit for *joie de vivre*: he is really driven to sack-drinking and hell-raising because, like Iago, he is a bored materialist.

People who are driven to drink may experience fabulous states of mind, but it is hard for them in sober retrospect to take these states seriously, since the fictions of intoxication so routinely fail to stand up to the critical eye of a hangover. Besides, there is some reason to believe that people who are driven to drink are less likely than others to enjoy the false consciousness of intoxication: being negative drunkards, they approach alcohol in the wrong frame of mind, perhaps suffering in advance the inevitable agonies of hangover, and so defeat themselves. The inhabitants of Gin Lane appear to have been driven to drink and Hogarth properly represents them as existing in hell. Dickens makes it hard for the reader to believe that Krook had discovered in gin a paradise he could not bear to leave.

No doubt the best way to enjoy the paradise of the alcoholic false consciousness is to arrive in it innocently unaware that its underside is hangover. This truth is memorably dramatized in the story of Aloadine's Paradise as medieval and Renaissance Europeans learned it from such reporters as William of Tyre, Marco Polo, and Samuel Purchas. Aloadine (Purchas's version of the name; Polo's is Alaodin) is better known as the Old Man of the Mountain, the common designation for leaders of the Assassins, or hashish-eaters, a sect founded in Persia by Hassan Sabbah late in the eleventh century. As Purchas tells the story, Aloadine enlists his intrepid young followers by causing "a certain drink to bee given to ten or twelve of them, which cast them in a deep sleep" so that they can be carried into the palace and woken. There they are sensually entertained by "goodly Damosels" that "the Fooles thought themselves in Paradise indeed." After four or five days of these pleasures they are again given the "certaine drink," carried out of the palace, and revived. Persuaded by Aloadine that they had truly been given a foretaste of Paradise and promised a permanent sojourn there if they give themselves completely to his will, they gladly become part of his ruthless army, the ferocity of which is in effect the expression of an intoxication that will endure until, presumably, the rude awakening of death.

So far as English literature is concerned, it is hard to find a better comic treatment of the alcoholic false consciousness than in Shakespeare's *The Tempest*. Here Caliban, the reluctant and half-savage servant to Pros-

pero, is discovered by the castaways Trinculo and Ste-
phano, the latter of whom has floated ashore on a butt
of sack. He gives some of the wine to Caliban, who, convinced that "the liquor is not earthly," worships its
bearer as if he were a god and proposes an insurrection
to liberate the island from the tyranny of Prospero. The
island itself with its ambience of music, magic, and
strangely exhilarating air is established as a psychedelic place. In this heady environment Caliban, with his
tipsy sense of elevation about his previous condition of
half-articulate servitude, is a comic repetition of Prospero, whose genuinely expanded consciousness and ability to control his environment are the consequences of
disciplined study.

It is to be noted that Caliban's vision of instant liberation (he envisions an erotic utopia in which he will pos-
sess Prospero's daughter Miranda and "people the island
with Calibans") is more the expression of a metaphoric
than literal intoxication. He is closer to Aloadine's Assassins than to Dickens's Krook. Having gotten high for
the first time in his life, he stays high all afternoon. Sack
ought to have quickly stupefied him or driven him ber-
serk, as it did those rum-frenzied Indians Benjamin
Franklin in his *Autobiography* refers to as forming "a
scene the most resembling our ideas of hell that could
well be imagined." At the very least Caliban ought to
have behaved like Cassio in *Othello*, who is off and roar-
ing after little more than one "craftily qualified" cup
of wine.

But this is frequently enough the way it is in literature: literal intoxication becomes metaphoric intoxication because the writer needs the release of intoxication
but not the messiness, incoherence, and stupefaction
that go with it. A realistically drunk Caliban would be
as useless to Shakespeare as a realistically drunk Falstaff. Thus literature, by so often detaching alcoholic euphoria from the unlovely or inconvenient side-effects,
has a certain tendency to idealize intoxication, and in

effect to reinforce the popular tendency to think of a depressant as though it were a stimulant.

One might speculate about the effects of this confusion on the story of Aloadine's reliance upon drugs to recruit and maintain morale. According to Italian scholar Leonardo Olschki (see his *Marco Polo's Asia*), the best contemporary Muslim historians, who would have had every reason to use such discrediting information against the Assassins, make no reference to it at all. Certainly there are problems with the popular accounts upon which Polo and Purchas relied. One is asked to believe that the concentrated ferocity of the Assassins over a long period of time is explainable in terms of an initiatory drug- or drink-induced deception reinforced later by a more or less frequent use of hashish. Perhaps the historians sensed a familiar trap here: that combination of naïveté and skepticism about the resources of the human spirit that so frequently results in truth-distorting fictions. One thinks immediately of the recent attempt to trace two thousand years of Christianity to a mushroom cult.

In any event, the historical fact about the Assassins is that they were a heretical and fanatical Muslim sect committed unconditionally to the will of a leader whom, says Olschki, they believed to be "the mythical and mystical Inman, the descendant of A'li and thus the sole possessor of the true knowledge of God." What they were intoxicated with, then, was that strongest of drinks, true belief. Olschki's conviction, and he marshals considerable scholarly support for it, is that the Assassins presented to medieval Europe a compelling image of utter self-transcendence through unconditional obedience to an unquestioned source of power or authority, and so became a factor not only in courtly love but in the development of religious, theological, and political totalitarianism. Thus, whether we begin with Norman Cohn and the liberation heresies in medieval Europe[3] or with Professor Olschki and the intellectual libertinism of the Assassins in the Persian highlands, we wind up with that ultimate intoxication that produces Dachau and Auschwitz.

Professor Olschki emphasizes the extent to which the disciplined terrorism of the Assassins was dedicated to a "noble" end: the creation of a universal unity of faith through the triumph of a dogmatic supreme authority. As a rule of thought and action, he says, their doctrine "implied the destruction of all intellectual freedom and of traditional Mohammedan individualism which for centuries had made possible the development and co-existence of numerous sects and the unhindered growth of simple devotion, as well as of philosophy and every other branch of knowledge."

Here we can see clearly enough that quality of intoxication, whether literal or metaphoric, that makes it the compelling human experience that it is. In its short-term efficiency as a way of handling an information overload it is hard to match. Intoxication is an expression of the urge to merge: positively, to experience Freud's oceanic sense; negatively, to obliterate the painful welter of information that threatens whatever integration one has managed to achieve. In Nietzschean terms, deriving from *The Birth of Tragedy*, this is a triumph of the Dionysian rapture ("whose closest analogy is furnished by physical intoxication") over the Apollonian principle of individuation so that the veil of Maya is torn "before the vision of mystical oneness." But since Apollo, the god of light, reigns "over the fair illusion of our inner world of fantasy" and is a god of illusion whatever his wisdom and beauty, it would seem to follow that to get beyond him is to get beyond information (which implies a lag, a disjunction between source and receptor) to a point or "ground" where one is the information. To sense oneself as synonymous with the information is the crowning achievement of intoxication. This is doubtless why all formulations that attempt to inscribe experience, at least temporarily, within a magic circle into which no other experience, perspective, or frame of reference can intrude are so

routinely understood in terms of the metaphor of intoxication. Here too is the justification for the use of the
metaphor of intoxication (infuriating to true believers)
in order to designate the states of mind that result from
the psychedelic drugs.

Nietzsche, says Norman O. Brown in his 1960 Phi
Beta Kappa address, "is the measure of the holy madness, of Dionysius, the mad truth." But if Brown is talking about the Nietzsche of *The Birth of Tragedy* something is missing, most specifically, Nietzsche's stress
on "that Apollonian illusion which saves us from the direct identification with Dionysiac music and allows us
to discharge our musical excitement on an interposed
Apollonian medium." This is a more complicated Nietzsche than Brown needs, at least for his 1960 address.
He wants a prophetic Nietzsche who points to a position
beyond which there is no position. That is, his address
is about the necessity and possibility of getting beyond
point of view, which is the objective of intoxication. For
Nietzsche this is like trying to get beyond interpretation
to fact, and if you are going this way Nietzsche is likely
to be discouraging company. Better to choose a more
forthright Dionysian—someone like Antonin Artaud, for
instance, to whom it was revealed in Mexico, long before Brown's address, that "madness, utopia, the unreal,
and the absurd will constitute reality."[4]

Brown's only reference to Shelley is his agreement
with the Shelleyan dogma that "poets are the unacknowledged legislators of mankind," but Shelley is
hard to beat as a celebrator of the urge to merge, to
achieve an ecstatic and erotic unity beyond the mortal agonies of definition, complexity, and contradiction. The man who wrote "Epipsychidion" with its intense glorification of a symbiotic relationship in which
the lovers, "confused in "passion's golden purity," will
realize

> One hope within two wills, one will beneath
> Two overshadowing minds, one life, one death,

> One Heaven, one Hell, one immortality,
> And one annihilation,

seems to have suffered as much from the need to get beyond point of view and to be the information as any writer in our culture. *Mutatis mutandis*, he would have made a superb court poet for Aloadine, whose young men might well have found his verses more enthralling than hashish.

Shelley wrote pure poetry in the sense that Robert Penn Warren has defined that term in his essay "Pure and Impure Poetry." Shelley is also a Platonist, after his romantic fashion. Brown too has no difficulty getting Plato on his side, especially the Plato who comes to him through the Renaissance Neo-Platonists: a Plato drunk on Dionysian wine, singing in dithyrambs, speaking enigmas and mysteries that "are intrinsically esoteric, and as such an offense to democracy." With Nietzsche it is another matter. The Socrates he finds in Plato is "the mystagogue of science," the celebrator of the victory of the particular over the general, the man who in collaboration with Euripides subverted Aeschylean art. In *The Birth of Tragedy* Plato's Socrates (for whom a later Nietzsche will substitute Christianity) performs much the same function that Clifford Chatterley does in *Lady Chatterley's Lover*, or that the Corporate State does in Charles Reich's *The Greening of America*. Clearly, Plato is not only the text with respect to which, as Alfred North Whitehead has observed, the rest of European philosophy is a series of footnotes, but the blank check which a bewildering variety of cashiers have filled out in terms of their own shortages. Even the Assassins, according to Professor Olschki, were able to find in *The Laws* a Plato they could use as a sanction for their regimen of blind obedience.

So far as the history of intoxication is concerned, one of the most suggestive interpretations of Plato can be found in Eric Havelock's *Preface to Plato*. Professor

Havelock does not mention Nietzsche, Shelley, or Norman O. Brown, but in effect he counters all three. To him the Socrates of *The Republic* is the means Plato uses in an effort to free the Greek mind from the imprisoning tradition of oral epic so that science and philosophy can happen. The world of oral epic is enclosed within a magic circle; at work in it, as in states of intoxication, is the protective impulse to close off all avenues of escape so that a *particular* world is apprehended as *the* world. To fight the good fight against poetry, then, says Havelock, is to be "a Greek Saint Paul warring against the powers of darkness." The fight is not against poetry apprehended as a vision among visions but against poetry apprehended as a vision that attempts in totalitarian fashion to resist all competing visions. Havelock's Plato champions sobriety and point of view, though not the perspectivism of Nietzsche in which point of view is itself a prison from which there is no escape. Such a Plato gives little comfort to those convinced that poets ought to be paid more attention to as unacknowledged legislators of the world.

Havelock's Plato would be of little use to Brown, either in the Phi Beta Kappa lecture or in subsequent works. Brown is of the brotherhood of Aloadine, not because he is willing to use violence to achieve his ends, but because he aspires to be the information, to establish a closed universe in which all language is metaphor and point of view is impossible, the sanction for which is an infallible revelation available only to an elite. This is to say that they both belong to that much larger brotherhood of inebriates, the Gnostics.

Gnosticism, says Eric Voegelin in *The New Science of Politics*, is the nature of modernity. Although he acknowledges the existence of earlier pagan, Jewish, and Islamic forms, the Gnosticism that interests him both as a compelling model and a continuing political force begins in twelfth-century Europe with Joachim of Flora, whose trinitarian eschatology "created the aggregate of symbols which govern the self-interpretation of modern political society to this day." In this eschatology history is conceived as a sequence of three ages "characterized as intelligible increases of spiritual fulfillment," the last of which, the Third Realm that is the age of the Holy Spirit, is terminal and millenarian. It assumes a paracletic leader, who may at the same time be the prophet of the new age possessing a special and infallible gnosis, and a brotherhood of autonomous persons. The impulse toward the Third Realm is totalistic and totalitarian: it aims, as did Aloadine's heresy, at a state of political, philosophic, and spiritual closure. The Third Realm, whether seen in the religious Gnosticism of Puritanism or in the secular Gnosticism of positivism, Marxism, and twentieth-century totalitarianism, is conceived of not as a realm among realms but as an end of realms, an establishment so intoxicatingly closed that it has cancelled out the possibility of finding a critical viewpoint anywhere outside it. Taking Voegelin's route, then, we arrive once more at Dachau and Albert Speer's inebriates with their attempt to counteract the hangover from a metaphoric intoxication with a literal one. For this is what Voegelin prepares you to expect in Western civilization: a succession of intoxication hangover experiences as one glorious gnostic dream after another is found to be a pipedream.

Voegelin's Plato, especially in *The Republic*, takes his stand against the "untruth of human existence as it prevailed in the Athenian sophistic society," whereas Havelock's Plato counts the Sophists "as his allies in the educational battle he is waging against the poets." However, both Platos oppose a false theological consciousness. Havelock's Plato is against the kind of closure that results from the poetic "spell of the concrete" in which time is a stream that cannot be managed as an abstraction, as it must be if critical thinking is to take place. The consequence is a kind of paratactic nowness that anticipates the nowness of the electronic global village. For Havelock the trouble with the world of oral epic (to put it in contemporary terms) is that once it closes warmly around you it becomes difficult if not impossible to distinguish rock poets from philosophers, with the implication that there is little hope that the philosophy of rock poetry will not steadily deteriorate. For Voegelin the quite analogous trouble is that legislators (*pace* Shelley and Brown) are too often poets: that is, they too often strive to construct a state that is "poetic" in its closed self-sufficiency, its unity, and its utter invulnerability to exterior critical positions. Even Nietzsche, the grand perspectivist in whose view there are only fictions, is driven finally, according to Conor Cruise O'Brien, to make an absolute of the poem of the state.[5] Perhaps this means that if we take Shelley at his word and consider *Prometheus Unbound* as a piece of unacknowledged legislation we can expect to find in it something like that gnostic celebration of a realm beyond realms that characterizes the political poems of Marx and Hitler.

Voegelin's book is now twenty years old. Some idea of the continuity between it and his present thinking can be gotten from his essay "Postscript: On Paradise and Revolution" in *The Southern Review*, Winter 1970–71. The immediate subject here is the effect of closure in Henry James's *The Turn of the Screw*, but the ultimate subject is the deformation of reality that results from "the fateful shift in Western society from existence in openness towards the cosmos to existence in the mode of closure against, and denial of, its reality." The study of this deformation entails an examination of closure in Milton and Blake, in the revolutionary consciousness as defined by Hegel, and in the ancient but continually compelling myth of the androgyne, in which tension- and conflict-causing opposites are brought into a symbiotic unity.

Voegelin, especially because of his interest in Henry James, can have the effect of emphasizing the place of a book like Quentin Anderson's recent *The Imperial Self* in the mainstream of Western political, philosophic, and religious thought. Anderson's subject is that form of American intoxication in which a glorified personal consciousness, particularly as seen in Emerson, Whitman, and James, is encouraged in its aspiration to close in on itself. For this consciousness organized society is the enemy against which it attempts to set up a counter-world in which it can expand autonomously. "All three imaginations," says Anderson, "are so commanding, tend so much to incorporation, that we may speak of them as performing a function for their possessors analogous to that of religion in other men. In all three the compelling character of history, generational order, places and things leaches out, tends to disappear." In effect he is very close to placing the Imperial Self in Voegelin's gnostic tradition, in which a dream world attempts to obliterate generational order and the compelling character of history. It should be noted too that Anderson is sensitive to the gnostic element in Brown: "he too reduces the stubborn opposition of Freud's world and accomplishes the subjection of imperial power, acquisitiveness, and heterosexuality to the individual consciousness."

But even with the advantage of prominent reviews in important journals, Anderson's often difficult book will exert little sobering influence against the intoxication of American Gnosticism. For every person who reads *The Imperial Self* a hundred will read Charles Reich's *The Greening of America*. In the apocalypse according to Reich there are all the classic signs of a gnostic enterprise, perhaps most conspicuously the Joachite sequence of three ages culminating in Consciousness III, in which the Holy Spirit (the "new consciousness" of which from the beginning Bob Dylan has been the true prophet) is triumphant in a realm beyond realms analogous to the Marxian State beyond states or to the Nazi Reich beyond reichs. The unitary revelation is codified in Reich's book, but its most effective existence is in the consciousness of a "brotherhood of autonomous persons" (Voegelin's terms work well here) who receive "the charismatic gifts that are necessary for the good life ... without the administration of sacraments"— or in contemporary terms, without the mediation of traditional institutions. The person who is informed with the Reichean gnosis, no matter how young and inexperienced he may be, possesses, says Reich, "an extraordinary 'new knowledge'"; he may not have all the facts about complicated issues but he still "'knows' the truth that seems hidden from others"; he is capable of ignoring established categories, for he sees "effortlessly," "with new eyes," the phoniness and dishonesty in politics that an older person would not see without years of reeducation.

Indeed, with Reich's Third Realm we are "dealing with some dimension utterly outside of the way most people in America have become accustomed to the world." Crucial to the new dimension are rock music, which "has achieved a height of knowledge, understanding, insight and truth concerning the world, and people's feelings, that is incredibly greater than what other media have been able to express," and drugs (the connection with Aloadine's hashish eaters?) which "add a whole new dimension to creativity and experience." All of this assumes both the sacred uniqueness of the person and "an extended family in the spirit of the Woodstock Festival." In fact, in Reich's context, Woodstock, like Aloadine's fabled Garden, is both experience and foretaste of Paradise; if it is not true—and Altamont, particularly as viewed by the editorial staff of the *Rolling Stone*, suggests that there may have been at least a minor devil loose in it all along—then his faith is in vain.

The gnostic revolution, says Voegelin, "has for its purpose a change in the nature of man and the establishment of a transfigured society." The expectation is chiliastic, not evolutionary; it may use evolutionary terms but it strains toward the Grand Finale, the Closure of a change beyond changes, a state impervious to criticism

because there are no positions left outside upon which
to establish a critical point of view. The new consciousness of Reich's Third Realm has a certain dialectic relation to that of the preceding two realms, but effectively the dialectic stops with it. Toward the end of his
book Reich does suggest that Consciousness III "will always be growing and changing" and that we should
look forward to Consciousness IV, V, and VI, "or if we
say that change is inherent in the definition of III then
new degrees of Consciousness III." But the tradition in
which he is writing is simply "wiser" and more powerful than this attempt to modify it. The possibility of
such a numerical progression therefore comes through
as an afterthought that has left little if any impression
on the reading public—for the obvious reason that the
main thrust of the book establishes the gnostic finality
of his Third Realm. The new consciousness is propheti-
cally celebrated rather than artistically rendered; there
is no excess in it, no flaw in its unity and virtue, no
worm in the apple; it can only repeat itself, assuming
that it will find in change itself a constant. It is the consciousness of an Outsider "genuinely free from the lures
and temptations of the Corporate State"—but an Outsider who, like Aloadine's heretics, aims to consume all
sides and so make the position of Outsider forever after
impossible.

   In all of this there is nothing strange for Americans,
whose very beginnings are tainted with gnostic intoxication. Columbus, like so many of his contemporaries,
had been influenced by Joachim of Flora. "Everywhere
in his writings," Charles L. Sanford tells us in *The Quest
for Paradise*, "one finds a compulsive conviction that the
prophecy about proclamation of the gospel to the ends
of the earth must be fulfilled before the approaching end
of the world." In his *Book of the Prophecies*, says Sanford, Columbus wrote that the Second Coming "was to
be preceded by the opening up of the New World, the
conversion of the heathen, and the destruction of Anti-

christ or Satan." Prophecies that do not sound as if they were secular versions of this grand expectation simply do not sound authentic to us; both our need of them and their availability might suggest that we are not simply hard drinkers but alcoholics.

Voegelin is certainly right when, in his *Southern Review* essay, he observes that the "pressure of the Edens surrounding us is enormous." Gnostic Third Realms compete for our attention from all directions, promising final unities in supermarket variety: the schizophrenia-generating family abolished; tyrannous genital heterosexuality replaced by androgynous equality, if not by nondivisive polymorphous perversity; sectarian politics consumed by ecstasy; individual and national distinctions merged in the global village; fragmenting specialism corrected by harmonizing comprehensiveness; work ended by play, nurture by nature, and time by now. It is hardly startling to find Annie Gottlieb winding up a *New York Times Book Review* essay on fem-lib literature by quoting approvingly the conviction of a sister writer that we are moving "beyond all known standards . . . to a species with a new name, that would not dare define itself as man." She is simply aspiring to the kind of gnostic closure (a species beyond species) that on a more prestigious level characterizes the visions of Reich, Brown, John Cage, Marcuse, and Buckminster Fuller.

Even B. F. Skinner, who in *Beyond Freedom and Dignity* is so often able to expose the tradition of autonomous individuality where it is most vulnerable, aims at a condition as utterly invulnerable to any critical point of view as that of Aloadine's Garden. His Great Good Place is as airtight as a well-made poem. Perhaps the book that presents it should be thought of as Skinner's *Prometheus Unbound*: as a passionate expression of the urge to merge, not through the agency of irresistible love but of environmental manipulation. In fact, Havelock's Plato might see that Skinner no less than Brown or Reich wants to confine us within a poetic circle in which we will be all the information there is and it will be us.

In time of course Aloadine's young men ceased to be intoxicated true believers and became simply hired assassins. Falstaff, the Lord of Holiday, was ultimately banished by a young king who had learned that to confound Holiday with Everyday was simply to lose the world. Caliban gave up his dream of being "king o' the isle," and confessed that he had been "a thrice-double ass" in mistaking a drunkard for a god. Abbie Hoffman, who seems to have reacted from Woodstock much as Nietzsche reacted from Bayreuth, is reported to have said of the culture in which he so lately flourished that its long hair is affected, its hip culture fraudulent, its music bad, and its dope lousy. As for Reich's young men, many of them had begun to experience the agonies of deintoxication even before *Greening* appeared, while for many others Reich is simply their Thomas Malory who fantasizes about a Golden Age of derring-do which, since it was mainly a fiction to begin with, can never really pass away.

But no matter; other distillers with other brews are selling in the alleys, if not already moving onto the streets. To be an American is to suffer from Woodstock-in-the-head, which is no doubt a paraphrase from something in Tocqueville. Even our century-long effort to sober up was a metaphorically intoxicating effort, so that temperance crusaders like Dioclesian Lewis, Carrie Nation, and Dr. Howard Hyde Russell were in effect acting out Emily Dickinson's great line: "I taste a liquor never brewed." The trouble with Americans is that having begun with the taste of such a rare brew they have ever since had a hard time defining themselves apart from the polarities of intoxication and hangover. In their morning-after moments—such as now, following the binge of Vietnam—the frightening thought that they might drink themselves to death often occurs to them, but they just as often decided not to go on the wagon but to change brands—now, for instance, Jean-François Revel for Charles Reich.

Revel with his position that "liberation must be complete, or it will not exist at all," his insistence that to survive we must have a utopian program and that the necessary revolution will take place in the United States, is bound to give more comfort to Noam Chomsky than B. F. Skinner, but his *Without Marx or Jesus* aspires, no less than Skinner's book, to imprison us within a gnostic Garden of Delights. Even if he is, as Mary McCarthy has suggested, less interested in flattering the United States than in shaking up an assortment of adversaries, he is nevertheless offering Americans an intoxicant for which they have demonstrated that they have little tolerance: one more vision of Manifest Destiny.

As for manifest destinies, not even Aloadine's Assassins were surer that they had one than our spiritual ancestors, the English Puritans, and it was against their threat, as Voegelin points out, that Thomas Hobbes erected his symbol of the Leviathan. This is the all-devouring political and social order which victorious Gnostics establish when they discover that they "can neither transfigure the nature of man nor establish a terrestrial paradise." The Leviathan, acting as if intoxication were its model, strives to create a new consciousness that can imagine nothing beyond the order that makes it possible. As an omnipotent state, Voegelin concludes, the Leviathan must ruthlessly eliminate "all sources of resistance and, first of all, the troublesome Gnostics themselves." Here then is the prospect one must contemplate: the possibility that contemporary prophets of a new consciousness who have managed to convince themselves and their true believers that they are in the vanguard of a Manifest Destiny may only be directing traffic into Hobbes's pocket.

Chapter 2
Salvation Unlimited

America, we know, is not simply a place in which one endures his fair share of the common burden of humanity while he works his way as best he can from the cradle to the grave. It is a church in which he hopes to find, not simply seek, salvation. Now more than ever it is quick salvation, almost as if we sensed (having taken the grim forecasts of the Club of Rome to heart)[6] that the time allotted for the fulfillment of the American promise is running out. Like that great spiritual forefather of ours, the legendary Dr. Faustus, what we want is more, and we want it with the least possible delay. Dale Carnegie courses and Toastmaster Clubs as means to self-realization and success through power over others may have worked well enough in their time, but their promise of a transformation of personality could be realized only through the disciplined effort over a period of weeks, even months. Such slow-paced improvement programs belong back in the middle ages of modernity, along with the homestudy courses offered by the La Salle Extension University.

Now we need and get, possibly because we need them, things like Erhard Seminars Training (EST), which promises to change one's life radically for the better in two successive weekend sessions; Assertiveness Train-

"Salvation Unlimited" first appeared in *Commentary* (April 1976): 52–56. Reprinted with permission.

ing (AT), which promises to overcome no less quickly that "inappropriate meekness" that stifles one's hidden potential; and the Maharishi Maresh Yogi's Transcendental Meditation (TM), which one can get the hang of in three one-and-one-half-hour sessions. Even prophets of doom have had to accelerate in order to compete for attention. Not long ago, for instance, Moses David, the guru of the fundamentalist Children of God sect, foresaw the possibility that the expected appearance of a comet "seven times as bright as the full moon" would precede by forty days "the end of things as they now are." Part of Charles Manson's power over his "family" seems to have derived from his ability to convince it that Helter-Skelter, like prosperity in the 1930s, was just around the corner.

All of this sounds immoderate to whatever slow-paced traditionalists are left among us. To be an American, however, is to be immoderate, to want Paradise Now, to put it in terms the Australian John Passmore used as he attempted to clarify the immoderation of the 1960s.[7] Of course, it is also American to counteract the immoderation with slow-paced, self-denying discipline. Hence Benjamin Franklin, Andrew Carnegie, and Horatio Alger, to say nothing of Theodore Roosevelt (if you want to make it big, you had better first submit yourself to the schooling of the strenuous life). Nevertheless, immoderation is the cardinal virtue that compels most of us, even when circumstances conspire to make us live moderately. We strain against the brakes of circumstance as if the senior Arthur Schlesinger was right when he argued that when the framers of the Constitution wrote of the pursuit of happiness they meant, and were understood to mean, not "something a people were entitled simply to strive for but . . . something that was theirs by natural right."

Certainly, not all students of the Constitution agree with Schlesinger, but vast numbers of Americans have always acted as if they do, which may have something to do with the note of urgent utopianism in the whole

American enterprise. No doubt there has always been among us a minority of Fabian gradualists content to sense themselves moving, however slowly, on an upward path. There is something in most of us, nevertheless, that sympathizes with those "strangers" on the *Mayflower* who made "discontented and mutinous speeches" and vowed, writes Governor William Bradford, that "when they came ashore they would use their own liberty, for none had power to command them."

God knows with what reluctance those forefathers of the dream of instant liberation and its materialistic counterpart, the dream of instant success, agreed to go along with the Mayflower Compact and promised "all due submission and obedience" to the offers and ordinances of the Plymouth Plantation. Their bodies may have lain a-moldering in the grave, but their souls have gone marching on to agitate the Great Awakening of the eighteenth century and the Evangelical movement of the nineteenth, both of which anticipated EST, AT, and TM in their tendency to measure the authenticity of personal transformation by the speed at which it happened. Their restless spirits were at work like yeast among the Transcendentalists (Emerson, Thoreau, and Whitman, like the *Mayflower* strangers, discovered how free they could be when there were none to command them) as well as among the many communal enterprises that enlivened the nineteenth century: Shakers, Ephratans, Zoarites, Hutterites, Rappites, Fruitlanders, Brook Farmers, Moravians, Fourierian Phalanxes, Nashobans, and the Owenites of New Harmony. All of these people had been inspired by men and women who, like Albert Brisbane, had been overwhelmed with "the depth and extent of the evil that preys upon Society," had seen "the necessity of a fundamental reform which will attack that evil at its roots and eradicate it," and believed passionately that their objective could be achieved quickly and permanently. Indeed, many of them agreed with John Humphrey Noyes, the founder of the Oneida community, and Ann Lee of the

Shakers that the millennium was Now. Meanwhile, their millennial expectations were being played over in a more mundane key by money-hungry robber barons and land-hungry westward-pushing pioneers.

But if the millennium is Now, as the Ken Kesey of Tom Wolfe's *Electric Kool-Aid Acid Test* and Jerry Rubin of "The Yippie Manifesto" were only yesterday prepared to believe, then what came before Now, having performed its task—or in another version, having labored long enough to prevent Now—could be dispensed with as the newborn chick dispenses with the shell out of which it is liberated. If the millennium is Now, or just around the corner—if we have arrived at last at the point where with one concerted mighty push we might burst into the clear sunlight of the freedom that has been our birthright all along—then it is understandable that Charles Manson should have been named Man of the Year by the Los Angeles *Free Press*, that Bernadine Dohrn should have celebrated the Manson atrocities as "far out!" and as something the Weathermen could really dig. For once the millennium is apprehended as a real possibility, not simply the stuff dreams are made of, all strikes, however extreme or violent, against established states of affairs tend to become equally virtuous. Ann Lee's sex-denying Shakers (who, apart from their doctrinal abstinence, anticipate the modern rock festival) triumph over time just as effectively as Noyes's sexually liberated Oneidans (who with their holy promiscuity anticipate the Manson family).

One might have expected that by 1960 Americans had bought so much snake oil in so many forms that they would automatically be suspicious of any nostrum that promised quick results. Such an expectation would have failed to take into account the accelerated tempo of post–World-War-II reality, in which it became easier than ever to identify salvation with speed. Speed is the least common denominator of EST, TM, AT, Esalen, Scientology, acupuncture, primal therapy, psychic healing, and psycho-cybernetics, to say nothing of light therapy, astral projection, witchery, sorcery, astrology, orgone energy, and Glen Turner's often-sued Dare To Be Great. Zen and Yoga in America immediately shift into overdrive and split into sects the way Protestantism did in the Reformation.

The psychoanalyst Elsa First has observed that "concentration practices of the TM type are considered the most elementary stages of meditation and merely a precondition for further work." This sounds likely enough, but who has time for, or can believe in, a form of salvation that takes time? The faster the pace of life and the greater the number of available options, the more one becomes aware of how little time one has and of the risks involved in serious long-term commitments. To go all out for one person or for a single program of salvation may only be a way of denying oneself the personality-expanding experience of other persons and other programs. Chronologically, the life span of the average American has never been longer; existentially, however, it has never been shorter. Hence that hounding contemporary fear, perhaps best expressed by the quick millionaires of the rock world, that one will through hang-up or rash overcommitment miss something. This fear is a factor in what Peter Marin, writing in the October 1975 *Harper's*, has referred to as "the trend in therapy toward a deification of the isolated self." Indeed, the "new narcissism," as Marin calls it, is itself a survival technique by which one refuses to join anything or anyone but himself lest some part of his human potential be foreclosed.

The ideal therapy for this assertiveness is the Janovian scream session or the encounter weekend. Critics who doubt that such hasty therapies have much permanent effect assume that participants seek a permanent effect. Actually, the very failure of such therapies to deliver on their promises, so that subjects are not denied the experience of newer and still more exciting therapeutic adventures, may be an important part of their appeal. A truly successful encounter might cut one off from EST, TM, or AT, and so leave one impoverished rather than enriched. With so little time who can afford to be cured?

In our kind of hyped-up society, in other words, normalcy can appear to be not only a drag but a trap: a reconciled, even-keeled state of affairs in which nothing of interest happens because all the occasions of interest have been removed. Who would aspire to the ruts of normalcy when that might mean giving up the creative reactions of the neurotic to the malfunctions and malignancies of the system? R. D. Laing[8] and others of his persuasion have opened out to us the superior pleasures of the melodrama of the emotional cripple as heroic and society-defining victim; and one reason why the victim is so hard to normalize is that de-victimization promises to be such a dull story. There is an "openness," a hypersensitivity to experience in the neurotic victim (so runs the romance of neuroticism that neurotics themselves are not reluctant to encourage) that makes it easy to identify *him* as normal, given our kind of world.

On the other hand, given a genuine desire to escape from the emotionally diminished world of victimizing neurosis, it is not hard to see the attraction of lithium carbonate, now being celebrated as a Cinderella drug in Dr. Ronald R. Fieve's *Moodswing*. Few of us would choose "the traditional and costly" way of the analyst's couch when a pill might do just as well and much more quickly. Traditional analysts, with their conservative tendency to favor earned solutions to human problems, may link this "third revolution" in psychiatry with all the false promises of Timothy Leary's LSD revolution, but at the moment the times are marching to a different drummer. The analysts are competing for a clientele that wants not simply quick salvation but the experience of salvation, which implies the freedom and capacity to keep on experiencing salvation in the greatest possible variety of forms. Such a desire, if it results in more sentimentalists and narcissists than the world can tolerate, may in time produce an abundance of fresh business for the analysts, but in the meantime the latter might be well advised to push lithium—taking ironic comfort, perhaps, from the thought that early in his career Freud himself had great hopes for the quick therapy of cocaine.

Relatively speaking, the narcissist lives a fast life. This is because he has joined nothing, least of all another person. It is the self-transcending commitments that slow us down, make us reconsider, delay judgment or satisfaction as we acknowledge the complicating presence of valued others or valued communal structures that we share with others. The proper symbolic expression for narcissism, as well as its most appropriate form of sex, is therefore masturbation, which might be defined as total sexual autonomy. Insofar as the times have defined salvation as quick and frequent orgasms, masturbation is in analogy with lithium, LSD, and the amphetamines. This is probably why our romance with masturbation is beginning to compete with our romance with homosexuality. Two of the most widely read novels in recent years, Philip Roth's *Portnoy's Complaint* and Erica Jong's *Fear of Flying*, have vigorous, if not always joyous, masturbators as central figures. To judge from a preview of it in *Esquire*, Gay Talese's eagerly anticipated masterword on sex in America will include a section in which an adolescent is caught up in an elaborate masturbation with a dream girl. Lonnie Garfield's *For Yourself*, dedicated to female sexual fulfillment through self-stimulation, was not only published on Valentine's Day by Doubleday last year but was chosen by the Book-of-the-Month-Club as an alternate selection. In the same vein, the *New York Review of Books* recently featured an ad for *Masturbation: A Woman's Handbook*, "a book by women for women" featuring "beautiful sex drawings." I can only wonder if it was written by that San Francisco woman who, according to an account in the *Berkeley Barb*, was not so long ago conducting a clinic in which her women clients were taught the ecstasies of vibrator-induced masturbation in one easy five-dollar lesson. All of which may suggest that we have kept in the closet too long (locked up there by the life-inhibiting biases of the Judeo-Christian morality) the most immediate and purest form of sexual fulfillment.

Masturbation as sexual fulfillment, apart from its occasional dependence on machinery, begins and ends in the self, is independent of complicating interpersonal communal and domestic involvements, and is thus simplicity itself. It might therefore be taken as a model for the popular salvational movement, especially since it is oriented to a greater intensity of life for the individual. EST, TM, AT, primal and encounter therapy—even when, like early Christian Gnosticism, they claim to derive from special insights—all appeal because of the simplicity of their practical formulation and the speed with which they promise to get results for the private individual. EST is typical. Its founder, Werner Erhard, like the philosopher-mathematician René Descartes, not only had a spontaneous experience of the truth to begin with, but, also like Descartes, was able to ground his revelation in an electrifying simplicity. As one of his trainers puts it: "What is is and what ain't ain't" because "reality is simple, clear, black and white." Similarly, nothing could be simpler than a therapy that gets you off the psychiatric couch and onto the floor where you can scream your way out of your hangups. And what could be a simpler way to experience community than through participation in encounter or sensitivity groups, in which the sensations of interpersonal relations can be briefly and intensely enjoyed without any of the long-term commitments, perplexities, and encumbrances of normal communal life?

But what, for that matter, could be more clearly in the American cure-all tradition—which, if it was often high comedy in the commune movement, was just as often low comedy in the bitters-and-tonic industry that flourished throughout most of the nineteenth cen-

tury? Products like Burdock Blood Bitters, Hoofland-
er's German Bitters, Hooker's Wigwam Tonic, Hostetter's Stomach Bitters, Hartman's Pe-Ru-Na, and Lydia
Pinkham's Vegetable Compound promised quick results
as a consequence of the simplest of techniques (swal-
lowing something) and in terms no less totalistic than
those enjoyed by TM, EST, and AT. Pe-Ru-Na cured tu-
berculosis, pneumonia, Bright's disease, appendicitis,
and heart trouble. Pinkham's Compound was an all-
purpose feminine reviver. Hostetter's Stomach Bitters
cured dyspepsia, ague, dysentery, colic, and nervous
prostration. Since most of these nostrums were heavily
laced with alcohol (Hostetter's Bitters was nearly ninety
proof, and Pinkham's Compound was twice as powerful as modern fortified wine) they could temper down
moodswing as quickly as lithium does. Being highly
regarded as virtuous substitutes for alcoholic beverages, they brightened the lives of many temperance advocates—not a few of whom, J. C. Furnas reports in *The
Late Demon Rum*, died of alcoholism without being
aware of ever having touched a drop. So they were
ripped off the American Way—as, presumably, were
those wistful utopians of Waldport, Oregon, who were
recently persuaded by two mysterious strangers (retail-
ers of cosmic Pe-Ru-Na) that they might very quickly
depart by spaceship for a higher level of reality.

One might conclude, given our salvational impulse
and the cultural conditions in which this impulse has
been at work, that America has always had a high potential for developing freak-show caricatures of itself,
that this potential is inseparable from its libertarian
impulse, and that it will be realized in proportion as
the culture speeds up, becomes more pluralistic and
therefore more complicated. But what may look like a
perverse effort to complicate life needs also to be seen
as at least partly an effort to simplify life by reducing it
to entertainment—a variety show in which the acts
change so quickly that spectators are left only with the
theme of a dazzling sequence of salvational events, no

one of which is especially significant by itself. What nonbeliever can take Dr. Sun Myung Moon's Unification Church seriously when it is being played over again, and in effect lampooned, by the Maharaji Ji's Divine Light Mission and Dixieland neo-Voodoo? The *National Observer* estimates that there are in the country about five thousand such cults that claim between two and three million adherents. No doubt these figures include many of those currently pursuing quick salvation in the hundreds of communes scattered about the country. No doubt, too, the lot of them are expressive of what Harvard Professor Krister Stendahl has called "a genuine hunger for mystical and religious experience." At the same time, however, they make up a rich national divertissement that counteracts the boredom that is the occupational hazard of an affluent and option-rich society.

Those who wonder why amidst so much salvational effort there is so little national sense of achieved salvation do not understand that in contemporary circumstances diversion is itself a form of salvation, and that nothing is simpler as a way of life than an openness to the possibility of being repeatedly born again. "Simplicity, simplicity, simplicity!" wrote the very complicated author of *Walden*. "I say, let your affairs be as two or three, and not a hundred or a thousand. . . . " But when your affairs are as two or three you are likely to be faced not with an infinity of possible salvations, any one of them available in disposable containers for quick use, but with your basic problems. Thoreau had in mind the undistracted life, the deliberate pace of which is correlative with a scarcity of options. But in America at the end of the twentieth century distractions are a guarantee that life is available in all its abundance. Governor Bradford's strangers seem to have gotten a message somewhat like that while they were still on the high seas and America was only a blank check each of them was eager to fill out in his own terms.

But more than that. The love affair with simplicity in

Western civilization, let alone in America, is a dangerous one. It leads one to believe that virtue and evil are
existentially disjunctive, intended in the order of things
to dwell apart from one another, as they were conceived
to be by the Gnostics. In this view evil is "out there" or
"in the others" or in the institutions that both structure
and contaminate our lives, so that it can be thought of
as isolatable. As a consequence, it is easy to think of the
pursuit of salvation as an uncomplicated and speedy affair, a matter of separating the dross from the gold.

In "Earth's Holocaust" Nathaniel Hawthorne sub-
jected this gnostic impulse to the same irony that he not
too much later directed against the Brook Farm experiment, in which one of his assignments was the community manure pile. In this cautionary fable the impatient
party of salvation determines to dispose of the world's
"accumulation of worn out trumpery" with a world-
wide busking, or bonfire. To this fire zealous reformers
bring everything that has ever in any context been accused of impeding the establishment of unadulterated
virtue: creature comforts, art works, literature, political and religious emblems, munitions, torture devices,
marriage certificates, money, legal documents, and business contracts. A young zealot cries: "Let mankind always do the highest, kindest, noblest thing that, at any
given period, it has attained the perception of; and
surely that thing cannot be wrong nor wrongly timed."
Hawthorne's own conclusion is more complicated: "How
sad a truth, if truth it were, that man's agelong en-
deavor for perfection had served only to render him the
mockery of the evil principle, from the fatal circumstances of an error at the very root of the matter."

America itself in one of its aspects is a grand busking
ceremony in which the corrupting trumperies of the old
world are thrown into the flames with the expectation
that they will be permanently disposed of. Indeed, the
impulse to the salvational busk (or its metaphorical
equivalent, the salvational bloodbath) is apparently an
ineradicable element in the American character. You

can hear it in Jefferson's famous letter to Colonel Smith, in which, referring to Shay's Rebellion, he says: "God forbid we should ever be twenty years without such a rebellion. . . . What signify a few lives lost in a century or two? The tree of liberty must be refreshed from time to time, with the blood of patriots and tyrants. It is its natural manure." Most recently the impulse was expressed in the (often quite literal) buskings and bloodlettings of the revolutionary Left and in the counterculture's efforts to live out the conviction that it is possible to disengage oneself quickly and totally from the trumperies of the "bad" America so that life may be all virtue and freedom.

The spirit of the busk (more than a little troubled, it should be noted) is also a factor in Ed Sander's *The Family*, his account of the Manson affair. What he has to say about Haight-Ashbury's 1967 summer of live-ins, be-ins, and share-ins suggests Marcia Seligson's truebeliever account of EST in *Cosmopolitan* no less than the advertisements for Hostetter's Stomach Bitters: "Potentially, flower-power was one of the most powerful forces of change ever seen in recent history." It was "a notable experiment" and "the politics of free." But evil came in from outside and ruined the great good thing of Ken Kesey's Merry Pranksters and made it evil. The very American thing about Sanders's book—the thing that makes it a better document than Vincent Bugliosi's later and factually superior *Helter Skelter*—is its often touching but always naïve bewilderment as its author discovers evil where it ought not to have been and at work in ways he cannot account for.

Three hundred years ago Cotton Mather, being a Puritan divine and therefore knowing where evil came from, was spared this bewilderment. He records in his spiritual diary:

> I was once emptying the *Cistern of Nature*, and making Water at the Wall. At the same Time, there came a *Dog*, who

did so too, before me. Thought I: "What mean, and vile things are the Children of Men. In this Mortal State! How much do our *natural Necessities* abase us, and place us in some regard, on the same Level with the very Dogs!" My thought proceeded. "Yet will I be a more noble Creature; and at the very time, when my *natural Necessities* debase me into the Condition of the Beast, my *Spirit* shall (I say, at that *very Time*!) rise and soar, and fly up, toward the Employment of the *Angel*."

This of course will no longer do. Mather, it is convenient and necessary for most of us to believe, is part of what the sons of Governor Bradford's strangers burned up in their own efforts to rise and soar. Beast and Angel have been disjoined for us, just as they are in Ed Sanders's book and just as they were for John Noyes's Oneidans. We can believe that either alone will save us; we can even believe that if we pursue the Beast vigorously and honestly enough the results will be somehow angelic. But if we have to believe that Hawthorne's "root of the matter" is the coexistence in us of Beast and Angel, then all our dreams of quick salvation will become pipe dreams and we will be left in that sobering and problem-heavy position, not of holding hands with angelic flower children, but of making water at the wall with Cotton Mather's dog.

Chapter 3

The Curious Analyzer

We remember only too well the macabre irony with which in the graveyard scene Hamlet contemplates Yorick's skull; how for him it mocks the vaunt and leap of life, whether manifested in the court jester, the beautiful woman ("let her paint an inch thick, to this favour she must come"), or the mightiest of rulers. Horatio's observations, being those of a straight man, are unfortunately less memorable. When Hamlet asks him, "Why may not imagination trace the noble dust of Alexander, till 'a finds it stopping a bunghole?," Horatio replies with his quieter irony, " 'Twere to consider too curiously to consider so." He is suggesting that his friend's analysis is over-ingenious, but he might also have suggested that it is rather old-fashioned. As Johann Huizinga helps us to see in his *Waning of the Middle Ages*, Hamlet's curious reduction of life to those grosser physical aspects of death that appear to invalidate it was supported by literary and social conventions over two hundred years old.

No matter. Hamlet never sounds more like our brother than when he is curiously considering: delving beneath the fair outer appearance of reality to discover the "things rank and gross of nature" that are the constituent truth about it. In him we find united the mod-

"The Curious Analyzer" first appeared in *Commentary* (May 1973): 62–68. Reprinted with permission.

ern psychoanalyst and the modern intellectual, both of whom, says Philip Rieff in *The Triumph of the Therapeutic*, "have the analytic method as the very basis and limit of their vocations" and as an integrating factor in a negative community from the vantage point of which all positive communities "appear either fraudulent or stupid." "Our" Hamlet is an instinctive demythologizer and iconoclast, a man suffering from epistemological shock who has become a relentless enemy of awe. But there is a heroic quality in the curious analyzing that follows from the shock. Like Melville's Ahab, he is not afraid to strike through the mask of phenomenal life or dive deep below its bland surface; like Byron's Manfred (or like Nietzsche or Sade, for that matter), he dares to think unthinkable thoughts because they are the only true thoughts; like Freud, he can stare the Medusa in the face. Because he is not taken in by the fictions that pass for reality, he can analyze the fraudulently healthy man to discover the real truth about him, which is the "hidden impostume" that will kill him.

This Hamlet thrives in an atmosphere of exposé and scandal. Like a familiar kind of literary intellectual, he belongs with an elite of inside-dopesters that has special access not only to the rottenness of Denmark but to everything under the sun. He like that literary intellectual is discontented not so much *in* as *with* civilization, the enemy that threatens his autonomy by attempting to co-opt him for comfortable establishment roles. What promises to comfort him by supplying social, aesthetic, philosophic, or religious comfort is automatically suspect, for authentic autonomous experience is uncomfortable. And Hamlet the literary intellectual expresses his alienated disgust with irony (his heroic armor) as he reports on his curious considerations. He can make authentic poetry out of "this brave o'er-hanging firmament" whose majestical roof is "fretted with golden fire" only if it is juxtaposed with the "foul and pestilential congregation of vapors" that give the lie to it. Because he has lost all his mirth (only the deceived can be truly mirthful) his humor tends to be black or sick. Like Lenny Bruce and his epigones, he seems compelled to degrade, demean, belittle, and debunk whatever threatens to keep his world in awe lest he lose his grip on a position of ascetic purity.

Since he is a puritan in a wasteland, our Hamlet suffers from sex nausea. He knows that "the power of beauty will sooner transform honesty from what it is to a bawd than the force of honesty can translate beauty into its own likeness." In his version of the *contemptus mundi* there is no better objective correlative for the disgust with civilization than the sexually irresistible but thoroughly corrupt woman. To see through her harlot's cheek to the Medusa face behind it, but without the buffering of Perseus's mirror-shield, is to display the kind of unflinching courage in the face of the appalling that we are expected to recognize in Celine, Artaud, Burroughs, Beckett, Albee, and Tennessee Williams.

It is a great convenience to us that our Hamlet is so close to madness. We know very well why Claudius believes that "Madness in great ones must not unwatched go." Hamlet's "turbulent and dangerous lunacy" threatens to subject the real lunacy of Claudius's establishment to a destructive analysis. Hamlet, in fact, makes a compelling prince in our romance of insanity, which according to Lionel Trilling ("Authenticity and the Modern Unconscious," *Commentary*, September 1971), is grounded on two assumptions: that "insanity is a direct and appropriate response to the coercive inauthenticity of society" and that "insanity is a negation of limiting conditions in general, a form of personal existence in which power is assured by self-sufficiency." Our Hamlet is mad, or on the dangerous edge of madness, for the same reason that some of our most compelling poets have been: as a means of validating his visionary insights. W. H. Auden has recently expressed a preference for a poetry "firmly rooted in staid common sense." One may assume that in it authentic personhood and commitment are not represented as hopelessly incompatible, and that it is neither obsessively analytical nor obsessively against awe. Our Hamlet would immediately recognize it as inauthentic.

I am using "our" Hamlet here as a means of approaching the curious analyzer in rather negative terms. Insofar as they are the right terms for him, his life is one of unremitting process, an endless discovery of illusion, an endless demythologization and iconoclasm as the seductive fictions play over the face of time. At his most extreme he will be a Prometheus bound by his own wish beyond all hope of unbinding, a hero of discomfort committed only to self-transcendence through suffering. Then the dangers are that he will become vulnerable to counter-analysis by deriving comfort from the myth of himself as a relentless demythologizer, or by failing to see the extent to which he may have been overdetermined by, even made the creature of, the icons he is set on smashing. His dilemma is that heroes are always prisoners of their story-communities and limited by the interdependence of themselves and their antagonists: what is Prometheus without the tyrant Zeus, to say nothing of the vulture that so accommodatingly and indefatigably feeds on his liver? Besides, it is the fate of the hero to inspire emulation and adulation, from which follow (it is the irony of what Trilling has called the adversary culture) the comforts of community and commitment.

Prometheus may want the authenticity of a Continual Refusal but it is likely that some higher need will use him in the interests of a Permanent Revolution. Thus Shelley releases him from his rock so that the Golden Age can begin. One might imagine that in this new and final order the loneliest man would be Prometheus, since he would no longer be permitted the authenticity of counterrevolution. Our Hamlet is in a similar lonely situation. Insofar as he is the prince of rejecters in a negative community, the play itself ought to be a disaster; but by being aesthetically successful, by demonstrating once more the possibility of a meaningful synthesis against near overwhelming odds, it brings comfort and so leaves him stranded. If our Hamlet were entirely successful in his curious considerations, he would destroy our faith in his creator. The Hamlet of most twentieth-century criticism is subordinated to the action or theme of the play, which is an aesthetic community; our Hamlet wants to reverse the order and in effect, by subordinating it to his own needs, to get entirely out of the play.

Fortunately, however, these negative terms are not the only ones available to the curious analyzer. There is a position of faith according to which analysis may be utterly relentless and yet ordered to comfort. To act as if the discovery of illusion were an end in itself—as if it had no story, no beginning, middle, and end—is to act heretically according to this true faith. To the extent that Prometheus is viewed as chained defiantly to the rock, he dramatizes the aspiration to the self-sufficiency of godhead. But according to the true faith, his proper destiny is to serve the needs of a community of the liberated in which perhaps everyone is a god. Actions motivated by the true faith may appear to be analytically sterile, perverse, or subversive with respect to established cultural values, but if seen with respect to their own teleology they are creative, integrative, and salvational. An old-fashioned radical like Trotsky could believe that the struggle against foul language "is an essential condition of mental hygiene, just as the fight against filth and vermin is a condition of physical hygiene." But for Herbert Marcuse (see *An Essay on Liberation*) the obscenities of the new radicals are "the elemental act of giving a new name to men and things" and fall in line "with the great design of the desublimation of culture, which, to the radicals, is a vital aspect of liberation."

To us living at the end of the twentieth century, Marcuse's reference is to a very old liberation dream. It envisages the creative and vital termination of curious

analysis prior to which all fearful depths will have been
plumbed, all frauds will have been discovered, all false
consciousness corrected, all garbage carted away and
burned up. Bertrand Russell puts it this way (Noam
Chomsky is quoting him at the end of his 1971 Russell
Lectures):

> Meanwhile, the world in which we exist has other aims.
> But it will pass away, burned up in the fire of its own hot
> passions; and from its ashes will spring a new and youn-
> ger world, full of fresh hope, with the light of morning in
> its eyes.

This is in the spirit of Shelley at the end of Act III of
Prometheus Unbound:

> The loathsome mask has fallen, the man remains
> Scepterless, free, uncircumscribed, but man
> Equal, unclassed, tribeless, and nationless,
> Exempt from awe, worship, degree, the king
> Over himself; just, gentle, wise. . . .

Or of Marcuse himself at the end of *An Essay on
Liberation*:

> . . . it [the condition of social redistribution and liberation]
> would mean the ascent of the aesthetic Principle as Form
> of the Reality Principle: a culture of receptivity . . . Not re-
> gression to a previous stage of civilization, but return to an
> imaginary *temps perdu* in the real life of mankind. . . .

So through analysis, sustained by a faith in the ultimate
direction of the process and implemented by what Max
Weber calls an ethic of intention, we have arrived at a
position beyond analysis, beyond fiction, beyond interpretation, beyond myth. There are no more hidden im-
postumes for Hamlet's curious considerations, no more
masks for Ahab to strike through, no more vultures to
feed on Prometheus's liver, no more Medusas to stare
down. We have bottomed out on solid ground at last. Or

to put it in the terms of Wilhelm Reich, father of the sexual revolution and most curious of analyzers, we have left the cultural periphery, passed through the horrors of the middle layer, and arrived at the core where the true blue orgonic cosmic energy streams free. The next and inevitable move is the joyful one Shulamith Firestone sketches in *The Dialectic of Sex*: for the first time to create a society "from the bottom up" and "to reestablish the earthly Garden of Eden." In this scheme of things even those who, like Freud, can see no end to discontent, or who, like our Hamlet, continue to defy and resist on their own egotistic terms, can have their uses: they have at least identified the enemy. You can be on the side of the angels without knowing it, as Blake believed that Milton was, though to him this meant that Milton was of the Devil's party.

It is the expectation of bottoming out at last that has sustained science in its curious analyses of the peripheral world of commonsense appearance. In the interest of its own moral, science has had to believe that no matter what Medusas it confronted, or what labyrinths it explored, or what monster forces it encountered at what depths beneath the comfortable fictions of daylight life, in the end all analytic operations would prove to have been on the right track, as if guided by a hidden hand. This is why C. P. Snow was able to maintain that scientists, unlike literary intellectuals, had remained on the whole happy analyzers, little troubled with the sense of themselves as members of an adversary culture. They have had the true faith, as Einstein had it when, unhappy with the implications of statistical probabilities, he observed that "God does not throw dice." Therefore they were in a better position to tolerate paradoxes and discontinuities, to say nothing of the increasingly disturbing political, social, philosophical, and religious consequences of their analyzing.

Despite the well-publicized rift between the two cultures, it is no doubt ultimately impossible to separate the scientist's from the literary intellectual's or social-

ist's dream of bottoming out at last providing one has
the courage to endure the incidental discomforts and
horrors. But long ago now the literary intellectual tried
to establish his faith on a different kind of bottom to be
groped for by different means. However, he remained a
truth-seeker at least as much as a maker. But in the very
nature of things he was much more likely than the scientist or the socialist (who had the advantage of thinking of himself as a scientific analyzer) to be demoralized
by the consequences of his own or anyone else's curious
considerations, by his Yeatsian apprehensions that the
center might not hold and that anarchy might be loosed
on the world.

But if it has become increasingly hard for the literary illusion-detector to keep the faith, he has remained
firmly attached to the dogma that the opposition to
comfort and awe is fundamentally right and that the
intrepid plunge into the depths, even if it means courting sinister powers, is the true way to liberation and
self-transcendence. One sometimes gets the impression
(in Burroughs or in Mailer at his most violent, for instance) that what is at work is a conviction that the
dogma will revive the faith if the dogma is pressed hard
enough. Hence our tendency to judge writers as if they
were old-fashioned heroes: putting more emphasis on
courage than on craft. Indeed, it is hard for us to get rid
of the suspicion that there is the same irreconcilable
conflict between craft and authentic experience that
there is between culture and reality, with the implication that if one expects to bottom out on the ultimately
real he must be prepared to let craft and culture go. In
this view the proper end of poetry is the end of poetry.
There have always been writers to whom this familiar
dogma has been unacceptable, or who, like Mann and
Conrad, have at least been of two minds about it. But
adversary voices are especially interesting now after
a decade during which so much encouragement was
given to the romantic faith in bottoming out and the

heretical faith in self-transcendence through discomfort. Thus A. Alvarez in his study of suicide, *The Savage God*, questions the therapeutic theory of art, whereby the artist relieves himself of his fantasies by expressing them, and suggests that the knowledge from the depths that results from the application of this theory "may change him irredeemably so that he becomes that image." W. H. Auden commenting on this passage in his review of the book, observes: "The moral, surely, is that one should be very cautious in what one chooses to write about." Joyce Carol Oates, in her review of the book, wonders whether the Aristotelian idea of the cathartic function of art might be mistaken and questions "our entire culture, which exhibits so proudly and, indeed, so lavishly, public images of violence, death, and comic horror in such billion dollar industries as the movies." Alvarez himself, speaking of Sylvia Plath's *The Bell Jar* and John Berryman's last poems, has confessed to similar reservations about what he once extolled as virtues in extremist poetry, "in which the artists deliberately push their perceptions to the very edge of the tolerable." The gains, he now believes, are not worth the terrible cost. To judge from the conversations recorded in *Reich Speaks of Freud*, even Reich had come to realize that the return to orgonic nature, to the core, "may be decades, may be centuries away" since if the corrupting armor of culture were removed "there would be chaos. Perfect chaos! Murder everywhere!"

This concern with the disproportion between gains and losses was a familiar one during the 60s as various critics reacted to anti- and countercultural extravagances—for instance, John Passmore, Daniel Bell, Saul Bellow, Seymour Martin Lipset, Robert Nisbet, Alfred Kazin, Lionel Trilling, Samuel McCracken, David Riesman, Nathan Glazer, Hannah Arendt, Conor Cruise O'Brien, James Cameron, and (though many of his most ardent admirers are likely to forget this) the late Paul Goodman. There are important differences of cultural commitment and critical stance among these writers, but it might be said that they have expressed a skepticism about the unqualified goodness of the analytical temper, however analytical they have had to be in their opposition to it, and a common concern with the preservation of culture. This means that they are in contention with a formidable piety: that all that is good or valid or personally authenticating comes from beyond or below culture. From the point of view of this piety Auden's moral that one should be very cautious in choosing his subjects is no less cravenly reactionary than C. S. Lewis's earlier moral: "To know how bad we are, in the mere condition of nature, is an excellent recipe for becoming much worse."

Both morals assume that there may be doors best not opened (it is too likely that behind them are destructive horrors) and depths best not plumbed (it is too likely that they have no bottoms or, worse, that their suspected bottoms are false). Such a position suggests a traditional fear of *hubris*, though it may have a piety of its own to make it more than a fear that one will not survive. But whether we are pious or merely prudent, we are familiar enough with the fear that science may be opening doors best kept closed, plumbing depths best not visited, analyzing arrangements best kept as they are. Thus George Steiner, after surveying "a revolution that concerns us all" in contemporary science, observes that trends in the life sciences cast doubt on our "confident assumption that the needs of man, that the requirements of social justice and personal worth, would prove to be in more or less natural accord with the discoveries of science." It is the shaking of this faith that threatens to leave us standing in Bluebeard's castle, says Steiner. "For the first time, the forward-vaulting intelligence of our species, so intricate and yet so vulnerable a piece of systematic evolution, finds itself in front of doors it might be best to leave unopened."

However, Steiner's reservations about the analytic, door-opening temper of science are rather tentative and probing; he is by no means certain that the roof fretted with golden fire will turn out to be a pestilent congregation of vapors. But criticisms of this temper are likely to be much more categorical if they have an ecological and countercultural basis. For Theodore Roszak, for instance (see *Where the Wasteland Ends*), science with its single vision "has led us not to the promised land but to the technocratic trap we find closing about us." Science attempts to be a school of consciousness that rules out alternate realities; it rolls across the globe "like a mighty juggernaut obliterating every alternative life style"; it is guilty of complicity in the rape of the environment by profiteering industrialists, myopic developers, and a greedily consuming public. Science as Roszak views it, then, has not only put us in Bluebeard's castle but is committed compulsively to opening all the doors.

For Roszak, objective knowing is alienated knowing, and the prime place of objective knowing is the research laboratory. He expresses the revolt against objectivity about which Robert Nisbet wrote perceptively in his essay "Subjective Si! Objective No!" Nisbet was concerned with the agreement among an increasing number of social scientists that their proper business was not to understand society but to destroy it in order to remake it. The result, as he saw it, was an epistemological nihilism in which salvation was to come not from analysis but from action following from one or another position of faith. More than sixty years ago the American historian Carl L. Becker suggested the possibility of such a shift in his essay "Detachment and the Writing of History." The time might come, he wrote, when objective detachment would be felt to be less important than caring greatly what happens—a time in which objective man might not be particularly adapted to survive.

Four years before Becker published his essay, Henry Adams in his *Education* had put the conflict between objective detachment and caring greatly in the form of a dilemma: "The historian must not try to know what is truth, if he values his honesty; for, if he cares for his truths, he is certain to falsify his facts." No one ever had less faith in bottoming out or in self-transcendence through discomfort—or is so close to our Hamlet in his alienation and profound disillusion. Arthur Balfour's 1904 announcement on the part of British science that "the human race without exception had lived and died in a world of illusion until the last years of the century" seems to have settled the matter for him. Bluebeard's castle held no further terrors. Like Flaubert, all Adams could do with his disillusion—but it was no small thing; it was even a comfort—was to make great literature out of it.

Adams's dynamo and Roszak's technocratic trap have a lot in common. "As Nature developed her hidden energies, they tended to become destructive," wrote Adams. "Thought itself became tortured, suffering reluctantly, impatiently, painfully, the coercion of new method." Nevertheless, if you take your stand with Adams, Roszak's position is one of pure illusion. What saves Roszak and many anti-objectivists from Adams's dilemma is the conviction that if one's faith is firm enough those facts necessary to validate it will be forthcoming (after all, one doesn't have to move very far from Adams's position to see that his book is itself a factual way of escaping from the dilemma). At the same time, Roszak shares Steiner's apprehensions about the doors in Bluebeard's castle which curious analyzers may be tempted to open. But Roszak is inclined to avoid the predicament by abandoning the castle for another domain entirely, in which, along with the "most ecologically involved young people in our society," we will learn more about our proper place in nature from sources of primordial wisdom (American Indian lore, Zen, and Tantra) than from Western science.

This hope of salvation through primordial wisdom— whether non-rational, supra-rational, mystic, gnostic, hermetic, demonic, diabolic; whether available through ascetic discipline, chants, fasts, diets, orgies, orgonic energy accumulators, erotic abandon, drugs, rock music, communal living, or a fortunate conjunction of the stars—is itself exacerbated by the analytic temper. One of Roszak's strengths is his knowledge that the aweless life is dehumanizing; another is the fact that he plainly cares very much. And certainly the wisdom that is primordial is not to be put down because it is primordial. But have not recent events demonstrated that he is standing in another kind of castle in which, at the prompting of curious considerations, all too many doors have been opened which had best been kept closed, or at least guarded more closely? To judge from the accounts of Ed Sanders and others, the members of the Charles Manson "family," for instance, were ardent devotees of what they and many others took (and still take) to be primordial wisdom. They had fashioned for themselves an escape from the technocratic trap that in time came to involve plans for a grand Helter-Skelter that would cure the evils of Western civilization by ending it.

Manson himself (like the late rock stars Janis Joplin, Jimi Hendrix, and Jim Morrison) comes on as an intrepid opener of doors—though it might be more accurate to say that he blunders through doorways inadvertently or carelessly left open by others. He seems to have been a proper Reichian orgastic man through whom the orgonic energy streamed unimpeded by character armoring: according to Sanders's evidence, he experienced three to seven orgasms a day over a considerable period of time. He even had a Reichian interest in infant consciousness as the beginning point for a spontaneous life beyond the imprisoning nuclear family and beyond culture. He believed that total paranoia was total awareness. He had true faith in bottoming out at last; indeed, he seems to have known where the bottom was: below that hole in the Hopi desert, to which he and his family, a saving remnant, would have access to eternal safety by means of a golden rope.

Manson of course does not invalidate Roszak. But by pushing the preoccupations of the adversary- and countercultures to extreme positions, Manson (like Sade before him) helps to expose them to the kind of critical analysis they might not otherwise get. He makes it easier to see the fascist potential that is in one segment of the counterculture—and makes one remember uneasily how important primordial wisdom was to Nazism, that other famous attempt to escape from the dilemmas of the analytic temper.

Nazi Man as totally committed man has helped to teach the post-World War II world the dangers of commitment; no doubt he is an important factor among those forces that have produced Rieff's Therapeutic Man who aspires to a mode of existence beyond the limitations of doctrine, integrating point of view, character set, or cultural configuration. He holds out the possibility of surviving with comfort and experiential variety in a world the curious analyzer has made all too uncomfortable. Bluebeard's castle holds no more threats for them than an amusement-park spook house—apart, that is, from the threat of personal extinction—for what is revealed behind the doors can threaten only committed people. Nor would they be likely candidates for Manson's family. Not unless they are posited on false assumptions about the human need for commitment and awe, in which case it might be all too easy to persuade them to enter into the spirit of Helter-Skelter and go down the golden rope.

Speaking of his Therapeutic Man, Rieff observes, "But the mind boggles at a culture made up mainly of virtuosi of the self"—just as, one suspects, Flaubert's mind boggled at the prospect of a culture made up of people modeled on the Frederic Moreau of his *Sentimental Education*. Certainly B. F. Skinner takes no comfort from such a prospect. For him the adversary- and countercultures are the plights visited on us because of our worship of the idols of freedom and dignity. However he may be pictured as a man plagued by his own Hamlet-like moments, even as a poet manqué, his book is a curious analyzer's offer of salvation from the discomforts of curious analysis. Skinner settles the issue of Bluebeard's castle by positing a Skinner Man to whom it would never occur to open doors meant to be kept closed. What he envisions, in fact, is a behaviorist version of what anthropologist Ruth Benedict has called a high-synergy culture, one characterized by a relative lack of friction between purely personal and communal needs. Skinner's strength is his sense of the inseparability of man from culture and his conviction that the dream of a postcultural autonomous person is simply the consequence of one of the more sophisticated games that culture plays with us. But his own utopia by aiming to be an end-state aspires to be a culture beyond culture, beyond ideology, beyond the discovery of illusion (because its own illusion would be impervious to question), beyond myth (by being unaware of its own myth), and in effect bottomed out at last. Nor is Skinner immune from the effects of Manson's mad caricature of a high-synergy culture, for Manson too had employed an effective system of positive reinforcing contingencies (combined, it must be admitted, with a few negative ones) in order to secure a position beyond freedom and dignity. Is Manson trying to tell us, then, that Skinner is simply offering to lower us into another Hopi hole where we will forget the golden rope that let us down?

It is possible, of course, that our fears of the curious analyzer are in part the consequence of considerations themselves too curious, so that we are led to imagine a future in which no significant force opposes him as he continues ever more devastatingly to cut the ground away under our feet. But suppose we had the power to act on such fears. Is it not conceivable that the refusal to open doors would have the effect of opening a trap door beneath us? And what are our poets and novelists to discover if they do not discover illusion, whether in the expectation of bottoming out or as a self-aggrandizing experience, or simply as a consequence of the artist's critical involvement with his time and place? Who can imagine George Steiner, for instance, agreeing not to open any doors that confront *him*?

Skinner suggests one solution: we will stop our curious considerations when our culture finds a way to distract our attention to other matters—just as Hamlet (a Hamlet it may be convenient for us to forget) stopped his curious considerations when the action in which he was involved found a way to distract his attention back to his princely duty. All our curious considerations have a similar dramatic potential to result in the kind of mess in the attempt to correct which we rediscover, for better or worse, the exhilarations of community and commitment. Discomfort, as Steiner observes, is the spur of life—though the consequences of this law in history are as often chilling as cheering. If it gives us those who keep anarchy at bay and make the center hold, it also gives us those passionate activists of the Right and Left, none of them "sicklied o'er" by Hamlet's "pale cast of thought," who demand that their motives be taken at their own evaluation, not reduced analytically to components they cannot manage without losing the fine edge of their fervor. So we are left to wonder whether the corollary to Steiner's law may not be that the dream of bottoming out is the spur of death.

In the meantime, and to speak practically, much that has not been able to survive the curious analyzer has not deserved to survive, and as a consequence much that is disposable has gone into the garbage bin of history. At this point there seems to be little reason to believe that the bin itself has a bottom: good news for garbage collectors but bad news for all who identify their discomfort with garbage. Animals have no garbage problem: so far as we can tell, they live contentedly beyond freedom and dignity and exempt from awe in a world of sensuous synthesis given to them by nature. Unaware of the qualification of information by time, they are beyond illusion and hence available to humans as symbols of a lost paradise in which nature and information were synonyms. But man becomes human at the point where he begins to question the given synthesis. What is crucial then, no doubt, is the context in which he analyzes and the degree of ironic restraint with which he resists the temptation to make analysis his idol.

The ascetic, in whom the analytic temper appeared long before it appeared in Hamlet, had to exercise this restraint lest he fall into heresy by identifying the given sensible universe, God's creation, as intrinsically illusionary and fraudulent, or into the sin of pride by glorying in his superiority to his deluded fellow men. The process of analysis for the ascetic who had the true faith was aimed at bottoming out on the ultimately real, just as it is for the modern analyzer who has the true faith, but the history of asceticism indicates that it has always been a process extremely difficult to control. Huizinga, to whose great book I would like to return, represents it as out of control in the decadent asceticism of the late Middle Ages, marked as the period was by its curious Hamlet-like considerations of the horrors of bodily decomposition in painting, poetry, sculpture, woodcuts, and sermons. In a passage applicable to our own analytic times, he refuses to see this preoccupation as truly pious:

> It would rather seem a kind of spasmodic reaction against an excessive sensuality. In exhibiting the horrors awaiting all human beauty, already lurking below the surface of corporeal charms, these preachers of contempt for the world express, indeed, a very materialistic sentiment, namely, that all beauty and all happiness are worthless because they are bound to end soon. Renunciation founded on disgust does not spring from Christian wisdom.

Nor does it spring from any genuine wisdom we know of, in whatever culture or creed, though disgusted renouncers are frequently enough heralded as wise.

Rather, it is that sentimental imitation of wisdom that in an excessively analytical time is too likely to draw whatever comfort it can from the overload of information about its own corruption. Huizinga sees this as a failure of imagination. The late Middle Ages, he says, "relished these horrors without going one step further, to see how corruption perishes in its turn and flowers grow where they lay." In the view that goes this one step further, analysis results in a more viable synthesis and returns us to awe, with respect not to a vision that denies the given sensible universe but to one that shows it in a new and richer dimension. Then the fact that the dust of Alexander might be stopping a bunghole is worth considering, truly enough, but only in a context that is no longer very interesting.

Chapter 4
The Promise of Dirty Words

When Barbara Lawrence's short essay, "Dirty Words
Can Harm You," appeared last year in *Redbook*, it was
no more likely to endear her to tough-talking feminist
extremists than to their male counterparts for whom
Portnoy's Complaint is in the grand tradition of liberating obscenity. Professor Lawrence argued that much of
our brutally frank and currently voguish sexual vocabulary is "implicitly sadistic or degrading to women: in its
intent to reduce the human organism (especially the female organism) and human functions (especially sexual
and procreative) to their least organic, most mechanical
dimension." At the same time, she was struck by the
irony that many teachers, critics, and writers who are
insensitive to this verbal degradation of women are
"eloquently angered" and "piously shocked" when eth-
nic or minority groups are similarly denigrated.

Barbara Lawrence has my sympathy and, with some
qualifications, my agreement. It may be an oversimp-
lification for her to imply a clear incompatibility between the familiar sexual crudities and the women's
liberation movement, but the crudities are likely enough
to be antiwoman in their immediate reference. The
problem is with the irony she points out. The inconsis-
tency is really there, but it is largely, I believe, a surface

"The Promise of Dirty Words" first appeared in *The American
Scholar* (Summer 1975): 385–404. Reprinted with permission.

matter, though nonetheless objectionable. Beneath the denigration of women, which is so out of agreement with verbal squeamishness elsewhere, is another, and in its implication even more disturbing, motive, which, consciously or unconsciously, uses the denigration of women as a means of expression. One of the best ways to see how this happens is to observe how one of our older contemporaries, Iago, behaves in Shakespeare's *Othello*.

Iago is not only a great denigrator of women, but he is also typical of the modern debunker. He is, as he says of himself to Desdemona, "nothing if not critical." His problem is how to maintain some kind of control in a universe that must be meaningless if he is to be safe, but in which he is continually threatened by mysterious, meaningful powers. He belongs with those characters in Shakespeare—for instance, Hamlet, Lear, Leontes of *The Winter's Tale*, Timon of Athens, and Thersites of *Troilus and Cressida*—who have temporarily or permanently lost faith and for whom the denigration of women is both symptom and symbol. Such persons dwell in their "critical" hell from which escape is made difficult or impossible by their fear of salvation. This hell, however spiritually sterile and even agonizing, lends itself to the illusion not only that it is all of reality but that it is quite controllable by those smart enough or tough enough to act on this information.

Iago demythologizes and denigrates in the interest of limiting and organizing his world. What threatens to complicate it, and therefore remove it from his control, is the possibility that apparent virtue is real virtue. Desdemona, as most of us know, is genuinely virtuous, a splendid variation on the Griselda figure (her best-known ancestress is the heroine of Chaucer's "The Clerk's Tale") who demonstrates her constancy in an extreme testing situation. She points to a moral, metaphysical, and theological order that threatens utterly to invalidate Iago's universe. There is therefore some desperation in him when he insists to the doting Roderigo,

"She must have change, she must." Later, when Roderigo exclaims that Desdemona is "full of most blessed
condition" and Iago explodes, "Blessed fig's end! The
wine she drinks is made of grapes," he is not simply de-
flating Roderigo's sentimentality; he is protecting himself from an alternative that would force him to revise
everything. He is what an unillusioned and smarter
Roderigo would be—a man "converted" to the dirty
and liberating truth that Desdemona is nothing but an
attractive cunt. This is the view to which Iago converts
Othello. Iago's need to convert others is at least as
strong as the need to "diet" his revenge; his disenchanted world is always threatened by the enchanted
believers outside, especially if, as he says of Cassio,
there is daily beauty in their lives that makes him ugly.

From Iago's point of view, of course, the impulse to
degrade and desecrate is liberating, and few people can
read or watch the play without sharing some of his liberated zest as he transgresses against, and transcends,
the moral and social norms that restrict his adversaries.
In the end, reality proves to be far too complicated for
him, but in the meantime he has the kind of freedom
from established limits that characterizes the animal
or human figures in animated cartoons—which is the
same thing as saying that he is in part a comic figure, a
practical joker who revels in the exhilarating game of
trying to outwit the mysterious, meaningful powers.
The most favorable position one could take toward him
would require pushing this liberational element as far
as it would go. In that case it would become clear that
we want to get rid of Iago for the same reason that we
want to get rid of Sade: we can't stand that much freedom and that much reality. We prefer to be captives of
value structures and self-transcending (therefore self-
denying) causes, even at the cost of living derivative and
hypocritical lives.

Considered in such extreme terms, it is easy to see the
true hierarchy of Iago's hates and degradations. Before
all else he hates civilization and culture for the intoler-

able burdens they are and the ego-diminishing service
they command after one has lost faith in them as meaningful enterprises. Desdemona throughout the play and
Othello before his fall represent civilization's effort to
maintain itself through a dramatic embodiment of necessary virtues. Together as happy lovers shortly after
their arrival in Cyprus, they exemplify that harmony of
complementary elements which mirrors the cosmos itself but which to Iago is the ultimate threat to his nihilistic integrity. Therefore he says in an aside:

> O, you are well tuned now!
> But I'll set down the pegs that make this music,
> As honest as I am.

His objective will be to liberate himself from all possible threats of this harmony by destroying its immediate symbols, and to do this he will convert Othello to his
own liberated and obscene view of Desdemona. In the
process he will demonstrate the extent to which a full,
free, authentic, and creative life can be associated with
repeated acts of degradation.

In this reading of the play, of course, Shakespeare is
really, if clandestinely, on Iago's side, giving expression
as best he can to his own radical unease with the culture. This is that blackly pessimistic but utterly courageous Shakespeare who, some critics are convinced,
captivated Melville and helped to shape that mighty degrader, that passionate and misogynistic antiestablishmentarian, Ahab. Such a Shakespeare may, of course,
be nothing more than a convenience created to validate
one of our post-romantic pieties. Shakespeare's good
men and women have an embarrassing tendency to accept the burdens of culture as the condition of human-
ization, not as its adversary.

It is possible to locate, however dubiously, "good"
Iago only because acts of degradation can be positive or
negative, oriented to a new and more valid order or sub-

versively, even compulsively, directed against all order. Positive or creative degradation can reduce rank, value, or prestige in the interest of a sounder, or more humane, or more rational or virtuous arrangement of priorities. We pull down false gods and smash icons in order to purify our worship. A significant consensus now, for instance, regards the American Revolution, the labor movement, the extension of the franchise to the propertyless, blacks, and women, and the early 1960s civil rights movement as positive acts of degradation, though each was once seen by its adversaries as shockingly and dangerously disrespectful of an established grading system. Put this way, the distinction between positive and negative degradation seems hopelessly relative. Degradation is simply inseparable from consciousness raising or growth in individual critical awareness. If we lived in a high-synergy culture in which, as Abraham Maslow puts it, "social institutions are set up to transcend the polarity between selfishness and unselfishness," we would have occasion to do very little degrading—but on the other hand we might have very little personal autonomy and we might even be comfortably fascist, Castorist, or Maoist.

But we live in a low-synergy culture in which social, political, moral, and religious institutions are widely felt to be fundamentally hostile to authentic, autonomous life—or hostile to an as yet unrealized order whose aim would be to foster such a life. Our time has much in common with that gnosticism of the early Christian centuries which—for all its psychological pessimism, its sense of the cosmos as prison, says Hans Jonas in *The Gnostic Religion*—still "holds out the possibility of stripping off one's own soul and experiencing the divinity of the absolute Self." Certainly we are familiar enough now with this nihilistic gnostic libertinism which permits a spiritual elite to use the natural realm indiscriminately out of a conviction that the latter has no positive relation with a higher order of reality. No doubt any culture will become low-synergy and gnostic in proportion as liberation becomes for it a primary object of conscious pursuit. The spirit of liberationism is necessarily defiant and transgressive to the extent that, as Jonas points out, "we find sometimes the freedom to do everything turned into a positive *obligation* to perform every kind of action, with the idea of rendering to nature and thereby exhausting its powers." In this view, the burden of culture and civilization is the cosmos "seen only in its aspect of compulsion which thwarts man's freedom." No longer possessed of the venerability of the Greek cosmos, says Jonas, it merits only contemptuous epithets: "these miserable elements," "this puny cell of the creator." Its nature is to be out of tune.

Iago, of course, must not be confused with Jonas's gnostic superstars, Simon Magnus and Marcion. He is a faithless Gnostic; this is why he seems so modern to us. His contemptuous epithets are in the interest of no grand metaphysical, theological, or mystical schemes. Although he may sometimes seem to be aware of an affinity with the Devil, it is hard to see in him an element of self-transcending service to an evil principle. All his actions are directed to the survival of the isolated self; he acts like a man driven by the fear that if he ceases to raise hell he will cease to exist. Hence he is a compulsive degrader who anticipates the fate of the modern *isolato* whose ideal, at its most extreme, is total autonomy. For him, therefore, acts of degradation become not only substitutes for virtue but indispensable means of self-definition and survival. One might even feel sorry for Iago. If he were alive today, his program of permanent degradation would have the support of an elaborate rhetoric of liberation and he would be able to see himself in some kind of self-transcending dimension.

An important difference between Iago and his modern descendants, however, is the fact that he not only does not need such support but would probably ridicule it if it were offered to him. To his critical eye, everybody's wine is made of grapes. He is in fierce competition with established virtue but is himself not much bothered by the need for moralism. For most modern degraders, on the other hand, the act of degrading has become a moral habit—in fact, a substitute for cultural virtue. Or to put it in the degrader's terms: thanks to the highly moral and even heroic work of the degrader, cultural virtue is now revealed to be the corruption it fundamentally is and always has been. The degrader, then, is the protagonist in a virtue story; he must depend on this story's action for his moral well-being. Only those transgressors whom Philip Rieff in his recent *Fellow Teachers* calls "triumphant therapeutic communities of one," those who in their nonheroic way have gotten beyond good and evil, appear to be living quite comfortably without the support of this story—though they can be accused of being freeloaders whose freedom depends on the moral effort of those who remain the story's captives.

The predicament of the faithless gnostic degrader is therefore his symbiotic moral dependence on what he degrades. Surely this dependence helps to explain why, three quarters of a century after the Victorian Age, we are still so conscious of the need to resist Victorianism. Our degradational and highly critical spirit could no more dispense with Victorianism than the world of Ingsoc in Orwell's *1984* could dispense with the legendary heretic Emanuel Goldstein, without whom Big Brother's world would deteriorate for lack of moral fervor. Late twentieth-century Victorianism has become a metaphor for culture, understood as the complex of all those forces that conspire to thwart the individual's aspirations to be autonomous—that aspire, in gnostic terms, to enslave his *pneuma* or spirit. This metaphoric Victorianism is the real enemy in two liberated products of literal Victorian culture: Oscar Wilde's 1891 essay, "The Soul of Man Under Socialism," and Mark Twain's famous and bawdy underground pamphlet, *1601*. It is the real enemy against which that late Victorian, Frank Harris, was tilting a half-century ago in his autobiography *My Life and Times*, just as it is the enemy (Jewish version now) against which Philip Roth is still tilting in *Portnoy*.

The metaphor of Victorianism is, after the fashion of metaphor, wonderfully economical. It organizes its attack on culture around sexual repression, just as Ingsoc organizes its attack on the forces that oppose it around the metaphor of Goldstein. An inevitable consequence is the eroticizing of both establishment and antiestablishment politics. The Nixon-Agnew-Mitchell hard line against obscenity and pornography (once a comfort but now, I imagine, an embarrassment to the Keating-led minority of *The Report of the Commission on Obscenity and Pornography*) was doubtless less important as a concern with literal pornography and obscenity than as a sign that Nixon, Agnew, and Mitchell were, like Frank Harris and Alex Portnoy, captives of the metaphor of Victorianism. For them, too, sexual liberation meant both the liberated *pneuma* and political liberation, but with the terms of the melodrama reversed so that they were the bad guys.

When Barbara Lawrence objects to the degrading view of women implied in the "'rich,' 'liberating' sexual verbs so fashionable today among male writers," she is in opposition to a powerful combination of forces. To begin with, she has against her something that probably has to be taken as a constant in our culture: men's fear of overdependence on women, of which male chauvinism and female chauvinism are symptom and countersymptom. This fear, grounded as it is on the male's biological and psychological dependence on women, can be subject to great complication and intensification, depending on the environment in which the individual grows up. He may come to fear that the dependence will be permanently crippling (especially if he has been induced to strive for a particularly chauvinistic male ideal). He may so strongly identify with woman the overwhelming and potentially destructive power of sex that woman becomes the symbol of all mysterious and threatening power (the malign Earth Mother). He may discover a powerful threat to his autonomy in his own capacity to idealize woman, so that she comes to represent the threat to him of all that he can idealize; or, to put it another way, he may discover that woman, as she exists in his imagination and emotions, is intimately involved with forces and processes that impel him to deny some of his deepest and most subversive impulses if he is to shoulder his share of the burden of human community.

I assume that somewhere along the line most men experience most of these fears to some degree, just as I assume that somewhere along the line most women, to some degree, experience a correlated body of fears—which is only to say that the effort to civilize and acculturate is an effort to survive in a precarious situation. All human societies attempt to domesticate these fears and the hatreds that are potential in them, so that they do not become too destructive to community-making. Thus, a society tries to keep the battle of the sexes, which is at bottom the battle for individual survival in the face of conflicting pressures, at the level of comedy, farce, and ritual gesture. Or put it this way: a certain amount of degrading activity—ranging from the merely tension-relieving, through the good-natured, comic, and farcical, to the ugly and vicious—is the inevitable by-product of any ongoing cultural process. The existing body of denigrating and desecrating obscenities in a society is a reflexive record of the extent to which it has been pressed by its pieties. *O Calcutta!*, for instance, records the power of the tradition of romantic love in our culture, both degrading and defining the image of woman in that tradition. (And insofar as that image has any base in the fundamental nature of woman, it is fundamentally degrading to woman.) Similarly, the numberless obscene post–Watergate Nixon jokes were a reflexive record of the force of democratic political ideals in America, and because they were largely sex-degrading male creations (which did not keep many liberated women from enjoying them) they were also degrading to women in Professor Lawrence's sense—though neither sex nor women was what they were really about.

The dirty words that Barbara Lawrence objects to always appear in contexts where they are the familiar cultural reactions to forces that threaten to overpower, overawe, or overabstract. There is a variety of reasons for them, some of which are bound up with the legitimate needs of literature (to say nothing of the exigencies of nightclub comics). Sociologically, they correspond to that "real language of men" with which Wordsworth believed he could re-identify only by smashing the icons of poetic diction. Hence, like many degrading gestures, they may function to keep the lines of communication clear, though their tendency to establish themselves as a new poetic diction is by now notorious. But the dirty words are also vehicles to carry the modern gnostic conviction that culture is basically evil—evil because it restricts free expression of impulse while it imposes ego-limiting commitments and roles, and imprisoning piety-fictions. When Professor Lawrence complains about those words, some of her opposition simply places her beside Nixon, Agnew, and Mitchell on Victorian grounds—in opposition not only to Iago but to the degradational gnostic morality of the whole liberation impulse. She puts herself on the side of Desdemona and the uptight culture-bearers, where she is in danger of being confused with those women who have made Marabel Morgan's *Total Woman* a best seller. Since she is a professor of humanities at State University, Old Westbury, New York, it also puts her on the academic hot seat—for the academy is still an enclave in which the metaphor of Victorianism is as important an organizer of information as the computer room.

Professor Lawrence speaks of her difficulty in persuading students that dirty words really can do harm. Caught up in their current romance with strong, funky,

gut-honest, liberating existential language, they have
nothing but scorn for "phoney-sounding middle-class
words like 'intercourse' and 'copulate.'" Anyone who
has attempted to teach literature to the young, anyone
who can remember his own youthful encounter with
modern literature will remember this romance (if indeed he does not remain its captive, out of a fear of ceasing to be young himself). In Western civilization, at
least, the young are naturally, and almost innocently,
degraders of pieties and violators of taboos as they
attempt to survive and define themselves in an environment of threatening and mysterious powers. Often
they learn from their elders how to put their transgressions in moralistic terms lest, in their efforts to be at
ease, they only frighten themselves more. In a low-
synergy culture such as ours, where acts of degradation
tend to be synonymous with virtue and dirty words turn
into holy words, there is a natural inclination to intensify the conventional cult of youth as a means of estab-
lishing a salvational image for adults. For much of the
New Left, for instance, the youth of Berkeley became
more authentically radical, and a more comforting symbol for sympathetic adults, as they escalated from free
speech movement to the dirty speech movement. Since
adults often connive at or actively encourage the degrading acts of the young (especially when it is convenient to reduce those acts to virtuous political motiva-
tions), they are often accused of corrupting the young.
This view lacks both charity and imagination. The "cor-
rupters," recognizing that youth can degrade with a li-
censed abandon not possible to adults, may only be ask-
ing the young to corrupt and save them. (And if, after
their fashion, the young promise more than they can deliver—or if, egged on by salvation-needing adults, they
promise what nobody could ever deliver—the adult disillusion and anger will be great indeed.)

Pornography, dependent as it is on images of youth-
fulness and on displays of sexual energy possible only to
the young, is one of the extreme forms of youth cult. It

is a kind of pastoral in which the sex-seeking male is liberated from the burdens of age and the burdens of community-making as they are experienced in loving relations between men and women. Male pornography degrades woman as a person in order to be free of her as a person, but ultimately to degrade culture; and the converse is of course true of female pornography. As the objective correlative of the masturbatory urge, it is the purest and most gnostic form of sex. This is what has made it so available in the past decade as an all-purpose liberation symbol, and why attempts have been made to see it as a serious art form. Insofar as it is believed to be genuine art, pornography can command respectful attention for doing what art is now widely respected for doing: for opposing culture in the interest of authentic "living." The moralistic rhetoric for this elevated (and ultimately political) pornography has been so well diffused in our culture that someone like Linda Lovelace, the star of *Deep Throat*, is able to say in her "exclusive intimate story," *Inside Linda Lovelace*: "I want to see the day when sex will be an accepted thing, and violence will be outlawed. I think children should be allowed to see sex openly if they can watch violence every day of their lives." She admits that she is not the most original thinker in the world, but she does not have to be. The pastoral myth of pornography, with its naïve assumption of the natural opposition between sex and violence, does her thinking for her.

But Professor Lawrence must also count among her enemies those women who are just as interested as are pornographers in degrading the traditional image of themselves as cultural burden-bearers. They may still feel just as uneasy, even as vaguely threatened, by the obscene and pornographic as they are by radical lesbianism, but they are so circumscribed by the degradational rhetoric of liberation that they can find no way to separate themselves from anyone who lays claim to it. Such women are victims of the package maneuver, an intimidating tactic generally employed with the effect of blackmail by those who dwell in the extremes of a movement, where on a clear day (and out there is always a clear day) it is possible to see forever. In this heady environment—in which, it was once thought, only the radical Right was at home—complicated issues are apprehended in stark either/or terms and thus make economically organized packages in which any one item is equal to every other item and to the package as a whole. Thus it seems only reasonable to say to half-hearted allies or potential converts, "Buy the whole package or nothing, and buy it all without question, or consider yourself a part of the enemy and damned."

In this particular package the necessary assumption is that all liberations are equal, while the correlative assumption, expressed in the metaphor of Victorianism, is that all restrictions are equal. Perhaps Lillian Hellman had the unworkableness of these assumptions in mind when, in an *American Scholar* forum of distinguished women, she remarked: "I think there is a difference between the women's movement and women's liberation. Liberation is a kind of silly word, a self-serving word." The trouble with liberation is not so much that it has become a cliché through overuse and abuse by a variety of movements, but what it has tended to do to its users. At this point in history, liberation may seem to have everything going for it as a rallying cry and as a public relations gesture. As are all super-honorific terms, it is strongly resistant to critical examination; like a setting hen, it warms equally all the eggs one can put under it. The problem, however, is with liberation as a goal or prime reason for action, as against liberation of some sort as the consequence of a particular action—the liberation, say, of one's capacities for full citizenship as a consequence of winning the right to vote. "Considered in a historical context," Sidney Hook has remarked, "the cry for freedom becomes meaningful only when it is a demand for specific freedoms justified by a consideration of the consequences of exercising them or denying them." A liberation movement

that is not bound to specifics is likely to have the ironic
and generally demoralizing consequence of discovering
simply what no one ought to have to look very hard to
find: the ineradicable restrictiveness of the human condition. In proportion as unspecified liberation euphoria
takes over a movement, restrictiveness becomes the real
enemy, and the movement embarks on a course of esca-
lating degradation in which it is overwhelmed and ultimately defused by the multiplicity of its options.

So we have one of the late-arriving benefits of an affluent, information-crammed, low-synergy culture: the
possibility of degradational activity as a sanctioned
and moralistic way of life. So too we have the inconsis-
tency that Professor Lawrence notes among her academic peers: their tolerance of obscenities that degrade
women alongside their intolerance of obscenities that
offend their liberal pieties. Iago's course of total degradation, in which the pegs that make the music possible
are all set down, is simply too frightening for most degraders. They need finally to believe that they are on the
side of some angels, which means that they need the
support of the rhetoric of liberation, even when for them
it is only an empty rhetoric that implies the gnostic
paradise in which they cannot believe.

I suspect that the dilemma for many of the women
(and men as well) who are uneasy with Professor Lawrence's stand against the liberating dirty words is that
they are just as uneasy with the ethos they rely on for
support against that stand. The promise of the dirty
words is relief from a cultural burden that is conveniently identified as a remnant of Victorianism—or,
more narrowly, male chauvinism—but that may have
been more accurately identified by J. D. Unwin in *Sex
and Culture* as the burden of opposing sexual permissiveness in the interest of conserving cultural energy
and maintaining civilization. Historically, this burden
has meant, among other things, the idealization of
woman as a quest figure along with the ideal of self-
abnegating male service as a correlative means of dra-

matizing necessary cultural virtues. It has made Desdemona possible and kept the Iago forces at bay—a fact that has been spelled out in fictions that range from the romances of chivalry to old-fashioned Western movies. But this has also meant, Unwin points out, "depriving the female of the species of certain rights which she seems entitled to enjoy."

Indeed it would be possible to argue from Unwin's study that women are culturally more important than men, that men know this and have therefore institutionalized women in a manner most likely to reduce the culturally destructive sexual rapacity of males and to compel their cooperation in community building. Obviously such an argument is no more attractive to women now than Unwin's forty-year-old prescription for the good society is attractive to either sex: complete sexual equality with economic and social organizations altered "in such a way as to render it both possible and tolerable for sexual opportunity to remain at a minimum for an extended period, and even forever." Such a formulation is not out of line with some of the conclusions in Robert Heilbroner's *An Inquiry into the Human Prospect*; but to a society in which faithless Gnostics have so much to say, it is simply modified Victorianism, and very nearly a prescription for hell.

As for the uneasy women, they are in the position of being promised relief from one burden on the condition that they accept another burden—that of the necessary degradation of their sexuality which goes with the demand that they accept dirty words (and the ethos that accompanies them) as holy words, giving up their traditional special assignments as culture-degraders. I suspect that the demand that this new burden be accepted is itself at bottom a not especially subtle form of male chauvinist liberationism. (One thinks of the extent to which Shulamith Firestone's vision of a sexual utopia derives from that male chauvinist Gnostic, Wilhelm Reich.)[9]

It is interesting to note that this burden is accepted in

some of the trashier magazines addressed to women
(*Loving, Revealing Romances, True Experiences, Daring
Romances, Exciting Confessions, Real Love Stories, Viva,
Playgirl*, et cetera) just as enthusiastically as it is offered
in counterpart publications addressed to men (*Mus-
tang, Gallery, Man's Delight, Oui, Penthouse, Debonair,
Cavalier, Swank, Playboy*, et cetera). An assortment of
these magazines arranged on a newsstand as a garden
of earthly delights (their pointless sexual segregation a
parody of old-fashioned modesty) asserts a transgressive togetherness whose basically male theme is that
the sexes that degrade themselves together will be free
together. At the same time, of course, these publications are American and are nothing if not moralistic,
with a great deal of talk about the imperatives of self-
fulfillment, of facing up honestly to one's natural impulses and deepest needs, of becoming a "total person,"
of refusing to accept the limited options imposed by
male chauvinism, of resisting the obscenity of Victorian
prudery, et cetera. Indeed the specter of Victorian prudery haunts the junk literature of male and female liberation the way sinister medieval monks used to haunt
gothic romances, so that one is constantly reminded of
Freud's dictum: "An obstacle is required to heighten li-
bido; and where natural resistances to satisfaction have
not been sufficient men have at all times erected conventional ones so as to be able to enjoy love."

To encounter sexual degradation on the mass-cult
level is to see what is true of it at any level: the inco-
herent nature of its attack on metaphoric Victorianism. This is another result of unspecified liberationism
and the impossible burden it places on sex. The psychiatrist Natalie Shainess has criticized the liberation-
oriented Masters and Johnson enterprise for having
"tended to detach the sex act from the words, feelings, and emotions of desire and love." One of the more
bizarre consequences of such detachment (Swift would
have been delighted to incorporate it in Book III of *Gulliver*) was the famous penis-sensitivity test performed

for the President's Commission on Obscenity and Pornography. Experiments of this sort suggest to Dr. Shainess a direct connection between our failure to learn
that "sexual expression is not separate but a part of
the person" and the fact that as a people "we have
become compulsive voyeurs" who make best sellers out
of books like *The Sensuous Woman, The Sensuous Man,
The Couple,* and *Inside the Sex Clinic.* In a concurring
criticism of our incapacity to see the cultural complexity of our degradational pieties, the psychologist Judith M. Bardwick writes of the many liberationists of
both sexes who "equate role change with freedom," unaware that the new roles, like the old ones, "will provide
frustration as well as fulfillment." This is to say nothing
of the simplifying moralism that pervades the ethos of
the dirty words as one finds it in so much of the literature addressed to men and women: that role itself, being a product of culture, functions only to frustrate and
restrict.

Dr. Bardwick and Dr. Shainess understand sexual relationships in holistic terms. From their position, the
cultural rejections demanded by the woman's new burden appear to be nonholistic acts of negative degradation—or, to borrow a phrase from the British scholar
Frances Yates, acts of "indiscriminate iconoclasm." Indiscriminate iconoclasts of necessity approach role with
a fanatic simplism. Dr. Bardwick's assumption is that
role is a constant of the human condition, as indispensable to communal relationships and unity as to
self-definition. The assumption implies a Renaissance
celebration of variety and contrast as principles of organization and intelligibility in the sensible universe
and as the basis of all grading systems. In this view, the
burden of civilization is inseparable from the burden of
role-playing, and transgressive gestures within a culture are necessarily role-degrading—whether as temporary relief from the pressures of acculturation, or as
efforts to adapt roles to changing cultural conditions, or
as efforts to achieve a condition of gnostic liberation

beyond role. The obscenities Professor Lawrence complains about are attacks on role. They get strong support (often, of course, unconscious) from the conviction that there is a radical disjunction between role and nature: that role is the immediate source of all that is divisive, unjust, and person-diminishing, and that if it can be effectively degraded out of existence, nature will be possessed or repossessed.

Yet it is role-organized culture that has made it possible to dream of a condition of personal autonomy beyond the reach of role and culture, so that nature had to be imagined as favoring an infinite variety of autonomous persons who exist together in complete harmony. Modern Gnosticism, being faithless and earthbound, is of necessity anarchistic. Unfortunately, even its anarchism is faithless, not only incapable of Proudhon's or Kropotkin's optimism about human nature but subverted by the cultural discovery that degradation under a moralistic cover can itself be a satisfactory way of life.[10] The sons of Iago are generally too symbiotically dependent on what they degrade to be counted on for a serious effort in any program of positive degradation. They are also sentimental degraders, trapped by the vitality they have been able to derive from acts of degradation.

Alex Portnoy is a sentimental and trapped degrader—a degrader of women, certainly, the most thoroughgoing in literature this side of pornography, but ultimately a degrader of the culture to which he is symbiotically joined. At the end of the novel, Dr. Spielvogel's observation, "Now vee may perhaps to begin," is the end of an elaborate joke; it is not possible to believe that Alex is going anywhere but where he has been, or indeed has any real desire to. His last intelligible words are, "But at least while I lived, *I lived big.*" Here one can see that a major factor in the popular success of the novel is the complex nature of the pleasure it offers the male reader. It is a drawn-out scream of rage against the con-

strictions of culture for which the reader comes prepared. The cultural scapegoats—the mother, all women
in their capacity to compel dependence or to demonstrate or suggest mysterious and threatening power—
are as familiar as the stereotypes of *commedia dell'arte*
farce. The language has that obscene and liberating
honesty of toilet-stall graffiti that has come to be one of
the marks of authentic literature; it gives integrating
shape to the mixture of pleasure and pain in the hell of
victimization with which the reader, insofar as he is
himself a compulsive degrader, is already familiar. It is
truly a *big* life in widely understood terms: erotically
and transgressively action-crammed.

Alex, as a trapped and compulsively degrading liberal, as a setter-down of the pegs upon which traditional
harmonies depend, is also an example of the inconsis-
tencies that bother Professor Lawrence. He is a denigrator of women who celebrates all the good causes. He
reads *PM*; he is an executive for the New York Commission on Human Opportunity; he is a defender of blacks
and Puerto Ricans against racial injustice; he hates
"America First"; he is capable in fantasy of dedicating
his life "to the rightings of wrongs, to the elevations of
the downtrodden and the underprivileged, to the liberation of the unjustly imprisoned." He is a negative degrader for whom the rhetoric of positive degradation is
simply another dimension of his hell. The "Good Alex"
who, it periodically seems to him, he might have been—
an impossible hyperbole constructed out of random
impulses which, if it could be realized in fact, would
result in a monster of virtue—simply defines his self-
degradation.

Alex is a caricature Everyman who is torn between
his good and bad angels and for whom those angels
have become hopelessly confused. What he would like
most of all is to get beyond guilt and shame. "Why must
the least deviation from respectable conventions cause
me such inner hell?" he complains. "Why is the smallest
thing I do for pleasure immediately illicit while the rest

of the world rolls laughing in the mud?" Why can't he
be like those lucky ones who "come down from the
crimes they commit [without] so much as a case of in-
digestion?" Why, in short, can't he be the Iago-opposite
to the "Good Alex"—the liberated, conscience-free transgressor, free of all angels, that his culture so infuriat-
ingly dangles before him as a real possibility? He has,
after all, says Morris Dickstein, inspired female writers
like Erica Jong and Iris Owens "to talk dirty and tell it
straight," to say nothing of having prepared the way for
the masturbatory adventures of Marilyn Coffey's *Mar-
cella*. Why, having performed such liberating service, is
he still bound to his rock?

As Alex sees it, his impotence is directly connected
with his Jewish conscience and its capacity to inspire a
crippling sense of sexual guilt and shame. His position
is the one Erich Heller suspects in Freud (himself anything but a shameless man): that the alliance between
sex and shame "far from being rooted in human nature
itself . . . results from some dark conspiracy." Heller's
own conviction (see his essay "Man Ashamed" in the
February 1974 *Encounter*) is that "the price of individuation is shame," which the Greeks elevated to the
status of a goddess (Aidos) and to which they linked rev-
erence, piety, and respect for their person. It is a fundamental disposition of the psyche, "the negation of which
leads to extreme states of inhumanity" (which is true
enough whether one thinks of Alex Portnoy or the sexual
atrocities of Nazi concentration camps). The manners of
shame may change, but it "cannot be done away with
by the machinations of history if human nature is to
have any definite attributes at all." For Heller it follows,
then, that "the campaigns of shamelessness, although
they may be waged in the name of liberating ideologies,
consciously or unconsciously have as their end the crippling of humaneness."

Heller's essay is eloquent and powerful in its wide-
ranging scholarship, but the position he argues for is
traditional enough. If the tradition is now largely un-

available to so many, the reason is that the present epoch, "quick in forgetfulness, obtuse to damnation . . . has sold all entrance tickets to the past." Jonas, having retained his own entrance tickets, reinforces Heller, especially in his epilogue to *The Gnostic Religion*, "Gnosticism, Existentialism and Nihilism." Unwin and Rieff also reinforce him, as they reinforce Professor Lawrence. Rieff, speaking of John Barth's *The End of the Road*, contrasts primitive man with the barbarism of modern psychological man who "throws no veils." "Be grateful for your inalienable sense of guilt," he writes. "Without an elaborately cultivated transgressive sense, there can be neither aristocracies of the feeling intellect nor democracies of obedience." All three offer cold comfort to Alex Portnoy: culture is a conscience-burden from which one is relieved only to pursue a lower state of affairs.

Heilbroner himself gives cold comfort to the likes of Geoffrey Barraclough, who view him with some dismay as a liberal conscience in a state of capitulation.[11] In the meantime, however, Heilbroner reinforces Heller, for there is an economic dimension to what has traditionally been known as shame. It is hard to read *An Inquiry into the Human Prospect* (or any of Heilbroner's recent work, for that matter) and miss its implication that shamelessness as part of a program of liberating and degrading permissiveness is a luxury that our culture will not be able to afford for very long. An Alex Portnoy is simply one of the expensive obscenities of history. Heilbroner discourages those "who would hope that the challenges of the human prospect would finally banish the thralldoms of authority and ideology and foster the 'liberation' of the individual," or who would assume that "man ultimately makes himself in a benign manner." He sees little reason to believe that man will be able to go on reveling in extravagant and heretical thoughts, or attempting to strip himself of all his false consciousness and divest himself of all the delusions and falsities that have misled him, without settling "into a state of existential despair, or [relapsing] into a suicidal solipsism." The postindustrial era Heilbroner envisages is one in which "men and women, much as they are today, will set the pace"; it will "stress parsimoniousness, not prodigal attitudes," as well as the "acceptance of communally organized and ordained roles." With its dependence on tradition and ritual, it will, he suspects, be relatively static. It will be close to that social condition in which, as Hugh Hefner has put it, a man will not have to choose between "enjoying life and having a social conscience, looking out for yourself and other guys as well," but with consequences for the impulse-releasing playboy quite other than Hefner had in mind.

What Hefner did have in mind, I think, was a society that would somehow manage to combine the benefits of a high-synergy culture (relative lack of friction between private and public demands) with the pleasures of a faithless Gnosticism. It would fulfill Wilde's requirement of relieving us "from the sordid necessity of living for others" but would not be presided over by the sentimentalized and liberated Christ upon whom both Wilde and Frank Harris ground their moralism. Its own need for moralism would be taken care of by its unremitting and zestful degradation of whatever in its environment opposed its only sanctioned form of transcendent aspiration: its commitment to that greater self one may become through the strenuous consumption of goods, services, experience, and other people. Such a society would revel in extravagant and heretical thoughts, but its reveling would be as sentimental as its Gnosticism would be faithless. It would be shameless, burden-rejecting, and service-abhorring, lest the autonomous individual be demeaned and diminished. In it Alex Portnoy would rise gloriously from his couch, prepotent and shriven beyond all need of further shrift. Spielvogel, like Othello, would lose his occupation. Iago would come into his own, recognized at last for the culture hero that he is, and Desdemona (transmogrified, perhaps, to a nude foldout) would be exposed as a meretricious cultural artifact.

Heilbroner with his "Malthusian forebodings" (as Barraclough has designated them) is about as likely as the Club of Rome to predict a long life for such a society. Marcuse, I imagine, would suspect that it smells too much of the "Pubertarian revolt" which he now believes the New Left must purge itself of. Its greatest contribution to any subsequent society might be, not its experiment in liberation, nor its collection of honest dirty words, but the Victorianism which in the interest of its own survival and enjoyment it had to keep alive.

Chapter 5

Honesty as a Policy

Disgust at duplicity, Benjamin DeMott has said, is "the deepest running tide anywhere at this moment." The observation leaves room for several possibilities: that there is more duplicity around now than ever before and therefore more to be disgusted at; that there appears to be more duplicity because we have learned to see more; that we see more because we need to see more; that the disgust with it is more symptomatic of the disgusted than it is indicative of moral decay. The availability of targets for disgust appears, in fact, to be a measure of civilization, although one would hardly care to argue that the more disgusting a culture is the more it is civilized. It is simply that relatively primitive peoples knit strongly into tribal groups seem not yet to have arrived at the point where they can indulge this passion. Perhaps it is best seen as a cultural luxury, like the capacity to wage atomic war. Indeed, it may be little more than a sentimental way for a people to pretend that it still has the moral fiber that it knows it needs but fears it is losing.

Nevertheless, Mr. DeMott is right: the disgust is widespread. We all agree with Iago when he says to an Othello far gone in suspicion of Desdemona: "Men

"Honesty as a Policy" first appeared in *The American Scholar* (Spring 1972): 251–64. Reprinted with permission.

should be what they seem;/ Or those that be not, would they might seem none!"

At this point in the play Iago's reputation as an honest man is still intact, although the audience knows that, his honesty being mere policy, he is only a clever imitation of Shakespeare's honest man. The latter really is what he appears to be, and above all he is loyal to his commitments. To honor them he may have to adopt a disguise, which if it is a kind of duplicity is not the kind Mr. DeMott is talking about. Shakespeare's kind of honesty assumes and is the expression of character, in the sense of a principled organization of energies and dispositions aimed at securing the subject's and society's best interests. It involves the conviction that the naked energies are naturally unruly, that attitudes ruled by passions are impermanent, and that the necessities for humane living are available only through disciplined effort. The fact that it is easy for us to believe that character so conceived is incompatible with honesty is one measure of the distance between us and Shakespeare.

Shakespeare and his age, however, were familiar with the opposition between character in the above sense and honesty in a sense close to one we are familiar with. Falstaff and Edmund, Gloucester's bastard son in *King Lear*, for example, anticipate a modern belief that character, understood as a predisposition determined by values held to be anterior to the individual, is hostile to an honest expression of impulse and is therefore against nature and hostile to life. Both figures are, of course, clearly enough identified as occupying heterodox positions, however attractively in Falstaff's case or as a consequence of whatever real injustice in Edmund's. In fact, a good deal of Renaissance thinking tends to be soft on honesty as it is understood by Falstaff and Edmund.

Nevertheless, the modern opposition between character and honesty comes most forcibly to our attention in Romanticism, however much it had been prepared for by Renaissance and Enlightenment optimism about human nature. The opposition is the expression of a complex of forces in which the person as we know him has to a significant degree emerged from the social units to which for so long he had tended to be subordinated. With this emergence, in part because of it, comes that valuation of the passional self that results in, and is in part made possible by, the polarization of honesty and character. It is now possible to say with Shakespeare's Edmund, and with less and less fear of being labeled heterodox, "Thou, Nature, are my goddess!"

It is apparent that in the raw passional energy he calls his goddess Nature Edmund has discovered something of the sense of liberation that goes with the cult of spontaneity—as one encounters it, for instance, in a modern romantic like John Cage when he urges us to "give up illusions about ideas of order, expressions of sentiment, and all the rest of our inherited claptrap." Edmund's hard-eyed and honest assessment of orthodox ideas of order as inherited claptrap also makes him an a priori caricature not only of such violators of inherited claptrap as Wordsworth, Whitman and Hemingway but of all those heroes of the New Left who have found in obscenity (with Marcuse's blessing) an honest and liberating response to the poetic diction of the establishment.

In Hemingway's *A Farewell to Arms* Lieutenant Frederick Henry has a metaphoric vision of language as an accretion of empty proclamations slapped up one on top of the other. This is the way traditional character formation tends to appear in the romantic world: as a meaningless repetition of gestures that not only thwart spontaneity but keep the right future from being born. Oddly enough, however, both Wordsworth and Hemingway admired examples of traditional character formation: compare the former's Michael or Old Leech Gatherer, for instance, with the latter's Santiago or Robert Jordan. The attractive thing about all of these people is their predictability, a quality they have in common with the poetic diction that both writers profess to abhor. Because figures of this sort are organized around unshakable convictions, they are intensely and honestly open to highly valued but very limited areas of experience. Being men of character, they are conservators; they tend to slow down the universe in which they live and breathe. They are in fact expressions of Romanticism's need to counter the high potential for dangerous excess in romantic values, and particularly in the romantic commitment to becoming rather than being. In other words, at least some romantics act as if there is no incompatibility between character and honesty in the sense of a capacity to be in accord with elemental forces. Probably they would agree with a recent remark by drama critic Eric Bentley: that "like other forces of freedom, spontaneity operates within limits, i.e., within an iron ring of unfreedom, of unspontaneity."

Nevertheless, romantics as a whole, especially modern romantics, do not take kindly to the suggestion that there may be an interrelation between spontaneity and the iron ring of unfreedom, and for the same reason they are unenthusiastic about character formation, which is likely to strike them as a bourgeois programming for survival. This is not to say that they are themselves invariably without it any more than their poems, plays and novels are invariably without structure; it is simply to say that they are radically uneasy with the anti-utopian, anti-spontaneous (and therefore anti-honest) implications of character and structure. They may have no personal experience of life beyond the iron ring (even states of entrancement or intoxication are ultimately experienced in relation to it); still it seems to them that the good man has no alternative to thinking of it as the enemy—even though to attack that enemy effectively may require a good deal of old-fashioned character.

There is good reason for this. Character as it has generally been known is a kind of specialization that is grounded on the experience of scarcity (there is never enough of anything to go around), the threat of information (at any given moment there is far too much of it available) and the related threat of time (at any given moment it is on the verge of moving too fast). Character formation is both a matter of vital economy (a limitation and concentration of attention and energy) and the product of a technique for achieving self-definition: it secures the self as an enclave of awareness and purpose from the sheer process and welter of existence in which it would otherwise be unselfconsciously lost. To put it this way is to emphasize that character as it comes to us out of our classical, Jewish and Christian past aspires to be an ideal combination of conservative and creative forces.

This paradoxical combination makes little sense to romantics like Cage or British psychiatrist R.D. Laing, who, like Whitman, commit themselves optimistically to time and change because of a conviction that the impulse (the god) behind them is utterly benevolent. Therefore, Cage can announce as a basic principle (see the long conversation with him in the Fall 1969 *North American Review*): " . . . choose abundance rather than scarcity. Be wasteful rather than pinchpenny. Get as much as you can out of all there is to be had. Have it even if you don't use it, or even if you use it badly as a gadget." Character achieves its economies in terms of a sense of values; but for Cage we must "give up first of all a sense of values," for values mean privacy, divisiveness and partition, all of which are hostile to an honest openness and togetherness and the release of creative force (Esalen is the natural prep school and Laing the ideal counselor for the kind of world Cage envisages). Character is steadfastness, principled resistance to the flow; in Cage's view this is fixity, and he sees "no reason to think that it's virtuous to remain one thing throughout one's life." Cage takes his stand with R. Buckminster Fuller: if you have to choose "between fixity and flexibility choose flexibility." The conviction that these really are the alternatives one must choose between, as if the well-choosing man could end up all flexibility, is one of the peculiarities of Cage's position, and possibly one of its causes.

Cage's implied ideal man sounds much like Robert Jay Lifton's Protean Man.[12] What characterizes the life-style of Protean Man is "an interminable series of ex-periments and explorations—some shallow, some pro-found—each of which may be readily abandoned in favor of still new psychological quests." His protean quality is a technique for survival in condition of great cultural flux. His submission to and determination by process might suggest the hero of a *Bildungsroman*. The latter, however, is a questing hero for whom a variety of experiences in strange environments is a necessary pre-liminary to an ultimate integration and identity that will stand against the flux. Protean Man is less a quest-ing hero than an experience hero in whom "idea sys-tems and ideologies can be embraced, modified, let go of and reembraced, all with a new ease that stands in sharp contrast to the inner struggle we have in the past associated with these shifts." Thus his aspiration to "ex-periential transcendence" by way of drugs, cars, motor-cycles and superorgasms uncontaminated by personal commitment tends to result in anti-heroic action and aims to secure nothing. The aspiration to secure some-thing implies an acknowledgment of Bentley's iron ring of unfreedom and the clinging to values that so offends Cage—whom Lifton, incidentally, sees "as an extreme exponent of the protean style."

Protean Man would thus seem to have much in com-mon with Charles Reich's Consciousness III Man, who, never having known the straitjacket of Consciousness I Man's character, is blessed with flexibility, honesty, wholeness and an immense capacity for social respon-sibility and love. Indeed, Consciousness III Man some-times comes across as Protean Man in his ultimate ideal development released by irresistible grace to love, creativity and imagination. Certainly Consciousness III Man does not represent a position or "set" arrived at or earned by inner struggle—at least not by *his* inner struggle.

But Consciousness III Man appears in the context of

prophetic and utopian vision: his existence assumes the inevitability of an entirely satisfactory (and pseudo-Marxian) end-of-process, a greening beyond which there is no fall of leaf, and in which it is hard to imagine that his creativity and liberation would have anywhere to go, any means of self-definition, and therefore any means of sensing his dispensation from the iron ring of unfreedom. Such an idyllic vision generates excitement in proportion as the satisfaction of experiencing it as an achieved reality is equated with the satisfaction of trying to make it such. Considered as a final state, it has the static quality and high potential for boredom that characterize all utopias. It would need, and would no doubt quickly get, an honest Iago to stir up the right kind of trouble.

This is no less true of R. Buckminster Fuller's "Planetary Planning," a long prophetic essay published in *The American Scholar* at about the time that Reich's book appeared. Fuller's vision is less parochial than Reich's: it foresees the greening not only of America but of Spaceship Earth. Fuller may, in fact, help one to see the extent to which Reich's book has implicit in it a parochial American dream of Manifest Destiny: the greening of America is the necessary and inevitable preliminary to the greening of the world. In keeping with his grander objective, Fuller's prophecy is worked out in terms of twelve periods or phases of consciousness. However, it is no less dependent than Reich's on the spontaneity and honesty of youth, whose rejection of specialization will be a rejection of the characterizing and genius-frustrating prison of the past. Before Fuller's Period Ten (the present age) has run its course it will prove an Eden for Protean Man: it will be a flux ranging between *becoming* and *became*; it will no longer need nouns, only verbs; it will "give every individual the freedom to reemploy his original unblemished childhood's faculty of thought and experimental curiosity drives in whatever way each finds to be most constructive."

But in the end Fuller, like Reich, is more celebrational than informational. If we really want to learn something about an important phenomenon in contemporary society we need to return to Lifton, whose optimism about Protean Man is significantly qualified. The latter suffers, Lifton warns, from a strong ideological hunger and "is starved for ideas and feelings that can give substance to his world"; he has a profound inner sense of absurdity; he is painfully ambivalent about technology and change—that is, he is as likely to commit himself to projects that promise restoration as to those that promise transformation. In fact, a Reichean enthusiast might argue that Lifton's Protean Man is simply Consciousness III Man in the act of being painfully born—if, that is, one could reconcile the notion of painful birth with Consciousness III.

It may be more to the point, however, to see both as extensions of the romantic ideal of the artist as sensitive reed, as the medium through which course, undistorted by characterological "preformations," those energies that are the radical stuff of experience. This ideal—implicit in much contemporary talk about honesty as well as in much social criticism and psychology—expresses an aspiration to a total openness to experience, to a generous and even heroic submission to the flux. Its inspiration is Edmund's goddess Nature: before anything else it is a commitment to experience. This is the goddess who, Edmund assures us, stands not "in the plague of custom," and has no awe "of honest madam's issue," but produces instead bastards "of fierce quality" against whom legitimate offspring engendered within a "dull, stale, tired bed" will never prevail.

Edmund's honest nature, as we have come to see, is Dionysian, even orgiastic in its implications; in time it will produce in one direction that brutally honest man, the Marquis de Sade, and in another that ecstatically honest man, Norman O. Brown. In whichever direction

one goes he is lured by the promise of an ultimate unity
and wholeness, for Edmund's goddess is a great prom-
iser of unity and wholeness. Indeed, she is the impelling
deity behind not only the electronic global village, as
simultaneously prefigured and caricatured by Woodstock, but also Brown's heaven-on-earth, in which, to
quote from *Love's Body*, "The antinomy between mind
and body, word and deed, speech and silence [is] overcome. Everything is only a metaphor; there is only poetry." It is hard to take a stand against such vatic utter-
ance, which assumes the irrelevance of the definitions
and distinctions of the time-bound and prose-dependent
world. One can no more argue with Brown than with
the Cumean Sibyl. One can only wonder whether in a
world where language has been reduced to metaphor
(reversing the direction of Orwell's "Newspeak" world),
it might not be hard to distinguish Brown's kind of transcendence from Sade's. Indeed, if one takes his stand
with Peter Michelson's *Aesthetics of Pornography*, it is
not too important to distinguish between them, since
they are both trying to liberate the human spirit from
the Establishment prison house.

In any event, in Brown, Cage, Reich and Fuller we see
the sensitive reed expressing its fear of specialization.
Specialization, like traditional character formation, is
at its best a principled selection among options and
therefore a reduction of them in the interest of an
economy of energy and action. In the view of the sensitive reed, this reduction is dishonest, not simply as lies
and hypocrisies are dishonest but as a refusal to submit
oneself generously to one's full potential for life is. This
view obtains despite the fact that our literature and
drama, if not our prophetic scriptures, continually demonstrate how likely it is that such submission will be
destructive and that its hero-victims will have to find
their transcendence in confusion and suffering, or in
rage directed against familiar scapegoats. The very ex-
cessiveness of this rage may suggest that beneath its apparent cause there are factors of which the individual is

aware only in an inchoate way if at all, and in fact dare not become fully aware lest he be demoralized. There is, for instance, the enraging suspicion, for most of us grounded in the painfully repeated experience of the unclosable gap between aspiration and achievement, that the effect of too many options is more likely to be restricting than liberating.

Midge Decter has shown this irony at work in her *Commentary* essay, "The Liberated Woman." Here the young "heroine" is largely emancipated from the traditional biases and has been led to believe "by those around her that there would be no let or hindrance to her achievement." What those around her have not told her is that the availability of a variety of options is meaningful only in terms of the principled economy of the personality that chooses which among them it will pursue. In this circumstance, bewildered and frustrated, she is attracted to the more extreme forms of the feminine liberation movement, the rages of which substitute for the organizing work once accomplished by character formation.

Rage as a major substitute for character formation is probably inevitable in a permissive, sensate and impulse-releasing culture. Such a culture has a low tolerance for frustration; indeed, it is likely to identify intolerance of frustration as a clear sign of honesty. Honesty and frustration thus feed on one another to make life more disgusting and unbearable; at the same time, they make it increasingly difficult to see the extent to which, as Bruno Bettelheim has pointed out, it is unbearable "because we have not learned to manage frustration." But to a neo-romantic, "manage" in this context can imply a crippling skepticism about Laing's "politics of experience"—that is, a lack of trust in the natural forces that are trying to manage one. So far as experience is concerned, Bettelheim and Laing belong to quite different political parties. The advantage in belonging to Bettelheim's party is that membership prepares one for the familiar contemporary sequence: intense and short-

term commitment to a cause, rapid escalation into violence, hardly less rapid descent into disillusion and
apathy as the disproportion between effort and effect
becomes painfully clear. Thus one of the most important human experiences, anger at corruption or injustice as a preliminary to determined corrective action,
is in the end simply another honest experience: the
sensitive reed turns out to be simply one more leaf in
the wind.

It is not hard to believe that Lifton's Protean Man
is dangerously rage-prone for the same reason that he
suffers from ideological hunger and tends to embrace
technical achievement—that is, in order "to combat
inner tendencies toward diffusion." The inability to
manage one's impulses, the sense of oneself as helpless
against interior forces, is itself enraging for many personalities, although the likely thing is that they will locate the enraging cause outside themselves—perhaps
in parents or teachers who, by having failed to help
them learn how to manage themselves, have in effect
left them naked to adversity. Ideological hunger is ultimately hunger for management, an appetite that fascism has a great capacity to feed. Consciousness III
Man, then, may be nothing more than Protean Man
wistfully and tenderly observed, with all the latter's susceptibility to the charismatic managers who are so eager to "characterize" him.

This is no less a possibility for Fuller's Period Ten
Man, especially since he lives in an age destined ultimately "to emancipate all humanity from physical
drudgery." For by now we have learned to expect that
Utopian Man will turn out to be Managed Man who will
have had imposed upon him the character formation
necessary to the utopian enterprise. It is this irony that
makes Ken Kesey's dream of controlling electronically
a world turned on with "Electric Kool-Aid" such a revealing caricature of the utopian impulse. Indeed, unless one approaches him in the spirit of a true believer,
the Kesey of Tom Wolfe's saga can appear to be a car-

toon version of the Leonardo-type so crucial to Fuller as he builds his twelve steps to the Heavenly City. It is worth noting also that the new consciousness we see in Fuller and Wolfe's Kesey operates like a charisma, especially on the young. In the world of the new consciousness, charisma, particularly in its capacity as an irresistible personality-organizing force, ranks with rage as a substitute for character.

Romanticism is so widely understood as a glorification of the honest private person that it is easy to miss in it a sinister antipersonal impulse. This impulse is expressed in the metaphor of the sensitive reed as well as in the image of the female dancer with the utterly inexpressive inward-looking face, an image that in its pathological phase, Frank Kermode points out, becomes the *femme fatale.* In both images can be seen the aspiration of the person to be annihilated as he becomes pure medium for experience, pure metaphor, the vessel for that holy madness of which, according to Norman O. Brown, Nietzsche is the prophet. Nietzsche is of course the grand champion of all efforts to leap beyond the iron ring of unfreedom, and it is Brown who makes clear how hostile to the private person is this dream of Dionysian transcendence. The great romantics knew this dream and feared it even as they were compelled by it, and the fear is part of their romanticism. The fear helps to explain the conservatism of Coleridge and the maturing Wordsworth, as well as the discovery by the Byron of *Don Juan* how to use style to manage the dangerous discordancies of his personality; it is also a reason why Keats in his letters has so many "unromantic" things to say about character, philosophy and the kind of mental discipline to which he gives the name "negative capability."

The irony that an honest submission to experience, ostensibly in the interest of an intenser and ampler life, can end in the destruction of the person—either by leaving him defenseless to the forces in himself or in his environment or by reducing him to experiential means—

is underlined by the fate of such pop art celebrities as the late Jimi Hendrix and Janis Joplin. The media clearly did not care to approve of the kind of excess that apparently figured in these deaths; nevertheless, they found it hard to keep a note of awe out of their reports. *Life*, for instance, referred to these young entertainers as "victims of an assault on the frontier of ever newer experience," as if they had put their bodies fearlessly and heroically on the line for us. There may be good reason to believe that the assault on this particular frontier is more likely to result in an impoverishment of experience than an enrichment; nevertheless, for much of the counterculture world such figures are message in the act of being medium. As an admirer has said of Andy Warhol, what they suffer as persons is irrelevant, perhaps even to themselves. Thus they are brought into line with, and at the same time caricature, what Lionel Trilling has identified as one of the major themes of modern literature: "the idea of losing oneself up to the point of self-destruction, of surrendering oneself to experience without regard to self-interest or conventional morality, of escaping wholly from the societal bond."

The reasons for the immense appeal of a figure like Che Guevara are not hard to see. He moves uncompromisingly against what his admirers believe to be a fundamentally corrupt and life-denying middle class and therefore sanctifies their rage against it, and at the same time he has great appeal as a superior kind of experience hero (although this is a trivializing interpretation to a true *Guevarista*). But at least as important is the fact that he represents in an acceptable modern context an old-fashioned kind of salvation for Protean Man. For Guevara, as is made abundantly clear in his *Diary*, was the Hero as Man of Character, the economy of whose life was determined by clearly defined principles and by an ascetic capacity for a disciplined denial of impulse. As a true revolutionary he could offer no homage to Edmund's goddess and little comfort to John Cage or Charles Reich. There is irony then in the acceptability of his legend to the impulse-releasing, permissive young, for whom figures like Allen Ginsberg and Timothy Leary are the logical heroes.

No doubt some of the young (perhaps bemused with Leary's reported determination to stay high and fight the revolution) conceive of a revolution as a Dionysian activity and therefore are able to imagine a triumphant Guevara as king of an eternal Woodstock. But surely many others have learned from Che, whether or not they can put the message into words, that the honesty of the contemporary world can be bad policy, since by insisting that the person submit himself to experience it ends up by incapacitating him to do anything about the social and political consequences of such submission. In a world in which because of technology the rate of change accelerates frighteningly, so that change itself often seems to be the only constant, Guevara demonstrates an activist's technique for salvation. This is the hero's single-minded and impulse-denying concentration on a high-priority objective that has the effect of drastically reducing the options and thereby slowing down the rate of change. To follow Che, unless one has great powers of self-deception, is to follow what for Cage, Reich, Brown and Fuller is a reactionary leader.

Che's kind of revolution, like Lenin's or Cromwell's or Robespierre's, is a puritanic state of affairs; it assumes a character set with a high degree of specialization and predictability, for instead of submitting honestly to nature in order that the best possible future may be discovered in experience, it aspires to force the future and determine experience. Neither Bacon nor Nietzsche is its philosopher. Morally and philosophically it is absolutist rather than relativist. Despite the comfort and inspiration it may derive from existential thinkers, its temper is authoritarian and essentialist. It may propose a general affluence and liberation of impulse as an ultimate objective, but its living fact, as Orwell suggests in *1984*, is more likely to be planned and spartan scarcity aimed at the concentration and conservation of power and energy and the de-acceleration of the rate of change in the interest of efficient management. Such a revolution would have to oppose the main drift of our romantic and sensate world. The "two, three or many Vietnams" that Che hoped for could hardly be achieved with a policy of honesty—not, at any rate, if it is our impulse-releasing kind.

Character then, as usual, offers to rescue us, but at great price. This is our predicament: on the one hand an honest, open and flexible commitment to experience with its tendency to make change an absolute and therefore to speed up time, but with correlative tendencies either to transcend time and personhood in forms often violent and destructive, or to succumb to the uncomplicated blandishments of the charismatic man of character; on the other hand, an inflexible, aprioristic, value-oriented, time- and experience-structuring organization of personality that so restricts options in the face of the increasing richness of living potential that it generates unbearable tensions and thus plays into the hands of charismatic and too often nihilistic experience heroes. In the end, the human condition and the human person appear to be too complicated for the simplistic policies either of character or honesty with which we are familiar. Each has a disturbing tendency to become the other through trying to exclude too much of the other, just as excessive specialization prepares for an impossible ideal of protean unspecialization in which distinctions vital to civilized life are lost.

This predicament is as old as the Renaissance, however it may appear to us to be peculiar to modern technological culture. Certainly it was recognized by the man who created Iago and Edmund. His continuing power over us has a good deal to do with his capacity to imagine fictions in which characters are tested against the conviction that to survive effectively in situations of adversity one must, in imitation of the playwright himself, be able to combine principled commitment with flexibility. Perhaps for us the comedies are more heuristic than the tragedies in this respect, not only because in the former the paradoxical interrelationship of freedom and the iron ring of unfreedom is dramatized with a clarity impossible in tragedy, but because the organizational success of the play as a whole is more likely to be repeated in particular figures. This is especially true of the heroines. Figures like Portia in *The Merchant of Venice,* Viola in *Twelfth Night* and Rosalind in *As You Like It* manage themselves so successfully and humanely in crisis situations that one wonders why feminine liberation publicists haven't made more of them.

Against such adversaries the mere flexibility of an Iago or the egotistic honesty of an Edmund is simply not enough. These wonderful women model an ideal personality type: they have character, but in them character is sufficiently flexible and adaptable so that they can honor their commitments without ceasing to be their own persons, for in honoring their commitments they honor themselves. In action, therefore, they demonstrate a strategy for the dilemma we know only too well: that in which sudden and drastic change of context makes it difficult to determine whether the best policy is an unwavering constancy to previously accepted principles or a complete and honest abandonment of them as so much inherited claptrap. The bias in contemporary literature against dramatic actions in which it is possible for such characters to make a convincing appearance is itself a clear sign of our bemusement by Edmund's goddess.

Part Two

Deconstruction and Reconstruction Fanaticism in the Eighties

Chapter 6
Call of the Wild

The late Henry Arthur FitzRoy Somerset, tenth Duke of Beaufort, must have given little comfort to English animal lovers. When his death at eighty-three was announced early this year it was revealed that the Duke had by his own estimation spent four thousand days in the saddle pursuing foxes, few of which, one must assume, evaded the pursuit. One must also assume that only the most knowledgeable traditionalist could remember a time when the hunting of animals in England could be represented not only as a necessary cultivation of military virtues but as a morale-raising demonstration of the triumph of human reason and skill over animal instinct. Fox hunters, fortunately, had the special advantage of being engaged with a creature that continued to get a bad press at a time when late in the eighteenth century it was no longer easy to use traditional justifications for other kinds of hunting. As Keith Thomas points out in *Man and the Natural World*, the fox was considered to be a subtle, pilfering foe, a conscious villain and midnight pillager.

Whether the Duke of Beaufort still thought of the fox this way two centuries later is doubtful, but his four

"Call of the Wild" first appeared in *Commentary* (July 1984): 52–55. Reprinted with permission.

thousand days in the saddle are an indication of the lengths to which humans will go to make possible a ceremonial encounter with the wild. Of course, long before that the English had learned how to encounter wild nature in the ceremonials of poetry, painting, and landscaping—though, as Thomas points out, "the taste for the wild and irregular was much more likely to seduce the well-to-do than the poor." One is tempted to say that this has been less true in America where there has always been plenty of wild and irregular nature left over after nurture has done its worst. But these things are relative. We are at least as worried about the survival of the wolf and the grizzly bear as the English once were about the survival of natural landscapes against the encroachment of formal gardens and symmetrically cultivated farm lands. After all, we had to adapt as best we could to the announcement by the Superintendent of the Census that as of 1890 we could no longer think of a frontier line separating the settled from the unsettled West—an announcement that raised the disturbing possibility that a wilderness experience crucial to our national well-being was about to end.

For Americans the childhood classic on the value of the wilderness experience was once Jack London's *The Call of the Wild*. In this 1903 novel the dog Buck, a thoroughly domesticated mix of Scotch Shepherd and Saint Bernard, is kidnapped from his California home and taken to the Klondike, where in the service of his master, John Thornton, he becomes a super sledge dog. Intermittently Buck experiences the call of the wild, and eventually, after the murder of his master by Indians, he answers the call and becomes the leader of a wolf pack, "his great throat a-bellow as he sings a song of the younger world." It is obvious to an adult reader, if not to a perceptive youngster, that Buck is no more a mere dog than Melville's Moby Dick is a mere whale or Faulkner's Old Ben a mere bear. He is, in fact, a quite sensitive human being who, one might say, disguises himself as a dog in order to liberate his Nietzschean potential from emasculating domesticity.

But one must say more than that. *The Call of the Wild* was ultimately chosen by the Boy Scouts of America for Every Boy's Library as one of those stories "in which the heroes have the characteristics boys so much admire— unquenchable courage, immense resourcefulness, absolute fidelity, conspicuous greatness." Buck, of course, has all these virtues, and through the alchemy of youthful imagination he no doubt comes across as a champion worthy of emulation, not as a subversive advocate of a reversion to primitive ways. London's novel, like Edgar Rice Burroughs's Tarzan books, belongs with the fictions of childhood and adolescence that put us in touch with that *mysterium tremendum* that exists beyond the threshold of conscious civilized life. One may hope that in due time its readers will move on to Conrad's *The Heart of Darkness* or Golding's *Lord of the Flies* and learn that the call of the wild can be a sinister siren call against which some hearers have very limited powers of resistance—perhaps even learn that the stories of Buck and Tarzan are adult fantasies of the utopianly liberated id.

Whatever one reads, however, the call of the wild, seductively varied as it is, is part of the mood music of our culture. London's canine hero is having ahead of time, for instance, the experience we see the enraptured German Nazis having in Leni Riefenstahl's 1934 documentary film *Triumph of the Will* or the no less enraptured young American Aquarians having in the documentary film of the 1969 Woodstock festival. More interestingly for the literary adult, Buck anticipates the experience of Connie Chatterley with the gamekeeper, Mellors, in D.H. Lawrence's *Lady Chatterley's Lover*. As the wilderness claims him for its own, Buck's experiences are analogically sexual (properly enough, since he will in time become the progenitor of a new super-breed of timber wolves): "Life streamed through him in splendid flood, glad and rampant, until it seemed that it would burst him asunder in sheer ecstasy and pour forth generously over the world." This is close to Connie's experience with Mellors in the Chatterley woods, especially in the section where in the wilderness of sex the shame bred by civilization is burned out of her and she is saved.

Connie anticipates O in Pauline Reage's *Story of O*, who also has the shame burned out of her in the process of demonstrating the paradox of self-transcending happiness in erotic slavery. Buck demonstrates this paradox as well when, his divided, civilized consciousness having been burned out of him, the wild possesses him as utterly as a master possesses a slave. Lawrence did not especially like dogs, but it is likely that he would have seen here an anticipation of his own conviction that our divided culture tempts us to define sexual experience as a culturally impeded effort to be overwhelmed by a wilderness force. One implication is that the truest freedom is beyond all consciousness of being free, which is the way it is with Tarzan in his jungle state, whether in Burroughs's version or in Hugh Hudson's new film *Greystoke: The Legend of Tarzan, Lord of the Apes*. This being the case, it is probably as safe to predict that some people will always be discovering Sade as a liberator from the tormenting false consciousness of civilization as it is to predict that other people will always be content to settle for fox hunting. Indeed, when communities attempt to ban or restrict pornography or prostitution, the problem often is not simply that other freedoms are involved but the opposition put up by the half-articulated conviction that the impersonal, or "pure," sex of pornography and prostitution is a manifestation of wilderness that merits the same conserving attention we give to wolves and grizzly bears. Something like this appears to have been on the mind of the late Jean Paulhan, member of the French Academy and editor of the *Nouvelle Revue Française*, when he wrote his preface to Reage's novel—along the way mak-

ing the point that women "never cease obeying their nature, the call of their blood, that everything in them,
even their minds, is sex."

Lawrence's Mellors, of course, is an imaginary figure
even though when he holds forth on the evils of civilization he sounds remarkably like his creator. His gene-
alogy takes us back to the medieval forest and another
legendary figure who is the subject of Richard Bernheimer's *Wild Men in the Middle Ages*. Bernheimer defines the urge behind this figure as "the need to give
external expression and a symbolically valid form to
the impulses of reckless physical self-assertion which
are hidden in all of us, but are normally kept under
control." The wild man lives shamelessly in the forest
like an animal for one of a variety of reasons, including unrequited love; he goes on all fours and has beast-
like long hair; his powers of speech are limited if not
nonexistent; he cannot control his passions and is excessively combative. Ultimately, the attitudes toward
him reflect the range of possible attitudes toward the
wild, the primitive, the natural, so that at one end of the
scale he is barely above the beasts while at the other he
is the eighteenth century's noble savage. In the beginning his opposite is the civilized courtly knight who is
often represented in tapestry and woodcut rescuing his
lady from the lusts of the wild man. A "major turning
point in the history of European civilization," writes
Bernheimer, occurs when "the wild man is sometimes
allowed to win in works of art describing the conflict."
At this point European society is getting ready for the
reversal in which the life of the wild man becomes the
ideal against which civilization is measured. In due
time it will be society that one has to be afraid of—that
"malevolent, partly insane beast," as Mellors the latter-
day wild man puts it.

There is an understandable tendency to take the wild
man out of the story world and locate him as a real

figure in the real wild, whether as a child raised by wolves like the famous wild boy of Aveyron, or by apes like Tarzan, or as a menacing man-beast like the Abominable Snowman of the Himalayas and the American Bigfoot, also known as Sasquatch. Hard information about such creatures is hard to come by since, like the Loch Ness monster, they live in fastnesses into which neither Boy Scouts nor fox hunters can penetrate, but they seem to lack utterly the virtues of Tarzan or Buck. Their escapades are grist for the coarse mills of the tabloids. The "Weekly World News" has recently reported that a seven-foot-tall monster with long reddish brown hair had run off with a woman who, her husband had reason to believe, was quite happy to be run off with. A bit later the same publication reported the appearance in China of hairy supermen, stronger than normal humans and more resistant to disease—which makes them sound like those possessors of pure Nordic blood who, Heinrich Himmler believed, could be found in the mountains of Tibet. An Associated Press release early this year refers to a Chinese Wild Man Research Institute that is looking into reports of gargantuan hairy creatures at large in the forests of Hubei province. Last summer it was reported from Peking that there were wild and very hairy women, one of whom had raped a peasant, living on the lower slopes of Mount Everest. The indications are that all such creatures are as shameless as Shakespeare's Caliban and as little bothered by the crippling restrictions of Christianity as the encyclopedist Denis Diderot imagined the Tahitians to be when, late in the eighteenth century, they came to his attention by way of the reports of the French explorer Antoine de Bougainville.

There is nothing formally religious in the call of the wild as it comes from London's dog or Lawrence's gamekeeper; nevertheless, it has always been easy for young readers of London's novel, to say nothing of older readers of Faulkner's *The Bear*, to sense that they are in a world of supernal realities. In this at least they have some affinity with Rousseau, Wordsworth, and Emerson. The romantic encounter with nature generally entailed the discovery that organized religion is a way of protecting people from the unmediated force of spirit. The call of the wild is thus an inciter of the urge to merge—to achieve, like Reage's O, a state of possession that is symbiotic rather than metaphoric.

To one who takes the call seriously it is always a summons to quit the realm of the civilized, divided consciousness and come home, as Tarzan does at the end of *Greystoke*. However, if one cannot literally come home to the wild one can at least have the moral equivalent of a return. Drugs, orgies, states of passionate and shameless abandon are such equivalents, and for some people they are more satisfactory than those calculated sorties into primitive areas made safely possible by sophisticated survival gear and an assortment of freeze-dried foods. Authentic encounterers of the wild must, like passion lovers, be willing to risk all, even rape by hairy wild women. It is to be expected that such people will have little sympathy for fox hunters, who conserve foxes not out of any genuine affection for the wild but for the pleasure of being able to assault it with safety.

The Greek Cynics were among the earliest of those who demonstrated a moral equivalent of being at home in the wild. They were as convinced as Rousseau or Lawrence's Mellors that civilization was an unnatural and generally bad state of affairs. For Diogenes of Sinope, says the late philosopher George Boas, "the natural was that which he could not discard and still live." Thus he and his followers had no alternative but to imitate the practice of animals in diet, sexual habits, scorn of privacy, and in the whole economy of living. However, this philosophy was lived out in full view of civilization, not out in the wilderness for an uncomprehending audience of wolves and foxes who needed no cynical schooling, since the idea was to dramatize the necessity of the burning out of shame. And where there is shame, as Mellors and Diogenes know, human beings are dangerously tame. The present miserable state of affairs will be over, Mellors says ironically to Connie, "When the last real man is killed, and they're *all* tame: white, black, yellow, all colors of tame ones: then they'll *all* be insane." The virginal Thoreau says in *Walden* that "he is blessed who is assured that the animal is dying out of him day by day, and the divine being established," but he is nevertheless in the Cynic tradition, his monastic cabin in the woods being the moral and critical equivalent of the wine jar in which Diogenes was supposed to live—and in which the latter too strove "to live so sturdily and Spartan-like as to put to rout all that was not life."

The aim of the Cynics was to break down the barrier between the wild and the civilized by reducing the latter to the former. They were meat-eaters, but like the animals they imitated they ate their meat raw. London's superdog was a meat-eater: "A carnivorous animal, living on a straight meat diet, he was in full flower, at the high tide of his life, overspilling with vigor and vitality." Burroughs's Tarzan "more than the apes, craved and needed flesh," ate all he could get, and developed into a "wondrous combination of enormous strength with suppleness and speed." Colin W. Turnbull tells us in *The Mountain People* that the brutish and mean-spirited Iks of Uganda had been happy and sociable people when they were hunters and meat-eaters. According to the Western historian Francis Haines, the Plains Indians, who were often admired by white men for their vigor and vitality, could eat ten pounds of buffalo meat per day per person when it was available. The English, says Keith Thomas, tended not to eat their pets and looked down on the wild Irish because they ate horses, but otherwise they were great meat-eaters, and in the eighteenth century "were notorious for serving their beef underdone"—impelled, apparently, not by an ingrained cynicism but by the "long-established habit of praising red meat because it supposedly made men virile and courageous." It is hard to imagine a fox hunter who is not a meat-eater, though there is no record of a fox hunter eating the fox: it is cut up and fed to the dogs, possibly in the interest of making them virile and courageous. Even Thoreau, that part-time wild man, admitted that his impulse to higher spiritual life was counterbalanced by a rank and savage instinct that once tempted him to seize and devour a woodchuck raw.

Vegetarians, on the other hand, believe that to eat animals, domesticated or not, is to violate a bond that unites humans with their creaturely relatives and guarantees a continuity between the wild and the civilized. Not for them Saint Paul's discouraging remark to the Romans: "One man will have faith enough to eat all kinds of food, while a weaker man eats only vegetables." Anthropologists now may disagree about the dietary practices of the first humans, but early primitivist thought, as Boas points out, tended to favor vegetarianism. For Empedocles, vegetarianism was linked with the pacifism of the Golden Age; the poet Aratus believed that men did not forge swords and eat meat until the Bronze Age; Pythagoras believed that people in the Golden Age lived on fruit, berries, milk, and wild honey; the Roman satirist Juvenal thought that virtuous people could get along on acorns, though it is doubtful if he was himself that virtuous. The early Christian theologian Tertullian, whose asceticism suggests Diogenes in one direction and Thoreau in the other, believed that there was no meat-eating before the deluge, and early Christian thinkers generally agreed with Milton that there was no meat-eating in Paradise. In seventeenth- and eighteenth-century England, Thomas points out, there was a growing tendency to think of meat-eating as un-natural and a cause not only of bad breath but of intemperance and aggressiveness in human conduct.

In our own time the ethical argument against meat-eating has been advanced by the Australian philosopher Peter Singer in *Animal Liberation* and by the American philosopher Tom Regan in *The Case for Animal Rights*. From such writers, as might be expected, we get a highly principled vegetarianism, but this is no less the case with such notables as Percy Bysshe Shelley, George Bernard Shaw, and Adolf Hitler, though the latter two depended at times on injections derived from the entrails of animals. In fact, Hitler, like Wagner whose music he so admired and Shelley whose poetry he seems not to have been aware of, saw a connection between meat-eating and the decay of civilization. Thoreau was an off-and-on vegetarian, not liking to eat "our kindred animal." Even Lawrence was persuaded briefly but to no good effect to try an arsenic-vegetarian cure. What Himmler's Nordic supermen ate in the Tibetan mountains is anybody's guess, but at least they were safe from the civilized depredations of the Beaufort hunt.

Vegetarians, being an alienated and embattled minority in what many of them consider a cannibalistic environment, tend to agree with cynics ancient and modern that civilization as we know it is a deplorable, power-abusing state of affairs. This was pretty much the opinion of the meat-eating Jack London, whose *Call of the Wild* belongs as much with the literature of utopia as does the vegetarian Shelley's *Prometheus Unbound*. Indeed, it is the combination of cynicism and utopianism that makes it so hard for many of us (as it is hard for Tarzan at the end of *Greystoke*) to decide in which direction we should go to get home at last. Perhaps this is why meat-eaters and vegetarians alike have been so prone to envisage home as an island—an island such as Diderot and his Enlightenment contemporaries imagined Tahiti to be, or as Margaret Mead much later imagined Samoa to be. On such an island it would be possible to sing a song of a younger, prelapsarian world, for nature would be uncorrupted by nurture and wild men and wild women would live in loving harmony with the unpolluted environment. In such a place, of course, fox hunting was no more likely to be permitted than in More's Utopia. Countless readers have found in Thoreau's *Walden* the moral equivalent of such an experience. For a long time Lawrence had an "island idea," his "Rananim," a place to which about twenty souls could escape "from this world of war and squalor" and find "some real decency," but by the time he came to write *Chatterley* he seems to have given up on the idea.

In the end, whether they are vegetarians or meat-eaters, those who are most sensitive to the call of the wild are most likely to respond to its promise of a symbiotic unity that will remove forever the burden of civilization with its dividedness, its sense of shame, and its confinement to the troubling ambiguities of metaphor. Perhaps civilization can be said to begin at the point where the difference between symbiotic and metaphoric states of unity can be recognized, for in the latter unity-in-diversity becomes possible along with privacy, self-conscious reflection, a sense of shame, and the discovery that we once may have been wild.

Our knowledge of the wild is of necessity limited since we must approach it, as Margaret Mead approached the primitive culture of Samoa, with our heads full of the structures of civilization—often long before we have learned that the critical instruments we use distort what we are measuring, if indeed they do not create it in response to our troubled, civilized need. One of the most effective instruments so far devised by civilization to define the wild is the tall tale, the kind of hyperbolic fiction employed in nineteenth-century America to define with a disclaiming humor the nature of frontier life. What we know about Diogenes, for instance, is a collection of grimly humorous tall tales, the most popular being the one that represents him going about with a lantern in broad daylight looking for an honest man— which if it tells us little about the historical Diogenes tells a great deal about those who value the story. *Tarzan of the Apes* and *The Call of the Wild* are tall tales told by writers who, if they have little of the humor that characterizes stories about frontier heroes like Davy Crockett and Mike Fink, have just as sure a sense of the fabulous. Burroughs admitted that the life of his Tarzan was wildly improbable, and there is good reason to believe that London knew he was telling his readers the kind of fairy story they (and he) liked to believe. Bernheimer's wild men and wild women are figures in humorless tall tales who need to be understood in relation to the extravagance and idealization that marks classical and medieval pastoral. And what is *Chatterley* if not the most humorless of tall tales?

The latter, in fact, was too tall a tale for Sylvia Beach, who said of it (after successfully resisting attempts to have her Shakespeare and Co. republish it in Paris) that it was all preaching. There is, God knows, preaching enough in the extravagant fictions that never seem to lose their capacity to thrill us (indeed, give some of us the only religious experiences we ever have) with their unfavorable comparisons between our own environment and nature in the raw, whatever that may be. Such fictions, of course, are more likely to entertain than to inspire corrective action, since the extremity of the terms in which they are conceived tends to discourage it. Once the story is over, all roads from Diogenes' wine jar and Tarzan's jungle re-doubt promise only more places where the meat is raw and the plumbing nonexistent. Meanwhile, their tall tales are means we use to keep from learning that our problem is not so much that civilization lusts against the wild as that the wild in us lusts against civilization. Perhaps fox hunting serves the same purpose.

Chapter 7
Cowboy

I once saw in the southeastern corner of the Villa Borghese in Rome an abbreviated version of an American amusement park. It had bumper cars, spaceships, and live Shetland ponies whose dung no one had bothered to collect. There was also a coin-operated mechanical horse. I watched it galloping in place as its small and excited rider pulled a toy gun from his holster and fired at his imaginary adversary—perhaps that Bulgarian desperado who a few days before had shot the pope. It occurred to me that in time he might become one of those motorcycle cowboys—urban rustlers, actually—who dart in close to the crowded Roman sidewalks and pick off women's shoulder bags. In any event, he took me halfway around the world to my own cowboy country in a way that nothing else in Rome did, not even the great equestrian statue in the Piazza del Campidoglio that represents a bareheaded Marcus Aurelius who, had he worn a sombrero, might have ridden with John Wayne in *Red River*.

No one is as enthralled with the legend of the cowboy as a child is. The young Roman was lucky; unlike so many American youngsters, he would not have to grow up to discover the discrepancy between the legend and the reality. I was spared that painful discovery by be-

"Cowboy" first appeared in *The American Scholar* (Summer 1987): 400–06. Reprinted with permission.

coming a part-time cowboy myself. At the age of ten, I spent a good deal of the summer on horseback carrying water to harvesters and driving cows in from pasture. For a dozen years thereafter, I spent the summers on the wheat and cattle ranches of southeastern Washington doing all those things that cowboys do, and more besides. Between summers I was back in the city doing such things as city people do. As a result I grew up with a perspective on city and country that was different from that of most of my contemporaries. In fact, I got to be rather smug about my ability to see past the stereotypical distortions that city and country took to be the truth about one another.

John R. Erickson makes it clear in his good book *The Modern Cowboy* that all cowboys are part-time cowboys—that is, they don't spend all their time superintending cattle on the wide open spaces where the coyotes howl and the wind blows free. They have to build and repair fences, clean the stables, slop the pigs, milk the cows, get in the hay, repair machinery, on occasion even perform such soft chores as feeding the chickens, gathering the eggs, and working in the vegetable garden. On the wheat and cattle ranches where I worked, I might spend many hours escorting cattle in and out of the arid summer pastures of the Snake River canyons, counting the herd, searching for strays, checking on the condition of water holes, and doing my bit with the branding team, but I spent many more hours doing the things that wheat farmers did when they still depended largely on horse power.

Between William S. Hart's *Hell's Hinges* (1916) and Lawrence Kasden's *Silverado* (1985), the Western movie is peopled mainly by cowboy types, but the viewer sees relatively little real cowboy life. In the scores of Westerns I have seen, no cowboy ever milks a cow, fixes a fence, hauls hay, or pitches manure out of a barn. Such pedestrian activities would be as inappropriate for the movie cowboy as domestic chores would have been for Homer's Achilles. To be interesting to the movies, the cowboy has to exist at the pitch of myth, which means that to define himself he has to get quickly into the right kind of trouble. The housekeeping chores that consumed so much of the real cowboy's life promised only the kind of trouble you need for comedy or farce, of which there is very little in the Western. From the Western you can learn how to foil rustlers, crooked bankers, greedy cattle barons, and rampaging Indians, or how to outdraw a gunslinger at high noon or face down a braggart in a saloon (meanwhile looking as hypnotically steely-eyed as Bill Hart does in *The Desert Man*), but not how to be a cowboy. For that you need a book such as Erickson's.

Of course, even real cowboys, like real policemen, real soldiers, real pro-football stars, or even real college professors, need to see themselves in legendary terms: it is a way of incorporating the inevitable humdrum of life into a significant pattern. Leslie Fiedler, being at the time a transplanted Easterner, though not even a part-time cowboy, wrote a famous essay entitled "Montana; or the End of Jean-Jacques Rousseau," in which he notes the paradox of real cowboys standing in line to see a Roy Rogers movie, apparently not bothered by the gap between reality and myth. By the time I read Fiedler's essay, I had become a cowboy emeritus, but I found those Roy Rogers fans easy to understand, albeit I much preferred Tom Mix and Hoot Gibson. Once I had become a real cowboy and prided myself on knowing the reality behind the myth, I became an avid fan of Western movies. I had no more trouble suspending my disbelief than do those wrestling fans about whom Roland Barthes writes brilliantly in *Mythologies*. The movies even glamorized the humdrum of my summertime world. The bank, the pool parlor (once a saloon), and the weather-beaten two-story hotel in my small ranch town all connoted the world of the Western movie, though nobody had ever robbed the bank, few people stayed in the hotel, and in the pool hall the lounging ranch hands drank beer or cola instead of whisky and played rummy, not poker. So, in the rock-ribbed desolate canyons, there was always the romantic possibility of rustlers, even though the likely thing was that the steers I was missing could be found a few miles away in a neighbor's pasture where the grass was greener.

No doubt there were fewer six-shooters in the real West than the movies have led us to believe. My grandfather, who after having been discharged from General Sherman's army came to the West in the days when it was truly wild and there were as yet no mythical cowboys, wore his gun only when he went into town, and he lived into his nineties without having fired it at anyone. However, when Leslie Fiedler came West in the early 1940s, the movies had made the gun standard equipment, and the owner usually kept it beside him even when he went to bed. Robert Warshow, in one of the best things ever written about the Western movie, wrote that the latter's "values are in the image of a single man who wears a gun on his thigh." I find it easy to understand why real-life gunless cowboys, to say nothing of Roman youngsters, continue to find irresistible this image of a gun-supported autonomy. Nevertheless, I never wore a gun when I rode into the canyons alone. Sometimes when I was with a friend, we did take along a rifle, hoping to shoot a coyote and share the five-dollar bounty, but we always missed.

The only man I knew who routinely packed a gun was the town marshal, a rangy Gary Cooper type who once in a drunken fantasy emptied his six-shooter into the woodwork beneath the counter of the town's only short-order restaurant. He was overpowered and locked up in his own jail overnight, certainly a departure from all familiar Western scenarios. Indeed, I was not to experience some sense of the swaggering security that gun toting gives one until, late in World War II in the jungles of British Guiana, I was required periodically to wear my forty-five pistol. Even then my sense of security was undercut by the knowledge that, like most Air Corps officers, I had never been able to qualify with the weapon.

If, as some credulous souls believed, the jungles were crawling with voodoo-worshiping cannibals and German spies who had been shipped up the Demerara River by submarine, they would have been in no more danger from me than the Snake River coyotes had been.

Robert Warshow, of course, in his essay is talking about the Westerner, and not all Westerners were or are cowboys, whether in or out of the movies, and as Henry Nash Smith reminds us in *Virgin Land*, until late in the nineteenth century, *cowboy* was likely to designate an armed, hell-raising desperado who would not have hesitated to shoot a pope if one had been available. In the movies, however, there is always the implication that any Westerner can function as a cowboy if he does not have more important things to do, which he generally does. In any event, insofar as the Westerner was a cowboy, the horse was as important to him as the gun, in fact as well as in image. Certainly no mode of conveyance ever gave a man such a sense of being comfortably and masterfully at ease in his environment as the horse did. To view the world from a horse's back when you are young is to view it from an Olympian height; a lone horseman coming into view at a mesa's rim is like the appearance of a god; and, as for a spine-tingling sense of speed, nothing compares with the pursuit of a steer while on a horse at full gallop. When, years later, through the fortunes of war I became a troop commander for the Air Transport Command and had my own jeep and driver, I experienced nothing like the mounted cowboy's sense of total command.

To understand this is to understand why horses in Western movies—Tom Mix's Tony, Gene Autry's Champion, Roy Rogers's Trigger, the Lone Ranger's Silver, Ken Maynard's Tarzan—could be as famous in their own right as the horses of Homer's superstars. Only the rustlers and the robbers of banks and stagecoaches had anonymous, and usually uncurried, horses. Even in movies where the cowboy hero wins the girl and is obviously on the verge of becoming a husband, you are more likely to remember the horse's name than the girl's. This means that such movies, unlike Shakespeare's romantic comedies, are generally only half-hearted celebrations of marriage; at heart they are less about the winning and civilizing of the West, which means making it safe for women and children, than about keeping it as a preserve for the unfettered male and his noble steed.

On the ranches where I worked, not only the noble steeds but all horses that were full-fledged members of the work force had names. This was a practical necessity, of course, but it was also an expression of the creaturely closeness between man and animal that is one of the many good things about ranch life. The intimacy, however, never extended to steers and cows, perhaps out of a sense that to name what is destined to be eaten is to flirt with cannibalism. This suggests that, if the Australian philosopher Peter Singer and his fellow vegetarians want to convert the rest of us, they might begin by agitating for a law that requires all edible animals to be named at birth. Ranch children are good models here; they name their pet pigs, calves, rabbits, and ducks, and they are notoriously reluctant to have their pets butchered.

My first horse was a geriatric blue mare named Bess who in crisis circumstances could be goaded into a belly-rumbling trot. The horse I rode in my last cowboy years was named Colonel, a neurotic eleven-hundred-pounder (the boss guessed he was part Hambletonian) who could outrun the fastest steer but could be spooked by a suddenly emerging ground squirrel or the mildest dog. His previous owner, who had ridden into the canyons to check his herd, was found dead there—of a heart attack, they said, but I suspected that Colonel, making one of his unpredictable changes of direction, had pitched him onto the rocks. Once when we were pursuing a steer pell-mell along one of the narrow cattle trails that terrace the shaggy sides of the breaks, Colonel detected a rattlesnake in the bush ahead of us. He was instantly airborne, and we landed without missing a stride ten feet below on the next trail. If he had thrown me to my death down that precipice he would not have mourned for me, as Achilles' immortal horses mourned for the slain Patroclus, but I loved him nevertheless and would no more have eaten him than Tom Mix would have eaten Tony.

The dismal truth was that my Colonel, unlike Tom Mix's Tony, had no character, and character was what the Western hero, on or off his horse, had in abundance. The movies in which he appears might be ambivalent about the value of civilizing the wilderness, but his values otherwise are traditional enough, and in their service he transcends himself, as heroes should. He has the stalwart individualism that Crèvecoeur and Emerson admired in the American farmer, even if the life of a farmer would be far too dull for him. Virginia Mayo, looking wonderful in frontier garb, sings in *The Big Land* that "she leaned on a man who bent like a blade of grass," defining by contrast the proper Western man who ultimately wins her. The latter, not unexpectedly, turns out to be Alan Ladd, who is anything but Robert J. Lifton's Protean Man.[13] Protean Man bends like a blade of grass on principle lest he be uptightly boxed in by a value system that wants to mortgage him to the past. In the Western, even the rustlers and the bank robbers, the men with the black hats and the scruffy horses, are boxed in, doing anything for a buck, on principle, with their own kind of heroic determination, which is not exactly what Lifton had in mind when he coined the phrase in the late 1960s.

As a matter of fact, a great deal of the attraction of the Western hero derives from the fact that he is mortgaged to the past. He might live on fast horses in a milieu of violent action, but culturally he lives in a slow world and his character tends to keep it slow. This was especially noticeable to a city boy returning annually from the speedy city, even though few real cowboys had character the way Bill Hart or Tom Mix had it. In time I came to suspect, however, that ranch people generally did not really have more character than city people, they simply had fewer opportunities to corrupt whatever character they had—which may be a rather negative way of conceding that Thomas Jefferson's agrarian bias had more behind it than wishful thinking.

In any event, the paradoxical combination of fast and slow in the cowboy's world may help to explain the lack of interest in politics I have noted among real and mythical cowboys. Both share the American's suspicion that politicians are out to change things, usually in their own interests, and that they threaten to increase the tempo of life in areas that, if anything, need to be slowed down. Once in the city I was invited to a party that turned out to have been organized by young communists. They were humorlessly and passionately in favor of very rapid changes, and the cowboy in me was immediately suspicious of them. Being at the time a month away from my return to the ranch, I could only wonder why anyone could want to be a communist and huddle together with others he called comrades if he could be a cowboy who prided himself on his ability to go it alone. Certainly both mythical and real cowboys had their share of that independence of spirit that in the thirties and forties made it so hard for some American writers to be the docile, true-believing Stalinists that they tried hard to be. It might not be too much to say that those who ultimately lost the faith were saved because they were cowboys at heart, mortgaged to a past that had taught them to be suspicious of all promises of a gloriously gregarious final roundup.

No doubt the cowboy's lack of interest in politics is connected with his famous taciturnity. In Emerson's essay on farming, in which you can find an early celebration of many of the virtues of the Western hero, he remarks, "Cities force growth and make men talkative and entertaining, but they make them artificial." Loquacity and politics go together, which is why, in the Western, politics is usually either missing or identified as one of the ways the glib city people waste their time and mess up the country. Politicians are fast talkers, which means that politics is fundamentally a shell game—a cowboy bias widely shared by city people. You cannot imagine Bill Hart, Buck Jones, or Hopalong Cassidy joining the Communist party, but neither can you imagine them campaigning for anybody. The act would violate their implied laissez-faire conservatism with its Rambo-like assumption that what the country needs is not politics but virtue—a dangerous assumption for a democracy in which it is so likely that, when the political talking stops, the rustlers begin to take over.

Of course, the Western hero, cowboy or not, turns out in the end to be a politician in his own fashion: he simply uses his six-shooter to settle problems about the just use and distribution of power, which, if they are not settled quickly, will soon overwhelm his ability to cope with them and thus cast him adrift into the culturally fast world that he abhors. This is also the politics of the not especially talkative rustlers, those greedy traditionalists who would very much prefer that the world remain as it is. But step outside the charmed circle of the Western, and this becomes simply the politics of the preventive first strike, which we have learned to see as one of the means that democracy uses to disguise its fear of itself as a virtue.

I learned early that ranch folk are not as taciturn as the movies or Emerson would lead one to believe—possibly because they had to rely less on that conversation stopper, the six-shooter. The town marshal could be noncommittal enough, but when I knew him better, I realized that he had little to say because there wasn't much on his mind. Certainly there were no political implications one way or another in his iron-jawed taciturnity: he had not been elected to his position but appointed, probably because he looked like a marshal to begin with and could supply a gun. Otherwise, ranch folk could be loquacious enough, however suspicious they might be of fast-talking city slickers. Sometimes I rode Colonel into town by moonlight just to listen to the garrulous old-timers, as they lounged outside the short-order restaurant, reminisce about the heroic olden times.

The fabled taciturnity of the Western hero and allied pastoral types in our culture appeals to a widespread conviction that actions speak louder than words, are more honest than words, and may very well be grounded on positions of philosophic integrity that a Socrates would quickly obfuscate with his verbosity. Thus it is easy for poets and storytellers, including moviemakers, to imagine that a cowboy, blessed with great stretches of time when he is alone with nature, cannot avoid dwelling on the eternal verities. This is the message one reads on Bill Hart's wonderful face, and the repetitions of it on subsequent if often lesser faces is one reason why Leslie Fiedler saw real cowboys standing in line to see Roy Rogers. As for myself, I liked the aloneness of ranch life but had little traffic with the eternal verities. Whether I was milking a fractious cow, finishing the spring plowing behind a not too reliable nine-horse team, or searching the treacherous canyons for missing steers, I had to keep my mind on the business at hand. The eternal verities I put on hold until I was back in college, where I was encouraged to read pastoralizers like Wordsworth and Rousseau, who probably would have liked Bill Hart.

A part-time cowboy was bound to be aware of the sartorial difference between himself and movie cowboys. I did not look even remotely like Roy Rogers or Tom Mix, or that commercialized Westerner, the Marlboro Man, who, give him his manly due, is about as concerned with the surgeon general's warning as Buck Rogers would have been. I wore waist-length denim overalls, not jeans (Calvin Klein and Ralph Lauren were a long way in the future), an undecorated blue cotton shirt, ten-inch boots (cowboy boots were too expensive and not very practical once I was afoot), a red bandanna that could be pulled over my nose when the dust was flying, and a wide-brimmed straw hat (the Marlboro Man would have been ashamed to wear it, but he did not have to endure the summer's heat).

I never wore the chaps that hung moldering in the barn (they were too hot in the summer) nor spurs (one touch of them would have sent Colonel into orbit). My belt and buckle lacked tooling and logo and simply held up my pants. Elaborate buckles, preferably engraved from models in the Cowboy Hall of Fame, are now de rigueur with Western buffs; the Gene Autry buckle even has the great man's signature on the back, and no doubt costs a good deal more than my entire outfit did. Sometimes I carried a lasso coiled on the saddle horn, but it was mainly decoration; I was about as accurate with it, in spite of sporadic practice on fence posts, as I would later be with the army forty-five pistol. It pleases me to learn now that, dressing without folderol, I dressed very much the way Erickson describes the modern cowboy—except that the latter is much more belt-and-buckle-conscious than I or most of my contemporaries could afford to be. When, during World War II, I saw *Oklahoma!* in New York, I saw my kind of cowboy clothes on stage, as I did thirty-five years later when I saw the splendid revival of the musical in London. The continuity was comforting: I was still in fashion.

To judge from his current advertisements, the millionaire designer Ralph Lauren appears to side with me rather than the Marlboro Man; his dungarees "are crafted in the spirit of an era when quality and durability were more important than fashion." They even feature "an authentic button fly," which identifies them with the world of Bill Hart in which zippered trousers would have been a sure sign of the effete Easterner. Lauren, I note in a recent issue of the fashion tabloid *W*, has himself become a part-time cowboy, having purchased a ten-thousand-acre cattle ranch in southern Colorado, where he spends as much time as he can, far from the plastic East where a man can lose his soul. He rides over his land on an expensive Appaloosa (in the Great Depression my unpedigreed Colonel cost less than a hundred dollars) and raises cattle without the chemicals or hormones that encourage dangerous accumulations of cholesterol in human eaters. He works the roundup with his crew, but I wonder if he has ever spent a dusty summer's day holding down fledgling bulls so they could be branded and turned into steers, or if he has committed himself morning and evening to the milking of a range cow that had delivered her first calf and was still wild as a mountain lion.

I detect in Lauren—pictured in a voguishly faded denim jacket with casually peeled-back cuffs, an open-neck plaid shirt, and a handsomely weather-beaten sombrero—not so much the real cowboy unself-consciously attired for the day's work as the city slicker trying hard not to appear like one. He displays, in fact, all the signs of the covert dandy who knows just how far he can go before he becomes the cynosure that the overt dandy is. He would not be caught dead looking like those flamboyantly attired artificial Westerners I once saw sitting on the top rail of a fence as that noblest of steeds, the Great Northern's Empire Builder, rolled into Montana's Glacier Park. I observed them with a priggish scorn that animated the newspaper feature I later wrote about them. Had they any idea how red in tooth and claw their cultish West could be? Had they ever seen a panicked horse pull its foot off to get free from barbed wire, or come up to a water hole at the head of a ravine to find beside it what the coyotes had left of a missing calf?

In Erickson's *Modern Cowboy*, the dandy impulse appears to be confined to belt and buckle, but it comes full flower in proportion as the cowboy becomes an entertainer, whether in the gaudy splendor of Buffalo Bill or the off-duty rodeo performer. Designers catering to the dandy impulse have been exploiting the cowboy for a long time but never so vigorously as now. In a recent issue of *Elle*, the Western motif is everywhere, most notably in a nine-page feature that models "cowboy chic" in its various guises. This is no less true of men's magazines such as *Esquire* and *GQ*. Dude ranches, with or without hot tubs and happy hours, never had it so good; and on Sunday morning television, old Western movies are as hard to avoid in my part of the world as Bible-beating evangelists.

Everybody, apparently, wants to be a part-time cowboy. Perhaps we suffer from the fear that if we let the cowboy go completely out of our lives we not only will lose contact with an important source of our national integrity but will have to face up to the technological complexity of our plastic and zippered world and get back to worrying about Star Wars and OPEC. Or, to put it more aesthetically, perhaps cowboy chic, like punk chic or safari chic, is an expression of the belief that self-identification and survival are ultimately a matter of style—and when in this need the ego becomes sufficiently inflamed, we have that hero of style, the dandy. Smart people like Ralph Lauren know this and get rich as they prove over and over again that the superintendent of the census was wrong when he declared in 1890 that the American frontier was closed.

Such speculations were far in the future as I spent my last days on horseback. The boss had been injured, and I found myself in charge of the last stationary threshing outfit in my part of the West, where combine harvesters had become as common as cheat grass. I rose at four in the morning, saddled Colonel, and rode out along the rim of the canyons while the dawn came up Homerically rosy-fingered. I could pick out cattle halfway down in the breaks and, far below them, the silver beaches along the river where the sand ran through one's fingers like sugar. At the outfit, I tied Colonel to the trap wagon, and for fifteen hours did all the things necessary to keep the wheat coming out of one spout and straw out of another—things that had no place in even the most pedestrian Western movie. At eight in the evening, after the crew had gone back to the ranch for supper, Colonel and I returned along the rim of the canyons as they filled up with night. The previous summer we had spent an afternoon down there looking for a valuable young bull that had gone roving, the way young bulls will. We found him at sundown, drove him all night, and locked him into the corral in the rosy-fingered dawn. I slept two hours and rose to spend the day with the branding team.

Colonel was fourteen that last summer, late middle age for a horse. He was losing the edge of his speed, and the ground squirrels no longer spooked him—sure signs that his cowboy days were coming to an end. When the harvest was over, he went his way and I mine. I thought no more about him until, returning from Europe many summers later, a change in routing brought me over my wild, rock-tumbled canyons. As I watched them from twenty thousand feet, I thought of that pregnant moment in the Western movie when a panoramic shot of the endlessly wonderful country is prologue to the appearance of that man of destiny, the lone and urgent rider. I felt then as if I had been the last cowboy.

Chapter 8

Untested Innovations

In Dr. Joyce Brothers's recent book, *How to Get Whatever You Want Out of Life*, there is good news: "Love, power, riches, success, a good marriage, exciting sex, fulfillment are not impossible dreams. They can be yours if you want them." And if, it should be added at once, you are willing to apply Dr. Brothers's surefire and scientific techniques. While she was writing her book a British psychologist was perfecting a battery-powered machine about the size of a shoebox that would make it possible to dream hitherto impossible dreams—that is, dreams of one's own choice. This is marvelous, even though the dreams do not translate into reality except insofar as they may improve the morale of one's waking life; indeed, it is almost as marvelous as Dr. Robert K. Graham's project to improve the breed by collecting and making available to women the sperm of Nobel Prize-winning scientists. Fortunately, the ultimate impossible dream, to shed weight not by pill, diet, or exercise but by sleeping in a slimsuit, is now offered as a reality by several manufacturers, whose magical garments cost between $7.95 and $14.95. If you keep in mind that the dream machine will probably cost $100, this is a remarkable bargain. But even more remarkable is that, according to advertise-

"Untested Innovations" first appeared in *Harpers* (May 1981): 69–74. Reprinted with permission.

ments in *The Star*, you may get everything that Dr. Brothers's book ($8.95, $2.50 paper) offers by wearing a golden horseshoe pendant ($7.00, $18.00 for three) or carrying Madame Zarina's Talisman ($2.00 aluminum, $4.00 bronze, $8.95 gold). What Dr. Graham will charge for his magical sperm has not been revealed.

Dr. Graham is reported to be a conservative and a churchgoing Protestant. Dr. Brothers suggests a mixture of Ralph Waldo Emerson, Norman Vincent Peale, and Dale Carnegie, but would probably prefer to be called a realist. Whatever else the British psychologist is, he is young and bearded. The purveyor of the golden horseshoes claims to be interested only in making money, which is probably true of the manufacturers of slimsuits. About Madame Zarina we know only that she is unavailable for comment, "though reporters have been dogging her footsteps for months." All of them, however, are optimistic and—if we remember that utopia can be defined as a state of affairs in which improvements come without trade-offs—they are all oriented to utopia. Swift's Lemuel Gulliver would have seen in them the same spirit he observes in the Grand Academy of Lagado, in Book Three of *Gulliver's Travels*.

In the Grand Academy Gulliver finds "Projectors" at work on schemes to extract sunshine from cucumbers; to translate human excrement into its original food; to turn ice into gunpowder; to weave cloth from spiderwebs; to improve speculative knowledge by an elaborate sorting wheel; to improve language either by reducing it to monosyllabic nouns or by substituting for nouns bags of material objects; and to bring about political harmony by cutting off and interchanging the occiputs of contending pairs of politicians so that both might "debate the matter between themselves within the space of one skull."

Gulliver observes all these projects with interest and with some sympathy; he had been something of a projector himself in his younger days. But even he seems to know that they are a waste of time and money, for he has some of Swift's conviction that a projector is one given to visionary schemes and activities—a fanatic specialist whose intense deformation of consciousness prevents him from imagining that the improvements he aims at might have undesirable trade-offs. It is obvious that if any of these absurd innovations were turned loose in society they would have disastrous consequences; they would not have been tested adequately outside the laboratory.

In these matters, as we know, Swift was a conservative literary intellectual satirizing the projects of the British Royal Society, some of which, given subsequent developments in science and technology, we are inclined to regard with more sympathy than he did. Nevertheless, it is hard today to read Book Three without transposing it into our own project-dominated world, in which the quick transition from golden promise to disconcerting side effects is the staple of the day's news. To go back to the 1939 New York World's Fair, with its utopian picture of the effortless World of Tomorrow (a projector's holiday if ever there was one), is like returning to one's childhood. Much more acceptable to current mood is Kirkpatrick Sale's conviction that "technofix," the expression of the belief "that all our current crises can be solved, or at least significantly eased, by the application of modern high technology," is more likely to compound our problems than to solve them.[14]

Sale's list of solutions that have not been tested adequately for long-range effects is familiar enough: synfuels that pollute the environment; a chemical-based green revolution that encourages monoculture, rather than a necessary crop diversity, in poor countries; tranquilizers that prove addictive; leaking nuclear power plants that threaten their human neighbors; miracle drugs that immunize the agencies they attack. Anyone can extend the list. Thalidomide, prescribed as a sedative for pregnant women, produces deformed babies. The risks involved in the use of contraceptives like the Pill and the IUD help drive up condom sales. While some researchers report a possible link between vasectomy and atherosclerosis, others discover that tampons may be dangerous to women and that saccharin may figure in bladder cancer. A team of Rutgers researchers led by Lionel Tiger experiments with macaque monkeys and finds evidence that contraceptive drugs may cause females to lose their sex appeal.

According to Paul Copperman in his book *The Literacy Hoax*, much of the decline of learning in public schools, particularly in the basics of writing, reading, and computing, is the consequence of such untested innovations as the new math, open-space schools, and formal systems of individualized instruction. In some areas busing, designed to facilitate racial integration, only increases racial tension. A federally mandated minimum wage designed to make sure that the young and the unskilled are not exploited keeps great numbers of them, especially blacks, from being hired at all. People who attempt to avoid the perils of smoking by taking up nicotine-flavored chewing gum may have to put up with hiccups, nausea, and dizziness, and if they switch to snuff to avoid one form of cancer they may only be courting another. Dr. C. Peter Erskine, professor of continuing medical education at the University of Wisconsin, maintains that even physical fitness has its trade-offs. Some joggers, he says, "are like narcotics addicts. When they can't jog they display classic withdrawal symptoms of irritability and nervousness. Their jobs, families, and friends suffer."

Given all this, it is understandable that so many of us are prepared for bad news as we contemplate present and planned efforts to technofix our world. What will be the trade-off in harm to the environment as we attempt to develop solar energy? Will an effort to solve poverty by redistribution rather than growth eventually make us all poor? What monstrosities will be visited on us now that the Supreme Court has ruled that a live, laboratory-made microorganism is patentable? The computer-science industry, honoring its marvelous microchip like a communion wafer, is as certain as a Lagado projector that the smart-machine revolution will enrich our lives and solve our most intractable problems, but who or what will solve the problems that the computer-science industry will cause but can't anticipate? Will the British psychologist's dream machine make waking life so intolerably jejune that it will become as addictive as cocaine? Will technological innovations in human conception make marriage obsolete and separate sex from procreation to such a degree that sex will cease to be fun? And what about that other electronic marvel, the vibrator, the do-it-yourself sexual microchip that is now the subject of a thirteen-million-dollar-a-year industry? Will the cohabitation of woman and machine, the "meditation of self-love," as Betty Dodson puts it in *Liberating Masturbation*, result in a hybrid form of syphilis immune to any known wonder drug?

It is of course just as normal now for us to have mixed feelings about recombinant DNA and the vibrator as it was for Robert Oppenheimer to have mixed feelings about what he and his fellow projectors were doing at Los Alamos with their nuclear marvel, that once impossible dream. The longer he worked on the bomb, it seems, the more uneasily aware Oppenheimer became of its likely frightful trade-off in human terms. Yet, when asked at his security clearance after the war why, in spite of his moral reservations, he had continued his work with the hydrogen bomb, he replied: "When you see something that is technically sweet you go ahead and do it and you argue what to do about it after you have had your technical success." It is this entrancement with the technically sweet that affiliates Oppenheimer's establishment at Los Alamos with Swift's Grand Academy of Lagado. And what is technically sweet must finally be tested in that truest of all laboratories, the everyday world.

The trouble is that since Los Alamos we have become much more systems-conscious, and ironically, the scientists themselves have played a major role in making us that way, or—in terms more acceptable to environmentalists and other humanists—making us think ecologically or holistically. The whole is the thing. The whole is always mysteriously greater than the sum of its parts, and the parts are interdependent and synergistic in their interactions. In systemic terms, two plus two may very well equal five, and neither "two" by itself deserves much attention, even though within the system (in banks and high school math classes, for instance) it may be necessary to ignore such holistic nonsense. Systems, we have learned to expect, have a certain tyrannical self-sufficiency, so that, as Barry Commoner says in definition of the third law of ecology in *The Closing Circle: Nature, Man and Technology*, "any major man-made change in a natural system is likely to be *detrimental* to that system."

Here is implied a potentially paralyzing position. If, as Professor Commoner says, nature knows best (he says it with more qualification than many who have come after him), we may have a prescription for a laissez-faire attitude that opposes any innovation whatever, since the testing of it in the laboratory of society might cause harm. This was not Swift's position, as Irvin Ehrenpreis points out in *The Personality of Jonathan Swift*. Swift's satiric attack on the projectors of the Royal Society comes out of his conviction that in the face of Irish poverty and slavery such technically sweet preoccupations were "frivolous evasions of real duties." In the interests of alleviating that poverty and slavery, he favored innovations that to the British were scandalously untested departures from all the systems by which they lived. Nevertheless, this is not the early eighteenth century, and it is now all too easy to believe that one of the surest ways to make a bad situation worse is by trying to improve it. Perhaps Professor Commoner's third law of ecology is simply a law of life itself, whether the systems in which it operates are seen in a social, political, psychological, economic, moral, aesthetic, or theological perspective.

Newsweek reports the reaction of one investigator to the findings of Lionel Tiger and others that the Pill may adversely affect the sexual impulses of women: "We're messing with things we know very little about." This is the apprehension one feels when one begins to suspect that the system in which one has been working has appeared clear, integrated, and predictable chiefly because so much has been censored out of it or because its relation with a larger system has been oversimplified or ignored. What makes good sense in a microeconomic system may make bad sense in a macroeconomic one. The good thing about Adam Smith, at least as some people read him, is that he keeps one from worrying about a possible lack of agreement between the two; to others, of course, such peace of mind is a sign that Smith ignores a more inclusive system. Moral Majority, Inc., the political action program of the electronic evangelist Jerry Falwell, takes the position that by ignoring traditional moral and religious absolutes, Americans have dangerously restricted the system in which they live. But Falwell's more comprehensive program has the technical sweetness that suggests the intense simplicities of those American millennialists about whom E. L. Tuveson has written in his splendid *Redeemer Nation*.

I find little awareness of mystery in Adam Smith or the Reverend Falwell, which suggests that they are projectors at heart. Nor is there any sense of mystery, in Dr. Brothers's book, about psychological technofix. "I don't believe in luck," she writes. "We make our own good fortune." Obviously, she is not one of those who have been dogging Madame Zarina's footsteps. In such optimistic systems as Dr. Brothers's, one is protected from mystery by the confidence that whatever at the moment seems uncertain or problematic will sooner or later become part of the clear picture. Such systems are threatened by innovations that assume that this clear picture is to some extent an illusion—innovations, like the golden horseshoe pendant, that generally take luck into account.

The watershed experience for Dr. Brothers was the winning of the "$64,000 Question," which she was able to do by making herself an authority on boxing. From that point on her life appears to have been an unqualified success, which may be why she is able to ignore one of the great themes in American literature: success as the untested innovation in one's life that is most likely to have unanticipated and undesirable trade-offs. If Theodore Dreiser or Stephen Crane or Sherwood Anderson or Sinclair Lewis or Ernest Hemingway or F. Scott Fitzgerald or Joseph Heller had written her life it would have come out quite differently. Most likely the winning of the "$64,000 Question" would have been the take-off point for a painful discovery of illusion and her essential kinship with Dreiser's Carrie Meeber, Fitzgerald's Jay Gatsby, or the hero of *The Education of Henry Adams*, who was jolted severely by Arthur Balfour's announcement in 1904: "the human race without exception had lived and died in a world of illusion until the last year of the century."

Such a doleful hypothesis, however, ought not to distract us from the fact that to mess around with things one knows little about is also the way of the heroic adventurer. If luck is on his side, the adventurer helps the rest of us to know more about things and the nature of their systems—or at least to know which projects are in violation of the inadequately known larger systems that contain us. Barry Commoner's understanding of nature is indebted to all those adventuresome projectors whose often untested innovations helped him to understand nature in more holistic terms. In response to those who claim that innovations in nature are inevitable he is now able to say what Jacques Barzun once said in response to the pseudo-naturalism of linguistic innovators: that we cannot "know what is inevitable until we have tried good and hard to stop it." Nevertheless, the ecological interdependency of adversaries, which itself may tell us something about the nature of nature and the nature of systems, suggests that we must manage to be what projectors themselves rarely are— discriminating and patient.

Literary intellectuals, or people who from a distance resemble them, are probably more systems-conscious than the rest of us, compelled as they are by their technically sweet aesthetic models. Their tendency is to regard the technofixing ambitions of projectors as Flaubert does in *Madame Bovary*. Charles Bovary, messing around with things he does not understand, attempts to correct the clubfoot of the stableboy Hippolyte by an operation that results in gangrene and the amputation of the leg; the clubfoot is eliminated much as the great fire of London supposedly cured the plague by burning up the rats along with everything else.

Flaubert presents this sorry business with the disgust that the poet and critic D. J. Enright has called the secret of modern fiction. Certainly the poems, plays, novels, and movies that literary intellectuals urge upon us amply express this disgust, not only with the human condition but with the efforts of projectors to improve it. This is especially the case now that literary intellectuals, picking up where Henry Adams left off, are having trouble believing that there is any significant connection between their verbal constructs and reality. Their morale, unlike that of Dr. Brothers, who has no such trouble, is low. The Marxist dream that once dazzled so many of them has proven, like thalidomide, to be one more untested innovation that, as the historian Eugene Genovese has observed, is dreamable only if you ignore all historical attempts to realize it. If literary intellectuals agree with Barry Commoner that nature knows best, it is less because they have any confidence in nature as a reliable system (what we call nature may be nothing more than a deconstructible verbal fiction) than because they are both disillusioned and disgusted with Commoner's opposition.

Fifteen years ago, Crane Brinton, in a special "utopia" edition of *Daedalus*, remarked that even in France intellectuals as a class were conspicuous in their despair, not only of progress but of orthodox democracy. Henry Adams himself believed that the machine the Founding Fathers constructed "was never meant to do the work of a twenty-million-horse-power society in the twentieth century, where much work needed to be quickly and efficiently done." Certainly, American democracy was an initially untested innovation—for its adversaries about on a level with something like Dr. Graham's sperm bank. Certainly, too, its trade-offs in contradiction, conflict, inefficiency, and confusion were often sufficiently great so that in time a choice between communism and fascism (those technically sweet solutions to the problems of democracy) seemed inevitable. The right choice promised a reconstituted and integrated society in which even intellectuals could be as optimistic about their various projects as Dr. Graham is about his. Thus we would have that paradoxical kind of conservatism that envisages an innovation so radical and utopian in its consequences that no further innovations are necessary or possible.

The issue of untested innovations is further complicated by the interrelated problems of pace and communications. If we consider these matters on the scale of Carl Sagan's Cosmic Calendar, the first humans appear on December 31 (having been preceded by the first worms two weeks before and the Big Bang twelve months before); since that date, technologically speaking, humans have gone from the wheel to the microchip. Whether the consequences of the latter innovation will prove more momentous than those of the former would appear to the layman at least to be an idle question; without the former the latter couldn't have happened. The late Gregory Bateson might have said that it isn't this simple; that a model of linear, causal progression fails to take into account "stochastic" processes that make it possible for events to evolve by startling leaps and bounds.[15] For Henry Adams the process was startling enough, however it was explained. "After [the year] 1500, the speed of progress so rapidly surpassed man's gait as to alarm everyone," he wrote, and society suddenly "felt itself dragged into situations altogether new and anarchic." In any event, if we set up another cosmic calendar to cover events that have transpired between the end of Sagan's calendar and the present, we would see a vast disproportion between the age of the wheel and the age of electricity, in which the microchip is currently such a dramatic development. Similarly, we would see a vast disproportion in the number of significant innovations to which humans have had to adapt, particularly in this electronic century, as the technological environment heated and speeded up at an exponential rate.

Nevertheless, it can be argued that even during the last few hectic days of the last month of this new calendar, we remain more at home with the wheel, our darling metaphor, perhaps because of what Adams called thought-inertia. The wheels go round in our head; we wheel and deal; our lives are determined in great part by big wheels; the stars wheel in their orbits as the electrons do in theirs; even the microchip, for all its solid appearance, is a matter of orbits wheeling within orbits. We innovate faster than we can integrate, which is to say that we have to live according to vastly disproportionate rates of change. This condition is older than most of us think; indeed, it is at least as old as Swift, for whom the fastest wheels were still carriage wheels. Adams blamed his eighteenth-century education for not teaching him how to exist in a world measured by the disparate paces of the Virgin and the dynamo, the technical sweetness of which, as he contemplated it in the

1904 St. Louis Exposition, symbolized the trade-off of accelerating historical forces. In him there was none of that Christian faith that sustained Swift, and none of the romantic confidence that faster is better which we find in Whitman's "A Passage to India," a poem that celebrates the "vast rondure" of the earth, accomplished by those stupendous innovations—the Suez Canal, the completion of the Union Pacific transcontinental railroad, and the Atlantic cable.

Most likely, Whitman would have reacted to the St. Louis Exposition as most Americans reacted to the 1939 Exposition of the World of Tomorrow: as an occasion for exaltation rather than education. Most likely, too, he would respond with enthusiasm to the one-world possibilities of recombinant DNA and the microchip. "Hurrah for positive science! Long live exact demonstration!" he exclaims in "Song of Myself," a poem in which there is even room for Dr. Graham's sperm bank: "On women fit for conception I start bigger and nimbler babes." Given his belief in phrenology and the comfort he took from the pattern of bumps on his own skull, he might even have been able to fit Madame Zarina into an odd corner of his ample universe. It was, after all, a universe in which a benign spirit was bound to turn innovation's apparently adverse trade-offs into long-term benefits—one in which Gregory Bateson would have been a more acceptable prophet than Arthur Koestler.[16]

But these are idle speculations. It is not, however, idle to remember that after he had confronted the dynamo in the St. Louis Exposition, Adams returned to Europe and bought an automobile, a dramatic embodiment of force he abominated, in order to study his "adorable mistress," the Virgin, whose force he never doubted "since he felt it to the last fibre of his being." Adams's auto was not only a transition between the wheel and the microchip—its wheels went around because electricity ignited the gases in its engine—but it was a perfect example of the seductive ambiguity of untested innovations, especially in communications. We expect unsettling trade-offs in any change within an established system, but it is hard, indeed often impossible, to resist the promise that the innovation is the only true way to higher integration, in which established systems will be illuminated as never before. Swift obviously learned something about the acceleration of forces and their consequences in his own world from the projectors of the Royal Society, so that his great book might have been subtitled *The Education of Jonathan Swift*. Thanks to the acceleration of time and force made possible by his automobile, which alone could unite the Virgin's places (Chartres, Rouen, Amiens, and Lyon) "in any reasonable sequence," Adams was able to study his mistress in ways not available to her medieval contemporaries, so that he was as dependent on the adversary forces' capacity to revise his education as is Barry Commoner.

But such a dependence might seem to imply a dialectic of progress, in which all education occurs in a system that forces revisions that are ultimately benign. Such a dialectic is a secular version of that millennialism that, as Tuveson indicates, worked its magic on the American mind for over three centuries. Adams was denied such a comforting philosophy. In his Virgin he found a grand vision of unity that, however fictive, was superior to anything that came afterward. Here, however, he may have revealed that he was at least a utopian manqué, with a utopian's attachment to a condition in which apparently beneficent innovations would have no trade-offs. There is a technical sweetness in his vision of the Virgin as a solution, embodied in time and place, to the problem of the one and the many, and this surely was a factor in his pessimistic "dynamic theory of history." "As nature developed her hidden energies, they tended to become destructive," he writes, but compared with the innovation effected by his adorable mistress, what energies would not have been? In the end, then, she crippled him as much as that other adorable mistress, the Bitch-Goddess of Success, has crippled so many of his fellow Americans.

In any event, to the seventy-year-old utopian manqué, still seeking education in the Paris of 1904, the pace of his culture was dizzying. "Forces grasped his wrists and flung him about as though he had hold of a live wire or a runaway automobile." But if he had been a true millennialist, time could not have passed too swiftly. For the faster the pace, the sooner the God-ordained utopia would arrive, after which, as Tuveson writes, "war and famine will cease; waste places will bloom; universal commerce will bless the happy time." No true millennialist could imagine progress, even technological progress, as anything but inevitable and beneficent; only the innovations of Satan and his agent, the Catholic Church, were threats, and these were doomed to fail as the WASP triumphant redeemed not just America but the world.

But as Professor Tuveson points out, disillusionment set in after the Civil War and continued apace into our century, even though millennialist faith influenced national expectations about the outcome of all subsequent wars. Nevertheless, says Tuveson, "like a recessive gene, in the right situation it could become dominant." His book may give most readers cause to hope that it will keep on being recessive.

At the moment, St. Augustine's sixteen hundred-year-old ironic and innovational distinction between the City of God and the City of Man (which the millennialists rejected categorically) is in favor again, though it has been widely downgraded to the distinction between an impossible dream and a nightmare. Throughout the land survivalists are arming, stocking up, and holing up, in anticipation not of an apocalyptic golden age but of various secular forms of doomsday: nuclear or volcanic fallout, earthquakes, runaway inflation, shortages of basic necessities, attacks by foreign or domestic enemies. The remnant utopianism we find in Dr.

Brothers or Dr. Graham, or in the Reverend Falwell and his numerous electronic evangelistic peers, either lacks theological sinew or has no sinew at all. With the collapse of the millennialist melodrama, the Pope, who can be assumed to be biased for Augustine, is released from the role of Antichrist, and Satan, that master of malign innovations and opponent of all true progress, is free again to do what he does best: pretend not to be there at all. Madame Zarina could be our last hope, but she wisely guards her mystery and eludes reporters—knowing, perhaps, that if they ever caught up with her in these skeptical times they would see her only as the Bitch-Goddess in disguise.

Chapter 9
The Devil and American Epic

Towards the end of his fine essay "The Englishness of English Literature" in the Winter 1983 *Daedalus*, the British scholar Peter Conrad contrasts English and American literature. He argues that "the characteristic gesture of English literature seems to be renunciation or wearied defeat" so that "its recurrent mode is pastoral; its recurrent mood is elegiac." America, however, "has always seen its destiny as epic" and therefore "has an unmisgivingly epic literature" that assumes as "its obligation the integration of a vast, uncharted national territory." One does not find in it the literal or symbolic "surrender of weapons" that marks the greatest English writers—Chaucer, for instance, with his nostalgic Wife of Bath, Shakespeare with John of Gaunt and Richard II, Milton with *Paradise Regained*, Wordsworth with *The Prelude*, Orwell with *Down and Out in Paris and London*.

Conrad's paradoxical thesis was on my mind one cold and wet London morning as I passed through Trafalgar Square heading once more for the National Portrait Gallery. High on his column, Admiral Nelson was obviously a man who would surrender no weapons, even if in the process of making that clear he had to surrender an arm and an eye. He suggests an epic destiny as much as the statue of Napoleon does on top of his column in

"The Devil and American Epic" first appeared in *The Hudson Review* (Spring 1987): 31–47. Reprinted with permission.

the Place Vendôme in Paris. In such company the band
of fundamentalist antinuclear singers below him among
the pigeons and the couchant bronze lions seemed utterly irrelevant.

They seemed no less irrelevant in the wonderful Portrait Gallery where—at least for an Anglophile American—the aura is celebrational rather than elegiac or
pastoral. Who looks more epic than Queen Elizabeth I,
or Sir Walter Raleigh, or Drake, or Mountbatten, or
Kitchener, or Edward VII—known as "The Peacemaker"
but here arrayed in gorgeous military regalia? Even his
father, Prince Albert, booted and spurred, right hand
resolutely on sword, appears capable of leading a second and successful charge of the Light Brigade. In such
company Sir Oswald Moseley and the Beatles become
part of the epic of England no less than Humphrey
Bogart, who is posed beside Winston Churchill.

Wearied defeat indeed! Here if anywhere is a place to
make one wonder if Professor Conrad isn't forgetting
the extent to which twentieth-century American writers
take a critical if not skeptical and downright disillusioned view of the epic strain in American culture. Stephen Crane, Theodore Dreiser, Eugene O'Neill, Thomas
Wolfe, Sherwood Anderson, Sinclair Lewis, E.E. Cum-
mings, Ernest Hemingway, and F. Scott Fitzgerald before World War II; Norman Mailer, Joseph Heller, Tennessee Williams, Philip Roth, Donald Barthelme, E.L.
Doctorow, Robert Coover, and Thomas Pynchon after it.
Where in such writers does one find the heroic elevation
of character and language, the narrative sweep, the confident and optimistic concern with events crucial to national destiny that are characteristic of epic?

But over the North Atlantic, sunk in the doldrums of
the long flight back to the New World that a not especially epic movie did little to alleviate, it became possible to see that Conrad might have a point. Americans
so far have had no difficulty sounding epically American
in their very skepticism about or enraged disillusion
with epical promises and expectations. Mailer's *The Na-*

ked and the Dead, Dreiser's *An American Tragedy*, Fitzgerald's *The Great Gatsby*, and Coover's *The Public Burning* are as much in the tradition of American epic as
Moby Dick and *Leaves of Grass*. As Daniel Aaron makes
clear in *Writers on the Left* and Paul Hollander in *Political Pilgrims*, many of those American writers who in
the thirties and early forties became communists or fellow travelers managed to sound epically American, and
even saw themselves as carrying the Declaration of Independence to its logical conclusion. Mike Gold, editor
of *The New Masses* and the party's "critical hatchet-
man," as Richard Hofstadter has called him,[17] was the
sort of person who had he lived in another century
might have earned himself a place in the American pantheon of legendary intransigents alongside Tom Paine,
Samuel Adams, and Henry David Thoreau. Gold surely
would have understood Ahab's epic need in *Moby Dick*
to surrender no weapons as he elevates the hated white
whale to the status of what Ishmael calls an "intolerable allegory."

The problem is that in America the epic impulse
has a way of disguising itself as anti-epic. This interdependence of what appear to be separate impulses was
made clear in two noteworthy 1983 television specials—
The Winds of War, the eighteen-hour version of Herman Wouk's novel, and the two-and-a-half hour finale of
M.A.S.H.
In the first of these Commander Pug Henry would
have recognized Ahab and Mike Gold as fanatic antici-
pations of persons with whom his position as naval at-
taché in Hitler's Berlin had made him all too familiar,
even if he would have been reluctant to dignify them
with the term "epic." The dimensions of the action in
which he plays a central role are, of course, unabash-
edly epic. He is a thoroughly reliable superachiever in a
typical modern crisis situation: one characterized by
sharply conflicting points of view, an overload of information coming from widely separated points of origin,

and dangerous accumulations of power combined with uncertainty about the intentions behind that power.

Henry's heroic connections are Virgilian rather than Homeric: his country's welfare comes first, his reason controls his passions, he is not defective in learning, he keeps the key issues of his world in perspective, he understands the relevant technology, he talks German to the Germans and Russian to the Russians. He is, besides, a concerned and understanding father and, under testing circumstances, a loyal husband. In short, he combines a capacity for unconditional commitment with knowingness, irony, and flexibility that suggests Shakespeare's Henry V, especially the Henry V whom Laurence Olivier presented immediately after World War II, when both British and American audiences were inclined to see a connection between their recent victory and the leadership qualities displayed by a young king who would have scorned the renunciations of wearied defeat as categorically as would Captain Kirk of *Star Trek* or Chuck Yeager, the test pilot hero of Tom Wolfe's *The Right Stuff*.

But if all this added up to a very attractive kind of modern epic hero for much of the TV audience, there were many who found Commander Henry at times embarrassing and even a cause of uneasiness. Harry F. Waters in *Newsweek*, for instance, was not about to take Pug Henry on Herman Wouk's evaluation. Unable to forget Robert Mitchum in his other personae, he wrote that the actor is "cast totally against type—and therein lies the power of his performance." For the "normally Bad Bob plays the quintessentially noble warrior," and his "inimitable, drowsy-lidded eyes" constantly signaled to Waters that Mitchum was aware of this gamesome paradox. His performance therefore "sets up a tension between actor and character that never ceases to intrigue."

In such a reading of *The Winds of War* the viewer is protected from the threat of the embarrassment of epic by proposing the possibility of behind-the-scenes anti-epic. It suggests a way of living with, even enjoying within limits, a kind of hero who if we took him seriously would place on us an uncomfortable burden of heroic emulation. Imagine the burden of taking seriously, as Wouk apparently intends us to, Pug Henry's words in his moment of erotic temptation: "I'm a family man . . . I'm a one woman man . . . and I've got a war to fight." In Waters's "subtle" and anti-epic reading this is "righteous drivel," and Mitchum is to be commended for bringing it off with a straight face. It is all too easy to imagine Waters's reaction if he were standing in front of Edward VII in the National Portrait Gallery.

It is also easy to imagine the reaction of Wolfe's test pilots and astronauts to Pug Henry, who would present them with the same disturbing paradox that John Glenn did: Henry appears to have the right stuff in spite of the fact that he has the wrong language, which means that he has the wrong style. In the American anthology of heroics this generally means that the stuff itself is less than genuine. The language of the right stuff, whether employed by fighter jocks, cowboys, hipsters, nightclub comics, or athletic superstars, is defined against the righteous drivel of all the non-elect others (politicians, government officials, the media, and the wildly cheering general public) who attempt to appropriate the right stuff by celebrating it. In them the vision of the right stuff inspires epic enthusiasms to which the inspirers must react in anti-epic style or lose their integrity. The day when the hero could frankly acknowledge his achievement, even boast about it, is long past. An heir to the post-romantic disjunction between language and action, the possessor of the right stuff is suspicious of language and therefore antipolitical. Like Frederic Henry in Hemingway's *A Farewell to Arms*, he is always being embarrassed by the righteous drivel of the old noble words. His position is that of those modern poets whose overriding concern is not to sound too poetical while winning a National Book Award or a Pulitzer Prize.

There was nothing subtle about the anti-epic of the two-and-a-half hour finale of *M.A.S.H.* that followed shortly after *The Winds of War*. A good deal of the appeal of *M.A.S.H.* throughout its eleven-year history has depended on its assumption that the conventional rhetoric of war is all righteous drivel. Its spirit, to use Peter Conrad's term, is that of the surrender of weapons, and its method of attack, as is so often the case in American anti-epic, is humor. This is a place for Falstaff, not Henry V; the latter has humor enough but, as he demonstrates in his great St. Crispin's Day speech before the battle of Agincourt, he is too inclined to the kind of righteous drivel that encourages a shouldering of arms. For Wolfe's fighter jocks the Korean War is the best place at the time to display the right stuff as they experience the *joie de combat*. For *M.A.S.H.*, however, the Korean War, and by extension all wars, is irrational, destructive, dehumanizing, and ludicrously ensnarled in the cross-purposes of its own operation. This being the case, the 4077th Mobile Army Surgical Hospital is fortunately situated: devoted humanely to repairing the violent effects of war, it can see war for what it is without endorsing what it is. It is apparently committed to the conviction that if both sides would surrender weapons all parties could go home and resume the good life.

But the irony is that when this conviction is dramatized over an eleven-year period anti-epic becomes itself a kind of epic with its own righteous drivel, not a little of which derives from the series' behind-the-scenes involvement with Vietnam, Watergate, and the human potential movement. Waters, to judge from his *Newsweek* story about the *M.A.S.H.* finale, missed this dimension. He took no note of the extent to which the program, by dramatizing the symbiotic relationship between war and comradeship, takes a benign view of war and at the same time represents the army as a place of adventure and discovery. There is a moment in the wrap-up episode when Colonel Potter speaks of going home at last to tend his garden. If one were inclined to look as critically at him as Waters looks at Pug Henry one might see in the Colonel's eyes (or should we say, in actor Harry Morgan's eyes?) a contradictory awareness that going home to the garden is going to be a sad comedown, that after a life of anti-epic elevation domestic peace and small-scale horticulture will probably be a bore.

Many viewers apparently believed that the wrap-up episode devoted too much time to the goodbyes, but given the under-theme of attachment to the army and the war, the emphasis on the goodbyes was right. The members of the 4077th had discovered one another as comrades in service of a self-transcending cause, and after such an experience the surrender of the weapons of their service signalized a point of no return. This is why veterans continue to congregate in celebration of "their" war—why, for instance, thirty thousand veterans assembled in Normandy to celebrate the fortieth anniversary of the D-day invasion—and why so many of them, without thinking of themselves as war lovers, are suspicious of pacifist attacks (themselves often quite warlike) on the armed forces. No doubt too this is why reruns of *M.A.S.H.* continued to be so popular: the faithful didn't want to let go of their anti-war.

Stephen Crane, like so many Americans who write interestingly about war, is easily put in the anti-war and anti-epic category. Who does not remember the bitter irony of the poem that begins, "Do not weep, maiden, for war is kind"? Early in *The Red Badge of Courage* it is clear that the traditional and epic rhetoric of war is righteous drivel, and war itself, as Tolstoy and *M.A.S.H.* agree, chaotic, meaningless, and unnecessary—except that in the novel it is also a vale of soul-making for some of those caught up in it. In Crane's other great "war" story, "The Open Boat," the enemy against which four shipwrecked men in a ten-foot dinghy must battle for their lives is again what appears to be a "flatly indifferent" nature. Nevertheless, the central character, the correspondent "who had been taught to be cynical of men," knows even at the time that the experience of comradeship in adversity "is the best experience of his life." Not only that, but at the end the three survivors know themselves to be an elite of interpreters of the great sea's voice. So nature has not been so flatly indifferent after all, and war really has been kind after its fashion.

"The Open Boat" is the story of an epical encounter of the human spirit with an elemental force, and the four men display familiar heroic characteristics. At the same time they are Americans, so like characters in *M.A.S.H.*, or like Tom Wolfe's fighter jocks, they use humor and irony as survival techniques; if they did not they would quickly go under. They are saved by style, as heroes generally are. But this is only so if you refuse to think of Crane as a Zolaesque kind of naturalist for whom the individual is completely determined by environment. Insofar as he is such a naturalist there is no room for epic or heroic in his story, and no place for nature conceived as an unsentimental teacher whose reiterated lesson is the interdependence of suffering and insight. If forces over which they have no control govern their thinking and conduct, Pug Henry of *Winds* and Hawkeye of *M.A.S.H.* are figures upon whom a flatly indifferent fate is playing a practical joke, and then the question is whether the authors who claim to perceive the joke are not having a joke played on them by a jokester beyond their ken. Certainly Crane did not think of himself in such depreciatory terms. For him the true writer was one who has chosen to shoulder arms in the good cause of opposing the forces of incoherence. According to his friend Joseph Conrad, he had many of the qualities of the old style hero, including "a strain of chivalry which made him safe to trust with one's life." Nevertheless, given the difficulties human beings get into once they take seriously what may turn out to be only the righteous drivel of the epic and the heroic, it is not hard to understand the appeal of the skeptics and relativists who have been replacing the old-fashioned author as believable interpreters of experience.

Of course, this is not the way it is with Waters and the authors of *Winds* and *M.A.S.H.*: all agree that Americans at least can have a significant degree of control over their lives, which is the indispensable assumption of both epic and anti-epic. In *M.A.S.H.* those who are responsible for shouldering arms are responsible for their bellicose conduct; if they were not, the antiestablishment virtue of Hawkeye and his friends would be undercut. And certainly in Waters's view Pug Henry, for all his righteous drivel, is no mere prisoner of circumstance; if he were, the virtue of the war against Hitler, at least as it is represented in the film, would be undercut—and there is good reason to believe that Waters does not want to go that far. Even Robert Mitchum is to be commended for being enough of his own man to resist being completely determined by his role. But then the self-invalidating capacity of naturalism has always limited its usefulness for the practicing critic; it forces him to surrender too many weapons, particularly the weapon of moral judgment.

Waters does not surrender this weapon in his attack on television itself, which in his view comes off a sad second best when measured against the virtues of *M.A.S.H.*, its own creation. He is as hard on the "plastic-phony" networks as Mike Gold was on Hemingway's *For Whom the Bell Tolls* for its mistake of not seeing the Spanish Civil War as a Marxist melodrama.[18] Waters quotes with approval *M.A.S.H.* producer Gene Reynolds: market research "usually says eliminate the pain. But you have to put the viewers through pain, conflict and obstacles. They have to go down the hero's thorny road to feel triumph in the end." If Alan Alda, Reynolds, and writer Larry Gelbert hadn't been willing to go down this hero's road, refusing to surrender weapons in defense of the integrity of their program, the CBS brass would have put into effect disastrous changes. In short, authentic anti-epic demands old style heroics and the willingness to run the risk of righteous drivel.

The corollary one may infer is that any human effort in the direction of peace that defines the will to power as nothing but an aberration, as a perverse refusal to surrender weapons, is doomed to futility. And indeed, the American's uneasiness with his historical impulse to epic is in great part an uneasiness about power: power after the Civil War as a corrupt exploitation of national resources; power in the 1930s as a capitalistic prelude to fascism; power since World War II as nuclear energy, the latter now having become the intolerable allegory that the white whale was to Melville's Ahab. Power is what the bullies have; perhaps if we get rid of or forswear power the bullies will be no more—with the implication, perhaps, that we will then all be peaceful and happy little guys together. And those who give up on power must begin to take the idea of utopia seriously or fall into despair. They can expect to get little comfort from programs like *M.A.S.H.*, which in the process of appearing anti-epic will be as much in love with power as with utopia. For utopia itself, unless we believe that it will happen automatically without any shouldering of arms against its adversaries, is a power-accumulating idea with its own epic potential. It is this fact that has led Ernest Lee Tuveson in *Redeemer Nation* to call attention to the resemblance between nineteenth-century American Millenarianism and Marxism, both of which, for all their historical determinism, see the approach to a grand end of things as "a continuing conflict between a monstrous 'conspiracy' and the party of the innocent and oppressed."

Huckleberry Finn's picaresque journey down the Mississippi River, the efforts of a little guy to disentangle himself from the corruptions of civilization, brilliantly dramatizes the American's uneasiness with power and the epic compulsions of his culture. Because Huck discovers comradeship while rejecting the combination of money and power so important to the standard American epic enterprise, Twain's novel is, like *M.A.S.H.*, anti-epic. The Duke and the Dauphin (farcical repetitions of the Gilded Age predator's insatiable appetite for money and power) advance the cause of anti-epic as their grandiose schemes end in pratfall. Epic is further undercut by the numerous deflations of Old World aristocratic and chivalric conventions, and especially by Tom Sawyer's own grandiose schemes—at the beginning of the novel as the quixotic leader of his Gang, and at the end as the entrepreneur behind the elaborate and romantic plan to free the already manumitted Jim. As he later tells his Aunt Polly, who cannot understand his motivation, "I wanted the adventure of it," and for that adventure he would have "waded neck-deep in blood." It is obvious that Huck with his "natural" conscience would not have used power so inhumanely. With the reader's approval, then, he can contemplate lighting out for the utopia of the Territory, where, free from the righteous drivel of civilization and the life-denying nag of its conscience, he can safely surrender all weapons.

In Tom Sawyer's version of epic, as in Mike Gold's, the grandiose idea is everything. He is himself an "author" in competition with the author of the larger work of which he is a part, and he is just as autocratic as authors generally are. His "novel" mandates the shouldering of all possible weapons and the reduction of all persons to means. His boyish entrepreneurship may amuse us, but insofar as we are individuals cherishing our own ends it is Huck's skepticism that we are more likely to sympathize with. One may believe that Commander Pug Henry, with his experience in pre–World War II Europe, would recognize in Tom the totalitarian's desire for a complete control of reality, but it is no harder to believe that *M.A.S.H.*'s Hawkeye would see in him an attractive candidate for service in the 4077th, where his talent for turning the daily humdrum into captivating escapades would be a surefire guarantee against boredom.

But neither of these possibilities should distract us from the fact that Tom as an ingenious and ruthless organizer of available power represents in the context of Twain's comedy the threat of technology just as much as does Melville's Ahab, who is no less a reducer of persons to means. It is technology in the dimension of adolescent epic adventure, however, that is especially threatening to any hopes of enjoying the utopian delights in the Territory or anywhere else, since Tom's technology implies that the pursuit of those delights can only entail another, and most likely, arduous adventure. This is why so much space has to be devoted at the end of the novel to the freeing of the already freed Jim.

Numerous critics have been unhappy with this escapade. Stephen Crane thought it absurd. In *The Green Hills of Africa* Hemingway says that if you read the novel "you must stop where the Nigger Jim is stolen from the boys. This is the real end. The rest is just cheating." But Tom is too important a character to be disposed of this highhandedly. William Van O'Connor has identified Tom as the Practical Joker of American literature.[19] Tom, however, is not joking; he is dead serious, which is what makes him so menacing and is why he must be brought back at the end and displayed for what he is. This is not to say that by so displaying him his creator has found a way to be at ease with technological power. Twain seems to have remained as ambivalent about technological power as most Americans. Indeed, he was as ambivalent about it as Wolfe's astronauts, who even while they are being glorified through an epical concentration of technological power have to live with the fact that they are only NASA's controlled minions, not full-fledged fighter jocks like Chuck Yeager. The likely thing, in fact, is that Twain would have sympathized with the West German Greens in their pastoral vision of a pre-industrial and non-nuclear life.

In our national life the adult analogues to Tom's grandiose schemes are those instances of "technological heroism" that Peter Conrad sees mirrored in our literature, whose epics "covet the status of grand industrial projects, bridging space and abbreviating time, engineering things into semblance of unison." The very language here suggests Twain's golden expectations for the Paige typesetting machine. One thinks of Whitman's "Passage to India" with its celebration of the "Rondure of the world" as a consequence of the technological heroism of the Union Pacific Railroad, the Atlantic cable, and the Suez Canal—to say nothing of the hundred-year-old Brooklyn Bridge and the moon landing of the astronauts, those fabulous examples of the American's metaphoric ability to bring together the distantly separated. Nevertheless, to live in America and in its literature is to hear behind Conrad's words the voice of the American's recurrent doubts not only about the uses to which his power is being put but about the goodness of that power itself.

Twain had lost faith in the goodness of technological power when in a time of financial disaster he came to write *A Connecticut Yankee in King Arthur's Court.* Here the Yankee, miraculously time-warped back to sixth-century Camelot, frequently suggests Tom Sawyer as he employs the marvels of modern technology in an apparent epic attempt to civilize England—which is just as reluctant to be civilized as Huck Finn is. Ultimately the Yankee and his few converts are unable to withstand the combined forces of the Church and the entrenched feudal order, and both parties, having shouldered all available arms, go down in a final bloody battle. The Yankee's enterprise would have been no less futile if the Duke and the Dauphin had been recruited out of *Huckleberry Finn* to manage it. Given the novel's dim view of the British aristocracy, it is unlikely that it was a subject of conversation when Twain, in England in 1907 to receive his honorary Oxford degree, chatted with that aristocratic peacemaker, Edward VII.

A Connecticut Yankee is generally thought of as satire, but the question is the target of the satire. The late Maxwell Geismar, writing anti-epically out of the liberational euphoria of the 1960s, sees Twain as an American prophet who in an admittedly uneven novel still brings off a powerful attack on the follies and corruptions of America and Europe, past and present.[20] But no satirist can be successful when he is as uncertain as Twain was at this point in his career about so many fundamental issues. In particular, he cannot make up his mind whether anybody can be guilty of anything since it is doubtful whether anybody can resist the combined forces of selfishness and environment. This is a damaging uncertainty if the novel is really trying to satirize an attempt to create a new human being and a new society by means of technological power.

Epic, anti-epic, and satire have in common the possibility that somebody can be guilty of something. This possibility may appear to be nonexistent in Twain's subsequent essay "What is Man?" in which, as in so much of his later unpublished work, free will is an illusion, human motivation is unqualifiedly selfish, and nature is not flatly indifferent but universally malevolent. Human beings, even Shakespeare, are only machines, which most of the time (like the accursed Paige typesetter?) don't even function very well. Unlike B.F. Skinner in his own anti-epic essay "What is Man?," Twain has no confidence that the right contingencies of reinforcement would make the situation any better. Whether humans shoulder arms, surrender arms, or beat their arms into ploughshares, they will probably make a mess of things. Indeed, Twain places even less value on the righteous drivel of autonomy, freedom and dignity than Skinner does.

Nevertheless, Twain remains always the outraged moralist for whom the idea of a guiltless universe is intolerable. As his famous "War Prayer" (his complete rejection of the spirit of Shakespeare's Henry V) makes clear, the irrational and violent conduct of the "damned human race" is the responsibility of the religious spirit and its perversions of conscience. In other and equally

characteristic moments (when in effect he is prophesy-
ing the antiestablishmentarian anti-epic of the 1960s)
he is just as capable of approving the most violent revolutionary conduct in pursuit of his own pieties. At such
moments he does not simply demand justice; he wants
justice as Hamlet wants it—in the form of adequate revenge. If, for instance, the atrocious Czarist government
can only be overthrown by dynamite, "then," he says,
"thank God for dynamite." Somebody must be guilty of
something.

Both epic and anti-epic are characterized by a unifying point of view with respect to the use of power. One
consequence of Twain's bafflement in his very American search for such a point of view is his romance with
the Devil—explicit in *Letters from the Earth* but clear
enough in published and unpublished work during and
after his dark period. The Protestantism of Twain's
background was itself quite capable of supplying an
epic and even, as we see in American Millennialism, a
utopian perspective, to which the inevitable counter-
perspective was that of the Devil. The interdependence of the two—a staple now in the TV evangelism of
Jimmy Lee Swaggart—is made brilliantly clear in Hawthorne's short story "Young Goodman Brown." Here
Goodman Brown walks into the forest where he encounters (or perhaps only dreams that he encounters) a community of apostate New England Calvinists that has
gathered to attend a black mass presided over by the
Devil. The latter gives his congregation this sadistic and
reductionist message: "Depending upon one another's
hearts, ye had still hoped that virtue were not all a
dream. Now are ye undeceived! Evil is the nature of
mankind. Evil must be your only happiness. Welcome
again, my children, to the communion of your race!"
The congregation reacts with a cry "of despair and triumph"—despair because of the lost establishment perspective, triumph because of the conscience-liberating
new perspective. That the Devil's words are epistemological nonsense (if everything is evil then nothing is

evil) is not apparent because the congregation has replaced one unquestioning faith with another. They are
in the Devil's bag, recruits for his own ongoing anti-epic
contest with the establishment God, just as Jimmy Lee
Swaggart might have predicted.

It is not likely that Twain would have shared Swaggart's unquestioning faith in the existence of the Devil—
or of God either, for that matter. Both figures, however,
seem to have been for him necessary fictions without
which reality lacked a critical framework. In any event,
it is not hard to see the attractiveness of the Devil's perspective to a bedeviled Twain: it promises an absolute
fix-point for the liberating discovery of illusion, just as
that "author" figure Iago does in Shakespeare's *Othello*.
Even if the right stuff is always the worst stuff and the
human race is damned, it can at least know the truth
about the damnation it is incapable of resisting. Even if
the truth is that all truths are equal, and therefore
equally deconstructible, so that the attempt to distinguish between dreaming and waking is the ultimate
folly, one can at least be dogmatically certain about that
and so have the comfort of standing on solid ground after all. In the meantime, the Devil cunningly sows confusion in humans' efforts to conduct their affairs by
making it possible for any establishment to identify its
critics, whether friendly or unfriendly, as diabolically
motivated.

In the satanic creed the language of all epic perspectives is righteous drivel—which is of course ultimately
true of the language of all anti-epic perspectives as
well, since any perspective is a way of hiding from the
absolute truth. Only the Devil is beyond mere perspective. It is Goodman Brown's bad luck—and perhaps ultimately Twain's as well—that he is denied the peace of
mind that is the bonus of this creedal position. Brown
does not belong to the Devil's community, he is only demoralized by the knowledge of its certainties; he knows
the despair, not the triumph; for even if the experience
was only a dream it "was a dream of evil omen"—one

of those Yeatsian dreams in which reality begins. Thus Brown is a useful hyperbolic indicator of the American's painful ambivalence about the use of available power (including the power of language), whether to thrive or survive. So Brown comes back to Salem utterly disillusioned, having surrendered all weapons—pretty much as Twain once planned to bring an older Huck and Tom back to Hannibal, Missouri. This means that Brown is so morally neutralized that he continues to do the Devil's work by offering no opposition to it.

The Devil, sensitive as he is to time, place, and circumstance, always presents himself in the most acceptable form. In Hawthorne's story he comes on disguised as one of David Riesman's inside dopesters,[21] since he promises his faithful the bonus of a penetration into "the deep mystery of sin, the fountain of all wicked arts," which are the source of all power. For him it is a customary disguise and a customary promise. The expectation of an enhanced life through participation in this power has always been the vital center of satanic cults, whether in medieval Europe, Puritan New England, or contemporary California. Thus even if, as Denis de Rougemont argues in *The Devil's Share*, the Devil's cleverest wile is to disguise himself as nonexistent, his no less clever caper, given the temper of the times, may be to identify himself as coming from where the action is.

But at the same time this very American Devil reinforces his authority by presenting himself as an intransigently honest perfectionist ("his once angelic nature could yet mourn for our miserable race") for whom absolute evil begins wherever virtue is to any degree less than it might be, and for whom all human motivation is morally invalidated through contamination by power. In or out of Hawthorne's story he stands ironically above the turmoil of time and misguided effort, knowing that all hopes to close the gap between good and evil are illusionary and that all conduct, however apparently righteous, can be reduced to hypocrisy and cowardice and must therefore be rejected in the most idealistic terms. This is of course the rejection of a failed and invidious utopian who is shrewd enough to encourage the utopian dreams of others, knowing that they can only increase the sum of disillusionment in the world.

We may have reason to think of this familiar Devil as the archetypal revisionist who wants all the power for himself. Certainly, in his disguise as the square-shooting, plain-speaking, and utterly reliable bullshit detector he is the formidable and morally indignant adversary of all human government, which in his categorical terms is nothing more than an attempt to monopolize power, and of all political activity, which is always selfishly manipulative and divisive. He is, in fact, the comforting idealization of our doubts about the worth of any effort to resist the entropic drift of things. The perfectionist Devil is, therefore, particularly hostile to democracy, which is committed to the belief that it is both necessary and good to strive for political power within the non-totalitarian guidelines of a constitution, even if the power is often abused, and good to ceremonialize its objectives and occasional epic achievements, even at the risk of righteous drivel.

This satanic opposition, high-minded as it is, is one reason why if Professor Conrad is right to recognize the American enterprise as epic it must also be recognized as a political and therefore uneasy epic, which is made particularly uneasy by an antipolitical utopian bias. You cannot be a democrat and believe, as Jean-Paul Sartre apparently did to the end of his life, that elections are "a trap for fools." To believe this is to imply that the proper aim of the good society is to get beyond politics to a state of virtuous unanimity—such as Sartre and numerous fellow travelers once believed to be the case in Soviet Russia. The perfectionist and totalitarian Devil, knowing how hard it is for humans to put up with disharmony, is of course a great propagandist for unity, though the unity he has in mind is the unity of a congregation for whom the fear of righteous drivel is the effective inhibitor of political conversation and therefore of all political action.

Given all this, the irony is the willingness of Americans to believe that politics, as the folk singer Bob Dylan has put it, "is an instrument of the Devil." Twain would have agreed. Justin Kaplan in his *Mr. Clemens and Mark Twain* refers to Twain's "lifelong contempt for politicians in general and Congressmen (the only 'distinctly American criminal class') in particular." His Yankee shares this bias as with high-minded duplicity he attempts to turn corrupt and backward Camelot into a Republic of Virtue uncontaminated by politics. "The country is the real thing, the substantial thing," he muses; "institutions are extraneous." Clearly, he is unaware that institutions are constituent of the country and depend, as does the country they constitute, on political action. Such political action is often, of course, just as corrupt and inclined to righteous drivel as Twain knew it to be. The problem is always how to keep the Devil from claiming the corruption as a validation of his own perfectionist demands and his own vision of a grand coming together of alienated and plain-talking souls. The problem, in other words, is how to keep the faith in circumstances where faithlessness is always trying to become a virtue.

Many of us are sufficiently infected by the habits of dialectical thinking to believe that the opposition between the epic impulse to glory in power and the anti-epic impulse to renounce power must, like the opposition between nature and nurture, point to some grand de-alienating reconciliation, in which Tom and Huck (joined perhaps by Pug Henry and Hawkeye) come together to establish the garden of America on a tension-free and non-epic basis. In the meantime, Freud being as usual a safer guide than Marx, we should probably expect to live with the discontents that derive from the tensions endemic to our democratic culture—prudently fortified by the well-grounded suspicion that the triumph of either impulse would be the Devil's delight. There seems to be some awareness of this possibility in the American public. If we were epically at ease with our power, if our epic and anti-epic impulses were not symbiotically joined, could *The Right Stuff* have become a best seller and *M.A.S.H.* have lasted for eleven years?

Chapter 10
The Doubtful Pleasures of the Higher Agape

Readers of Joseph Conrad's *Heart of Darkness* will remember that Kurtz before the darkness claimed him was a spellbinding idealist. Among those over whom he has cast his spell is the young Russian whom Marlow, the narrator, meets not long before his own encounter with Kurtz. Once, says the Russian, he sat up all night with Kurtz talking about everything, including love. "Ah, he talked to you about love!" says the amused and skeptical Marlow. "It isn't what you think," the Russian protests. "It was in general." The exchange is preparatory for the moment when the two of them are confronted by the menacing community of the stretcher-borne Kurtz and his adoring savages. "Let us hope," says Marlow, "that the man who can talk so well of love in general will find some particular reason to spare us this time."

Marlow, of course, has good reason to be worried, having already learned how incompatible with love-in-general love-in-particular could be for Kurtz. When Kurtz came to Africa he had a commission to write a report for the International Society for the Suppression of Savage Customs. This report, Marlow tells us, ran to seventeen closely-written pages of "burning noble words" whose "moving appeal to every altruistic

"The Doubtful Pleasures of the Higher Agape" first appeared in *The Southern Review* (Winter 1988): 134–44. Reprinted with permission.

sentiment" made Marlow "tingle with enthusiasm." The report, however, was utterly without practical suggestions, unless a note, apparently added later in an unsteady hand, could be taken for one: "Exterminate all the brutes."

Conrad expects us to see that while love-in-general may be complementary with love-in-particular (as they are in Marlow himself) the much more likely thing is that they will be experienced existentially as incompatibles, so that in practical situations the second interferes with the first and must give way to it. This means that Kurtz's love-in-general must be distinguished from the kind of loving traditionally known as agape, which, as Webster defines it, is "spontaneous self-giving love expressed freely without calculation of cost or gain to the giver or merit on the part of the receiver." This is a hard kind of loving, understandably much undervalued by those who, like Nietzsche and his epigones, had little confidence in what the Third Earl of Shaftesbury and his epigones believed to be an innate human propensity for altruism. The imperatives of agape can still complicate life as painfully and fruitfully as they do in Conrad's novel or Shakespeare's *King Lear*. Yet ever since what the Harvard political scientist Judith N. Shklar has called "the birth of historical optimism" in the French Revolution, it has been easy enough to be so intoxicated with a vision of love-in-general that, as was the case with Conrad's young Russian, it becomes the Higher Agape.

"This man has enlarged my mind," the Russian says of Kurtz. One of the functions of the optimistic mind-enlargers, who for better or worse change history, is to reduce, if not obliterate, the conflict between love-in-general and love-in-particular. Lenin is a classic example. The bunch of roses he was given when in April, 1917, he arrived at the Finland Station in Petrograd (still clutching it, he delivered a fiery speech from the top of an armored car) might have encouraged humanitarian expectations in some of his listeners. However, as

Paul Johnson points out in *Modern Times*, Lenin's humanitarianism was an abstract passion that "embraced humanity in general" while the embracer had "little love for, or interest in, humanity in particular." Hence his reluctance, as reported by Gorky, to listen to music because it disposed one to be stupidly nice to particular people. Hence, too, Hitler's scolding of General Heinz Guderian because the latter wanted to pull back his battered troops from the gates of Moscow. Guderian was too deeply impressed with the suffering of his soldiers, Hitler said; he ought to "stand back more" since "things became clearer when examined at longer range." It is the examination at longer range that so often makes possible the ruthless single-minded economy of love-in-general, that intoxicating form of self-transcendence that can make blood baths, gulags, and guillotines appear even to particular victims like loving instruments of mind-enlarging experiences.

The Russian tells Marlow that Kurtz once threatened to shoot him unless he gave up his ivory—despite the fact that the Russian has nursed Kurtz through two illnesses. At this point in his career Kurtz's idealistic love-in-general has flowered into self-deification. His failure, or inability, to honor particular creaturely bonds is familiar enough in our post–French Revolution World. One thinks of the ease with which in the interest of a Higher Agape Lenin, Stalin, Hitler, Mao, Pol Pot, and Castro disposed of those who had once been close to them. Indeed, the Reign of Terror has come to mean that breakdown of love-in-particular that we associate with historical optimism: the Higher Agape demands the Higher Fidelity, which is often enough what infidelity becomes when examined at longer range.

The analogy with the artist is very close here. For him the imperative of love-in-general takes the form of a self-transcending commitment to his artistic vision. In fact, there is a pronounced aesthetic bias in historical optimists like Marx—who, like Kurtz, had once been a poet. They envision the good society as one in which the particular persons will exist uncomplainingly and without friction in the interest of the whole they make together, as if they were components in a poetic or musical masterpiece. Not only do we easily excuse the artist who sacrifices love-in-particular (especially that of wife, children, or mistress) to his art, but we tend to suspect his authenticity in proportion as he flinches from such a sacrifice. About this kind of aesthetic Machiavellianism we are inclined to say of the artist what the Russian says of Kurtz: "You can't judge Mr. Kurtz as you would an ordinary man." This is no doubt why life with a true artist can so often be the "loving" Reign of Terror that life with Robespierre, Lenin, or Hitler could be.

Artists are particularly susceptible to the allure of historical optimism with its aesthetic vision of a triumphant love-in-general. William Wordsworth, looking back in *The Prelude* over his own youthful entrancement with the French Revolution, refers ironically to "speculative schemes—/ That promised to abstract the hopes of Man / Out of his feelings." The particular abstracting scheme was as unifyingly intense as that of a great poem, so that in retrospect he is able to say, "Bliss was it in that dawn to be alive." Indeed, when one remembers how many writers subsequently became blissfully alive, either as participants or bemused visitors, in revolutionary Russia, Spain, China, Cuba, or North Vietnam, one may suspect that for such personalities historical optimism is an aesthetic trap in which terrorist conduct is nothing more than the editorial excision of superfluous or awkward sentences whose nonbeing is then celebrated in the perfection of the whole—as Hitler expected to celebrate the nonbeing of the Jews in a revitalized and bliss-pervaded Thousand Year Reich.

"One must not be sentimental in these matters," Goebbels observes in one of these aesthetic contexts (he is, in fact, referring in his diary to Hitler's Final Solution). "No other government and no other regime would have the strength for such a global solution to this question." Goebbels here is captivated by the

Higher Agape of his Master's long-range idea. That Master, according to his biographer John Toland, said to Himmler that the idea was "extraordinarily humane," and in his final testament—written shortly before he died, like Kurtz with his "immense plans" still unrealized—again asserted its humaneness. Marlow early in Conrad's novel has his own comment on ideas of this elevation. What redeems the ruthless conquest of the earth, he says, "is the idea only. An idea at the back of it; not a sentimental pretense but an idea; and an unselfish belief in the idea—something you can set up, and bow down before, and offer a sacrifice to. . . ."

Marlow here is talking about a long-range idealism that has no more to do with love-in-particular, which in the perspective of the worshipful idea is a contemptible short-range affair, than with terrorism. Terrorism enters the picture when you are a nonworshipping outsider threatened by the idea rampant and you see how irrelevant to it your particular love is, including the love of your own skin. Besides, terrorists always have the advantage of their victim's knowledge of how hard it is to put worshipful ideas into practice if they are not permitted to exterminate some of the brutes who grossly stand in their way. Even those who have lived as captives in what unbelievers call a terrorist's world sometimes return with a new respect for the Higher Agape of their captors. The priest Lawrence Jenco who was held captive for nineteen months by Lebanese Shiites "expressed sympathy for the young men who imprisoned him and called attention to the fact that they thought of themselves as freedom fighters, not terrorists." The Greek prelate Hilarion Capucci, after visiting the jailed Georges Ibrahim Abdullah (ultimately sentenced to life imprisonment because of complicity in terrorist murders in Paris), declared that Mr. Abdullah was an idealist, not a terrorist. The same distinction helped for a long time to make the United States a sanctuary for members of the Irish Republican Army, and at the same time made it harder to protect society from such homegrown idealists as the Weatherpeople. When stories and photographs of such people emphasize their common humanity—they cherish their wives and children, love their parents, brothers, and sisters, have hopes for a better life, et cetera—the comforting implication is that their Higher Agape does not necessarily rule out love-in-particular but simply puts it temporarily on hold. Unless, of course, it is assimilated to love-in-general as it is in the motion picture *Reds*, where the lovemaking of the ardent revolutionaries John Reed and Louise Bryant happens in rhythmical rapport with the music outside that celebrates the Russian revolution.

Bertrand Russell gives a good example of the ease with which idealism can swallow terrorism and regurgitate it as the Higher Agape. Who when he was alive was more the inspiring historical optimist? In his vision of the future—a vision that suggests the memorable vision of the New World that bedazzles the Dutch sailors at the end of *The Great Gatsby*—he saw the evil of the world passing away, "burned up in the fire of its own passions" so that "from its ashes will spring a new and young world, full of fresh hope, with the light of morning in its eyes." Russell had seen the beginning of the Russian Revolution in pretty much the same terms, and is remembered for his humanitarian involvement with the Peace Foundation and the Tribunal that proposed to try the American war criminals for their atrocities in Vietnam. Yet, says his biographer Ronald W. Clark, after World War II, and before the Russians had the atomic bomb, this same Russell could suggest the advisability of a preventive war against the Soviets, the good effects of which would be the extermination of the brutes who threatened the emergence of the new and younger world. When in June of 1971 Noam Chomsky delivered the Bertrand Russell Memorial Lectures at Cambridge he was adamant about the culpability of the American terrorists in Vietnam but made no reference to Russell's anti-Russian terrorist proposal.

Most likely his audience would not have accused him of avoiding an embarrassing subject. After all, with the Americans they were in the world of the most immoral terrorism, whereas with Russell they were in a world of a Higher Agape that only the truly barbarous would misunderstand.

Or were they in the world of the Higher Chauvinism, which, whether sexual or political, is a perversity of idealism? Chauvinism may appear to be the ideal solution to the conflict between love-in-general and love-in-particular since it assumes the willing and absolute subordination of love-in-particular to a grand idea one can bow down before, offer sacrifice to. Russell, the lover of many women (including perhaps T.S. Eliot's wife), once admitted that it was against his nature "to remain physically fond of any woman for more than seven or eight years"—which suggests a chauvinistic subordination of women to the grand theme of his own free development. Kurtz is a chauvinist, and his "Intended" back in Europe, whose people had disapproved of him because of his poverty, gives all the signs of becoming the sort of wife who would be content to be loved within the limits of her husband's higher commitments. The young Russian with his self-transcending and mind-enlarging idealization of Kurtz is a chauvinist. Eva Braun was content to remain Hitler's Intended, serving with him his chauvinistic and monstrous love-in-general until, shortly before the Wagnerian *liebestod* of their suicides, he was free at last to marry her, as if released by a long pending divorce from a previous wife. His longtime great love-in-particular, his dog Blondi, predeceased both of them, dying of the cyanide given to him to test its authenticity. So Blondi too was in his brute way a chauvinist.

Chauvinism as a reconciler of love-in-general with love-in-particular is, of course, most effective when it has charisma on its side, as Kurtz and Hitler did. Max Weber defines charisma as a "certain quality of an individual personality by virtue of which he is set apart from ordinary men and treated as endowed with supernatural, superhuman, or at least specifically exceptional qualities." Thanks to it, human effort can be concentrated, for better or worse, on the long-range perspectives necessary for institution building. In the disenchanted times that have followed the excesses of the charismatic historical optimists it is easy to believe that charisma exists only in the eyes of the beholder. Russell, with his roots in the eighteenth-century Enlightenment, tended to look at it this way—which did not keep him from having at least as much charisma for a beholder like Noam Chomsky as Fidel Castro once had for Sartre.

In the Marxist scheme of things we will be saved by the inexorable process of the shrewd spirit of history, not by charismatic leaders, despite the fact that wherever the spirit of Marx prevails charismatics spring up like mushrooms after rain. The effigy of Marx in London's Highgate Cemetery projects at least as much charisma as Lord Nelson does on his pillar in Trafalgar Square. History in its shrewdness can use the most unlikely means to remind the skeptical of the reality of charismatic power—producing with didactic generosity figures like the Reverend Jim Jones and the Reverend Sun Myung Moon with their message that without the Higher Charisma of the Higher Chauvinists there can be no access to the Higher Agape. And for better or worse charisma is not always one of those personal properties that gets buried with one's bones. It may even be retrospectively enhanced, as it is with those neo-Nazis for whom the Führer is forever.

In Conrad's young Russian we see the spiritually lonely seeker who, with no protective base in a particular love, is especially susceptible to a charismatic chauvinist like Kurtz. Such an inability to stand the alienated loneliness of individual liberation is, of course, a great advantage to the historical optimists in their recruitment efforts. Traditionally, their antagonist is that institutional expression of love-in-particular, that haven in a heartless world, the family. Therefore Orwell in *1984* quite properly represents the family as the natural enemy of the totalitarian state, which, wanting to be all the heart there is, must chauvinistically celebrate the Higher Agape of love-in-general. So the family gets a bad press in proportion as the utopian impulse takes over, as it did in such almost forgotten classics of the early 1970s as David Cooper's *The Death of the Family*, Shulamith Firestone's *The Dialectic of Sex*, and Jill Johnston's *Lesbian Nation*. Such books, picking up where the Marquis de Sade left off with his *Philosophy in the Bedroom*, argued that the New Person must be liberated from the prison of the sexually monogamous family if the regenerated world is to happen. The late Rajneeshpuram community in Oregon, says Frances Fitzgerald in *Cities on a Hill*, was a "liquid family" in which children "would have mothers, but they would not know who their fathers were," and in which the New Person was not fettered by fixed character or the selfish sexual monopolizing of the traditional family. Ms. Fitzgerald shows the same utopian impulse at work in the gay world of San Francisco's Castro district, where the Higher Promiscuity of "impersonal sex" soon led to the *liebestod* of AIDS.

Of course, such flowerings of the Human Potential Movement are familiar enough now, so that one reads about the Castro district with the same sense of déjà vu that one reads about the Beach Boys rock band in Steven Gaines's recently published *Heroes and Villains*. According to Gaines, the drummer Dennis Wilson, having become enthralled by that dialectician of sex and charismatic embodiment of the Higher Agape, Charles Manson, was interested in joining the latter's liquid family. "You're not allowed to have crushes," Manson warned him. "Everybody is supposed to love everybody." Here "impersonal sex," always highly valued in the straight no less than in the gay world as an escape from the restrictiveness of love-in-particular, was raised to an institutional level, with some promise of offering competition to the romance of whoredom that since the Romantic Age has captivated so many artistic personalities.

Those who are otherwise susceptible to the promises of the historical optimists are often ill at ease with the person-annihilating side effects of the charisma they see at work in a Marx or a Manson. In that event they might take comfort from the vision of the best of all possible worlds available in Oscar Wilde's famous essay, "The Soul of Man under Socialism." Wilde wants private property converted into public wealth and a substitution of cooperation for competition, but none of this means anything to him if the result is an authoritarianism that stifles "the great actual Individualism in mankind generally." Surely here we have a historical optimist who, recognizing spellbinders like Kurtz and the Bhagwan Shree Rajneesh for the authoritarians they are, would champion love-in-particular.

But Wilde's socialism assumes a relief "from the sordid necessity of living for others," so that the love-in-particular it points to is as impersonal and isolated as masturbation. It assumes that love-in-particular can happen in a vacuum apart from the caring and burdening relation with other persons who are valued more for themselves than for their subsidiary value to some transcendent end. True agape, unlike the Higher Agape, is always anti-utopian, in great part because it does not accept Sartre's inverted utopian formula that hell is other people. And the antiperson and antifamily nature of Wilde's socialism is reinforced by the fact that it is an aesthetic utopia in which the state is to make what is useful while the individual makes what is beautiful, to the end that all people "will have delightful leisure in which to devise wonderful and marvelous things for their own joy and the joy of everyone else." Indeed, the aesthetic nature of his socialist utopia is modeled on Wilde's characteristic delight in paradox, the compulsion to which overrides all other considerations. Thus it has great practical value not as a prescription for a better world but as an example of the tyranny of the aesthetic. Paradoxically, the essay even bites its own tail since it propagandizes a state of affairs which, being impervious to paradox, would surely bore its author.

But the most useful thing now in an otherwise dated essay is that it gives us entertaining evidence of the extent to which utopias tend to be not only tyrannously aesthetic but antipolitical and therefore antidemocratic. For Wilde the true personality of man will not be discordant. "It will never argue or dispute. It will not prove things." As for democracy, "it means simply the bludgeoning of the people by the people for the people." The disturbing thing is not simply that many people living in democratic societies believe this but that they believe it because they are, like most historical optimists, aesthetic utopians.

To see the extent to which aesthetic utopianism is a factor in American democracy one has to recall the etymological connection between "aesthetic" and "feeling," especially with respect to those refined feelings we associate with the arts and the intensity of pleasure they give. Wilde's utopia is dedicated to the pursuit (in the sense of practice, not quest) of such pleasures. The senior Arthur M. Schlesinger has called our attention to the fact that behind the hallowed phrase "pursuit of happiness" in *The Declaration of Independence* there was a sizeable body of opinion that, as John Adams put it, "the happiness of society is the end of government," so we have evidence of historical optimism in America well before the French Revolution. None of those who believed this, says Schlesinger, "thought of happiness as something people were entitled simply to strive for but as something that was theirs by natural right." Wilde couldn't have agreed more. If this is what democracy is all about, Sade could have signed *The Declaration of Independence* as boldly as John Hancock did.

Unfortunately, as the idealistic historical optimists have by now made clear enough, totalitarian entrepreneurs quickly see to it that the highest of all pleasures is the experience of love-in-general as the individual sub-

mits himself without reservation to the long-range aspirations of self-transcending social idea. This is why
the Marxist-inspired societies can be called pleasure-
oriented, and why they can even be admired for the success with which they combine privation and creaturely
self-denial with the practice of that pleasure that is beyond the sufferings of alienated loneliness. Hence the
upbeat nature of the official literature which in Marxist
societies reeks with the love-in-general that is both the
cause and effect of a regimented pursuit of happiness.
Pravda, despite Mikhail Gorbachev's much publicized
policy of openness and candor (*glasnost*), remains the
classic example of a "good news" newspaper, and to appreciate it as such it needs only to be put alongside any
American paper. The most prominent feature of a typical issue, that for January 7, 1986, for instance, is a four-
column picture of two smiling women who are "advanced milkers" on a Chuvashi dairy farm renowned for
its high yield of milk. Not only do these fair and happy
milkmaids dominate the front page but they set the tone
for the entire issue. What is said about them—that they
"simply love their work and perform it conscientiously,
putting their hearts into it"—is being said about Soviet
workers generally, and may refer to the cows as well,
since conceivably their contentedness derives from a
bovine awareness of a generous giving for the common
good. Here is that reconciliation of love-in-particular
with love-in-general that Americans associate with advertisements for such pleasure-pursuing reconcilers as
Coca-Cola and Winston cigarettes. It is no wonder that
aesthetic personalities like Wordsworth who participate
in the dawning of such enterprises find it blissful to be
alive.

The blissful pursuit of unalienated pleasure is incompatible with democratic politics which, being a process
of divisions and discordances, is aesthetically offensive,
if not downright "cheesy," as *The New Republic* has contended about the 1986 elections. For some idealistic
Americans, then, the process of politics is tolerable only

in the context of a utopian expectation that politics is simply the means employed by the cunning of benevolent historical process that aims at a final apolitical and unanimous condition. Politics in this view is what bourgeois capitalism was to Marx: a necessary but by-the-way thing to be endured in the expectation of something far better. This suggests that democracy depends not simply on the ability to reconcile love-in-particular with that impulse to love-in-general without which no society can succeed, but on its capacity to live with that unpleasurable tension between the two that condemns us to the competition among "bad news" newspapers. Any loss of nerve invites in the epigones of Kurtz with their documents (rarely restricted to seventeen pages) in which burning noble words appeal to every altruistic sentiment.

Voltaire, as we know, made his contribution to historical optimism by way of his attack on the Old Order, but, as we also know, his *Candide* is not uplifting reading for historical optimists. Coming as it did after the shattering effect on its author of the Lisbon earthquake and the Seven Years War, it gave little comfort to those who had based their theodicy on the altruism of Shaftesbury and the optimism of Leibnitz and Alexander Pope. Indeed, says one of his recent biographers, Voltaire wrote to a Genevan clergyman "that the myth of the Fall of Man, whether Christian or otherwise," made more sense in human terms. Perhaps this is why he permits Candide and Cacambo to spend only a few weeks in the utopian land of El Dorado and sees to it that they leave with no particular regrets, as if to make the point that in a land where the pursuit of pleasure is unqualified and all people, having read their *Pravdas* without irony, are of the same opinion, even the Higher Agape would be a bore. On the other hand, when the novel at the end has Candide say "we must cultivate our gardens," we can assume that it is not saying that ultimately we must choose between our desire to return to El Dorado and the boredom of private horticulture.

Where people in particular are free to tend their gardens love-in-particular has a chance to survive against the self-abnegating compulsions of whatever Higher Agape demands the sacrifice of their particular loves. And those people who cultivate their particular gardens best do so with a sense of human limitation, having learned the dehumanizing consequence of ignoring the myth of the Fall of Man. In American democracy, of course, the image of America as a garden (perhaps one intended by the Great Source of all agape to replicate that original garden before the Fall) has always been a complicator of the national effort, both expressing and encouraging, as it does, our historical optimism and keeping alive our hankering after the aesthetic utopia. And the historical optimism goes with a threat of demoralization: if we have to give up on the dream of the ultimate garden we may let the one we have go to weeds, or even turn on it vengefully, as Kurtz turned vengefully on the African natives who fell so far short of his noble burning words.

During a visit to the United States a few years ago the playwright Eugene Ionesco noted how frequently on the liberal left he found a guilt for American conduct at home and abroad combined with a conviction that "Marx still lives." The combination is a familiar one; Marxism has always been an inspirer of guilt. Indeed, one of the functions of the Higher Agape anywhere is to inspire guilt. If Kurtz's seventeen-page report had arrived at European headquarters it might very well have made people in high places feel guilty enough to take action, in which case one could only hope that the action would not be so long-rangedly idealistic that it would do more harm than good. Guilt-prodded love-in-general, especially when fortified by the aesthetic imperative, can be a ruthless tyrant.

But American guilt is a lot older than Marxism and perhaps should be seen as a cybernetic reaction to the fear that the pursuit of happiness will combine with an excess of love-in-particular to reduce the American

Dream to a nightmare of selfishness. So we have our own built-in capacity to bow down before a Higher Agape, and with it a democracy-thwarting capacity to denigrate political activity unless it can be seen as a way of arriving at a point where it is as irrelevant as it is to *Pravda's* fair and happy milkmaids.

Chapter 11
The Politics of Transfiguration

If we knew that T.S. Eliot had often stood in the checkout line in an American supermarket where his practice was to snoop-read the tabloids, we might have a footnote for the well-known line from "Burnt Norton": "human kind/Cannot bear very much reality." Where might the poet have found better evidence of the human appetite for the fabulous as an escape from the unbearably boring, frightening, or anomic in the human condition than in *The National Enquirer, The Examiner, The Star, The Globe,* or *The Weekly World News*? Imagine him "With his features of clerical cut, / And his brow so grim" noting such typical stories as these:

> Woman gives birth to 69 babies in 30 years.
> Two-headed boy found in jungle.
> Wife feeds evil hubby to the sharks.
> Voodoo drug brings dead back to life.
> 3,000-year-old time capsule predicts modern events.
> Ghouls sell drops of Elvis's sweat.
> Baby is born with tattoo dated 1917.
> John Lennon speaks from the grave.
> Woman is pregnant by creature from outer space.

Perhaps the clerical features soften as it occurs to him that these startling departures from quotidian norms

"The Politics of Transfiguration" first appeared in *Stanford Literature Review* (Fall 1987): 183–94. Reprinted with permission.

are no more remarkable than the fact that in his poem the oracular words are spoken by a bird. In context, however, it is a bird of a higher order, perhaps even the order of magic realism, whereas the tabloids are junk literature for the masses. In fact, *The Star* in a three-page ad in *New York* magazine claimed more than twelve million readers. This is tough competition for high-order birds. Wordsworth, himself a bird lover, had this kind of competition in mind when in the Preface to the second edition of his *Lyrical Ballads* he complains about "frantic novels, silly and stupid German trage-dies, and deluges of idle and extravagant stories in verse," which, catering to a "degrading thirst after out-rageous stimulation," lack a "worthy purpose."

A half-century later Walt Whitman had the same vul-gar competition in mind when in the Preface to the 1855 edition of *Leaves of Grass* he complained about the "nui-sance and revolt" of a corrupted popular taste "which distorts honest shapes or which creates unearthly be-ings or places or contingencies." Imagine a poet who be-lieves that "all beauty comes from beautiful blood and beautiful brain" being confronted on every newsstand with the likes of soap-opera star Joan Collins or pop-rock stars Michael Jackson, Boy George, Prince, and Madonna. Or imagine Thoreau, disgusted as he was with the American's avidity for outrageous stimulation, reading in *The Examiner* that an African woman who had been raped by a baboon gave birth to an ape. It would confirm once more the conviction he would later express in *Walden*: "I am sure I have never read any memorable news in a newspaper."

To a class that was being introduced to fiction I once read ten sensational headlines half of which had actu-ally appeared on the front page of one tabloid or an-other and half of which I had invented. No student got a perfect score and all chose "Man Lives with Live Frog in His Belly" as "real." One point to the exercise was that the tabloids create an atmosphere in which it is difficult to distinguish between statistically unlikely events and utterly inconceivable events: news that an Italian priest is proposing the late Grace Kelly for sainthood will validate any number of belly-dwelling frogs and jungle-dwelling, two-headed boys.

Of course, the same point can be made about medieval and Renaissance travel literature. In Sir John Hawkins's account of his second voyage to the West Indies you may read about trees that rain continually and islands that disappear as you approach them. Sir Walter Raleigh reports that in Guiana there are men whose heads grow beneath their shoulders, just as Shakespeare's Othello claims. Sir John Mandeville claims that he had fought for the Great Khan, lived in Prester John's court, and drunk from the Fountain of Youth. For Marco Polo the ferocity of the Assassins who followed the Old Man of the Mountain is explained by hashish and an initiatory experience in an artificial paradise in the mountains of Persia, where, without knowing it, they prepared themselves for a subsequent appearance in Coleridge's poem "Kubla Khan." One who had fed on such marvels might be forgiven for believing Baron Munchausen's account of how the Siberian weather froze the notes in his servant's French horn. A naïve enough reader might even find Swift's Gulliver as credible a traveler as Drake or Magellan.

A version of Gresham's Law is involved here. If the fabulous is too indiscriminately apprehended it may cease to be a factor in human consciousness and the quotidian humdrum will overwhelm all. Thoreau who knew this foresaw dire consequences. "Shams and delusions are esteemed for soundest truth," he writes in *Walden*, "while reality is fabulous. If men would steadily observe realities only, and not allow themselves to be deluded, life, to compare it with such things as we know, would be like a fairy tale and the Arabian Nights' Entertainment." Or, we might imagine him implying, life would be as fabulous as he is making it appear in his book, which, unfortunately, few people will read because the false fabulous has given them a false consciousness. If one's standard of the fabulous is a two-headed boy found in the jungle, Thoreau's report of the battle between the red and the black ants in his woodpile may seem to be very jejune stuff.

To a proper reader, of course, the report of that battle in the chapter "Brute Neighbors" is anything but jejune—is, in fact, a brilliant demonstration of the fabulousness of reality, and even reinforces Whitman's conviction that when "histories are properly told there is no more need of romances." For Wordsworth, too, the realities of his pastoral world are truly fabulous. Poems like "The Idiot Boy," "The Thorn," "The Old Cumberland Beggar" and "Ruth" would lend themselves to tabloid headlines as nicely as Thoreau's battle of the ants. The exploitation of metempsychosis in his ode "Intimations of Immortality from Early Childhood" ("our birth is but a sleep and a forgetting") might have been a supporting reference in a recent *Examiner* story in which the television superstar Jaclyn Smith reveals that her son is the reincarnation of her grandfather.

My classroom experiment with the true and false tabloid headlines was also heuristically useful in making the point that most of the stories in the course, indeed, most of what we know as imaginative writing, could be reduced to tabloid headlines. Such a reduction would be a way not to belittle literature but to make it clear that great writers tend to agree with Thoreau that reality is fabulous, even when—like Maupassant and Stephen Crane, whom we happened to be reading—they were realistic revisionists unhappy with traditional definitions of the fabulous. Crane's *The Red Badge of Courage*, for instance, is very close to Thoreau's account of the battle of the ants in its skeptical attitude toward the traditional fables of warfare with their irrational all-or-nothing heroics, and close to it, too, in offering itself as a revisionary fable.

We like to think of realism as a necessary cooling off of a fabulously overheated world, the way Comte thought of his positivistic religion of science or Sartre thought of his attack on the cultural fictions that make false consciousness and bad faith possible, but the great realists stick in the mind because they have been able to reveal the fabulous in a new and exciting perspective. They suggest that there is no sharp line of demarcation between the realism of Crane and the magic realism of Gabriel García Márquez. They are like the Flat Earth Society, which, in order to counter the Copernican fable of a global earth, must posit an equally fascinating fable of a flat earth ringed with ice fields. But they are also like Marco Polo, and the later great Renaissance explorers, who went into a world which by trustworthy report resembled a horrifying freak show of human and animal monsters set in an environment of boiling seas, fiery equatorial calms, treacherous winds and whirlpools. Their own revisionary report of this world is no less fabulous, thanks in part to their employment of techniques refined centuries later by the new journalists and nonfiction novelists, to say nothing of the tabloid hacks. This is why Ed Sanders's account of Charley Manson's bloody escapades in *The Family* and Tom Wolfe's account of Ken Kesey's psychedelic adventures in *The Electric Kool-Aid Acid Test* find congenial company in those great collections of English Explorations made almost four centuries ago by Richard Hakluyt and Samuel Purchas.

In these matters, fortunately, my fiction class had in hand a splendidly clarifying novel, Muriel Spark's *The Prime of Miss Jean Brodie*, which is concerned not only with the importance, in both literature and life, of transfiguring the commonplace but with the importance of distinguishing among transfigurations. One might say that Polo and the Renaissance voyagers were teachers who, in reporting what they believed to be the truth, transfigured an established world the shape of which was the consequence of previous transfigurations. But as Spark's novel shows, it is not that simple, for there is a certain congeniality among transfigurations. After the enthralled reader reads Polo on the court of Kubla Khan, which he knew at first hand, the reader is hardly inclined to be skeptical about Polo's account of the legendary Old Man of the Mountain, whom Polo knew only by report.

Similarly, the fabulous moon landings (media-constructed hoaxes in the opinion of the Flat Earth Society) help to make tabloid reports of the shenanigans of space aliens believable. In the supercharged atmosphere of the 1960s, the established "liberating" transfigurations of middle-class reality helped to validate for their followers the "New World" visions of Manson and Kesey, making it easy for them to believe not only that reality could be fabulous but that its very fabulousness was a proof of its authenticity. Transfigurations tend to resist the distinctions that threaten them, which is no doubt why some of my students were reluctant to see the charismatic Jean Brodie as a dangerous teacher who has to be gotten rid of, despite the novel's attempts to show that her charisma is grounded on the transfigurations of fascism.

For the noisy modern Greeks in the late spring of the year it was politics that was transfiguring the commonplace, not the old discredited gods. My wife and I abstracted ourselves from the politics as best we could (not easy in election week) and lived in the ancient time among the ruins at Athens, Sunion, Corinth, and Delphi where it was possible to imagine that the awesome pillars of dilapidated temples still supported a sacred canopy. Yet one must acknowledge that if the truth were told from an available perspective, the ancient Greeks subscribed to a tabloid theology. The erotic adventures and misadventures of Zeus, Poseidon, and Apollo, for instance, are rich as Ovid's *Metamorphoses* with headline possibilities for *The Weekly World News*. Think of Poseidon, whose temple broods brokenly over the immensely blue Aegean, disguising himself as a stallion to mate with Zeus's own sister, Demeter, she at the time being conveniently disguised as a mare. Think of Apollo's vengeful treatment of Cassandra and the Sibyl of Cumae after they had rejected his offered love, the former becoming a prophetess whom no one would believe, the latter being cursed with extreme longevity without the youth to enjoy it. Or think of Zeus who anticipated our own randy tabloid visitors from outer space as he impregnated mortal beauties with such superachievers as Perseus and Heracles. Under his dominance Mount Olympus was an even more fabulous place than the paradisical valley ruled by Marco Polo's Old Man of the Mountain.

Zeus's world would in many respects have been congenial to the Shiite Terrorists who, shortly after we departed safely for Paris, began to monopolize the media with their hijacking of TWA flight 847 from the Athens airport. Perseus and Heracles were only the sons of a god, but the Hezbollah Shiites, like the followers of Manson and the Reverend Jim Jones, were the Party of God. The difference is important. There is some critical distance between bastard sons and father, but the Hezbollahs were locked like ideologists in a closed system with a totalitarian deity so that violent transfigurations of the commonplace were inevitable. They take us back not to Polo's Old Man of the Mountain but, according to the Italian historian Leonardo Olschki in *Marco Polo's Asia*, to the Shiite Hassan Sabbah whose fanaticism centuries ago was a violent threat to traditional Mohammedanism.

Hassan's power over his Assassin followers, who fascinated and terrified even Christian Europe in the early Middle Ages, depended not on drugs or bamboozlement in a Playboy-type paradise but, Olschki writes, on Hassan's ability to inspire his followers to a blind obedience (subsequently emulated by European courtly lovers) with an interpretation of reality "mystically connected with the godhead." They were fanatics with a purpose, as all true fanatics are, and they were as ascetical as our

own hyperathletic New Puritans, to whom bourgeois
creature comforts are obstacles to self-transcendence.
Thoreau saw them all for us in analogy as his red and
black ants, neither faction manifesting "the least disposition to retreat," battled to the death in the jihad of
his woodpile. Perhaps at the end of the year one could
see the long reach of Hassan's fundamentalism in the
bloody atrocities at the Rome and Vienna airports, believed to have been masterminded by the Palestinian
super-terrorist, Abu Nidal. But it would have been just
as easy to see it six months before in the Egyptian government's efforts to censor erotica out of that fabulous
Arabian classic, *A Thousand and One Nights*. Surely, if
he had the power to do so, Hassan would have censored
the libidinous Greek mythology, however he might have
sympathized with the single-minded terrorist ferocity
of an aroused Zeus or Poseidon.

The terrorist expert Robert H. Kupperman of George-
town University said after the hijacking that we will
continue to be plagued by terrorists for the next couple
of decades no matter what we do to defend ourselves.
Hodding Carter, spokesman for the State Department
during the Iranian hostage-taking, pointed out that tril-
lions of dollars of defense spending "is nothing to a
couple of guys with hand grenades, who are more than
willing to die and will strike anytime." We are targets
for terrorists, Ronald Steel wrote in *The New Republic*,
because "to much of the world we are an omnipresent
giant intervening everywhere" with money, weapons,
and even troops.

All of this is no doubt true, but there is another and
perhaps even more disturbing truth behind it. The terrorists will continue to menace us (and preoccupy the
fascinated media) because of their refusal to live in an
untransfigured and anomic reality. Something in all of
us responds to a willingness to put all in hazard in the
service of a self-transcending cause, whether we see it
in the Bassanio of Shakespeare's *The Merchant of Venice*, in Hassan's Assassins, about whom medieval Eu-

rope had such mixed feelings, or in the yuppie junior executive who neither smokes nor drinks and daily runs five miles before breakfast. To understand this is to understand the consanguinity among Khomeini's Iran, the IRA, and the MOVE group blasted out of existence in Philadelphia in the spring of 1985. But it is to understand also why television wrestling is currently so popular, why the Liverpool soccer fanatics, in a prelude to the hijacking, were moved to kill forty-one Italian spectators at the European Cup matches in Brussels, and why so many otherwise law-abiding citizens support the cocaine traffic. The many ways of belonging, at least momentarily, to a Party of God for whom everything comes lucidly and purposefully together, range from the vulgar through the drugged to the murderous. Most of them would, I imagine, give little comfort to a fabulist like Kurt Vonnegut, Jr., who has announced that he is mad at the universe "because humanity turns out to be such a failure." Could that young Norwegian who, shortly after the 847 hijacking, surrendered his own hijacked jet for beer, thereby desecrating the grand theme of the Hezbollah terrorists, have made Vonnegut even madder?

Perhaps more than anything else it is the need to feel intimately at home in a potentially cold and anomic universe, threatened everywhere by the entropy of the commonplace, that makes a heterogeneous family out of the ancient Greeks, the Shiite hijackers, and the tabloid millions. One can sense something of this at Delphi, standing in the hard Greek sunlight at the oracular shrine with the fabulous Mount Parnassus shouldering up a sky uncontaminated by the pollution of Athens and as Blue as Poseidon's Aegean. Here people—free men and women as well as slaves—once felt at home in the transfigured universe, just as, the historian Theodore Roszak has argued, millions still feel at home in it because astrology has saved them from the disenchantments of modernity by connecting them "with ancient and cosmic images."

The tabloids, too, help their millions feel intimately
at home in a universe threatened by disenchantments.
They may appear to be committed only for profit to
the exploitation of the sensational, even if it is perverse
and monstrous, but in effect they bring news from a
thrilling universe in which supernal powers are always
at work, if sometimes bewilderingly, and in which there
are clear signs that virtue will ultimately triumph, if
only after evil has put up a good show. Here one can be
on first name terms with the makers and shakers of the
culture—Lucy and Johnny and Di and Liz and Jackie
and Dolly and Mick—and here life-enhancing and sta-
tistics-defying events may happen to the least of us at
any moment: we might even be invited by Robin Leach
to participate in the life-styles of the rich and famous.
Here one is excitingly safe from the epistemological
confusions of postmodern and deconstructionist culture. Here it is possible to say, as the media superstar
Cher has been reported as saying, "I feel I know God
personally, and I am one of his favorite children." Could
the Shiite Party of God say more?

Thomas Burnet, the seventeenth-century divine who
supplied the motto for Coleridge's "The Rime of the
Ancient Mariner," knew why terrorists and tabloids belong in the same family. "I readily believe," he says in
the famous quotation from *Archaeologiae Philosophicae*,
"that there are more invisible than visible things in the
universe." Therefore, "it is sometimes good to contemplate in the mind, as in a picture, the image of a greater
and better world; otherwise the intellect, habituated to
the petty things of daily life, may too much contract
itself, and wholly sink down to trivial thoughts. But
meanwhile we must be vigilant for truth and keep proportion, that we may distinguish the certain from the
uncertain, day from night."

If we are to be truly human, in other words, we must
honor a perspective in which reality is fabulous lest
the vital umbilical between secular and sacred be sev-
ered; but it is no less important, as Spark's novel

maintains, to distinguish among fabulations, especially given their propensity for an indiscriminate congeniality with one another. Bruno Bettleheim is on Burnet's side when in *The Uses of Enchantment* he points out how important it is that fairy stories not "confuse the child as to what is real and what is not." Children, he says, are not confused—are, in fact, educated about important realities in the human environment—by stories frankly set in fantasy land, but are confused by those which mix "realistic elements with wish-fulfilling and fantastic devices."

There is no such confusion in Coleridge's great poem. The fabulous voyage of the Ancient Mariner is not a poetic substitution for the historical voyages (fabulous enough in their own right) of Magellan, Hawkins, Cook, and Shelvocke, reports of which Coleridge had read. His imagination was omnivorous enough but it was ironic, not totalitarian; therefore, his poem asserts an enriching interdependence of poetry and history in which the integrity of each is respected. If we wish to understand Eliot's talking bird in "Burnt Norton," we must be able to believe that the poem acknowledges an order of reality in which birds do not talk—which is the way children understand talking animals in animated cartoons. Cervantes' *Don Quixote*, Flaubert's *Madame Bovary*, and Melville's *Moby Dick* are fabulous stories about people who truly enough have lost their ability to keep proportion so that they cannot distinguish among fabulations. Such people get into the right kind of trouble for good stories, and, as their creators might concede, deserve tabloid headlines. Their stories are about the significance of the fact that the characters themselves do not know this, or do not know it until the knowledge comes too late to spoil the story. But at the same time such characters dramatize the recurring predicament of human beings confronted with that ambiguous congeniality of fabulations which makes it so hard to distinguish between certain and uncertain.

The tabloids have as hard a time distinguishing among

fabulations as does the Shiite Party of God. For both, realistic elements are mixed with wish-fulfilling and fantastic devices so that no proportion is kept. This is also true of all the totalitarian societies we know; certainly it is true of Gustav Husak's Czechoslovakia as we see it in Milan Kundera's *The Book of Laughter and Forgetting*. Husak, at a festive ceremony at Prague castle, is represented as the president of forgetting, the "president of the eternal, not the ephemeral," who weeps at the music of pop singer Karel Gott because his music is the music of forgetting, and who weeps too for the attending children because "childhood is the image of the future." Husak is of the Party of God, a God who has been denied his integrity in the process of being incorporated in a secular fabulation. Having forgotten so much, Husak does not know that he deserves a tabloid headline as much as Don Quixote and Emma Bovary do. By the same token he cannot know how vulnerable he is to the novel's perspective in which he is like a figure in an animated cartoon who does not doubt that his adored children will continue to take him literally—as indeed they must if he is not to become the victim of forgotten transfigurations.

One must assume that the Thoreau who described the battle between the red and black ants would have reacted to the martyrdom-courting Hezbollahs with scornful irony. Whatever lesson the ants had taught him, however, was forgotten or bracketed when he became captivated by John Brown's tabloid-style promise of a blood bath in which the sinful, slave-cursed land would be purified and transfigured. When Brown was captured after the fiasco at Harper's Ferry, Thoreau wanted him to hang, certain that a martyred hero would serve the cause best. Perhaps there had been something of the Shiite fundamentalist in Thoreau all along—something which affiliates him with such fabulous ascetics as the Greek cynic Diogenes, Hassan's Assassins, and Flaubert's Saint Anthony.

Certainly some of his contemporaries—Henry James, Sr., and Robert Louis Stevenson, for instance—thought Thoreau acted as if he were a one-man Party of God—and like all Parties of God he had little use for democratic politics. Election week in Athens would have disgusted him as much as it would have disgusted the Shiite Hijackers or Abu Nidal's terrorists. From the point of view of any Party of God, which above all wants the simplifying and unifying transfiguration of a fairy story, democratic politics does a poor job of distinguishing certain from uncertain, day from night. This is why, when the State fails to measure up to a Party of God's highest expectations, bombs and blood baths are so likely to be the moral imperatives. When Thoreau wrote "Civil Disobedience" the moral imperative for the good man hounded by the bad government was simply to wash his hands of it. Later, apparently, John Brown made him see the superiority of the Hezbollah way.

Historically, of course, democratic politics, whether in America or in post–World War II Greece, has often enough employed the transfigurations characteristic of tabloid style. Thoreau, then a recent Harvard graduate and a sometime teacher, would have seen it in this guise in the boisterous 1840 presidential contest between Whigs and Democrats, when the claim that President Martin Van Buren ate from gold plates and perfumed his whiskers with cologne enlivened the campaign, even if it did his cause no good. But if the democratic process is affected by tabloid style it also counters and domesticates that style for the same reason that it counters and domesticates the wistful Parties of God that both enliven and threaten it with visions of a sublime unanimity. In the always volatile democratic mix, then, it may be that the tabloids are in effect a sociopolitical version of T.S. Eliot's "objective correlative" for a public state of mind that might otherwise find the fanatic fabulations of potential terrorists irresistible. Grant this and the tabloids have something of that

"worthy purpose" which Wordsworth believed distinguished his *Lyrical Ballads* from all those stupid German tragedies.

Perhaps Eliot's talking bird would have been more
useful to us if it had said "boredom" instead of "reality"
and let it go at that, particularly since our problems
with reality are so hard to separate from our problems
with boredom. Certainly, American politics for Thoreau
lacked the transfiguring excitement that would have
made it tolerable. In this respect he was like so many
literary intellectuals, his spiritual heirs, for whom—as
was apparent once more at the forty-eighth International PEN Congress in New York—the arts model a
level of clarity and existential intensity against which
the everyday routines of democratic politics are appallingly jejune. Perhaps their susceptibility in the thirties
and forties to a Marxist-Leninist vision of a transfigured
world needs to be seen as a kind of bovarism the tabloid
dimensions of which in time have become embarrass-
ingly apparent.

In the good society, we like to believe, there would be
no boredom—a definition which Kundera's Husak and
Orwell's Big Brother, to say nothing of Olschki's Hassan, would have no difficulty accepting. The totalitarian
ways of avoiding boredom are familiar enough: censorship, scarcity, surveillance, ceremonial cooptation of
the person (only the person alone can be bored), and terror: terrified and terrorizer are symbiotically immune
to boredom, as those travelers who experienced the hi-
jackings of the Italian cruise ship Achille Lauro, or that
ill-fated Egyptian jet liner, might be the first to agree.

This may be why the test of a free and open society is
its disciplined capacity to endure the boredom of the
untransfigured commonplace—not so much because the
commonplace is in itself boring but because the insistence that it be at every moment glorified with an entrancing intensity of meaning violates the reality of the
commonplace, the nature of which is to test as it resists

all impetuous demands that it be at every moment fabulous. Perhaps this is only to say that a free and open society depends as much on the ability to keep proportion as it does on hope. Those who, lacking this ability, live in the expectation of irreversible transfigurations of the commonplace, recruit all too easily into the most available Party of God.

Chapter 12
The Perils of Poetry

As the year begins one learns from *Advertising Age* that advertising is approaching a time of challenge when budgets and media will be closely scrutinized and new creative strategies must be developed. Media experts believe that advertising expenditures will continue to increase but much less dramatically than during the golden years of the early 1980s (in 1983 the one hundred top advertisers spent $11.67 billion). Nevertheless, the general picture, at least for the layman, is that of an industry that has never been healthier or more effective. Timex, in fact, had enough confidence in it to spend a million creating its spectacular underwater ad for the 1986 Super Bowl, where it was televised at a cost of $1.1 million per minute. In 1967 that Super Bowl minute would have cost only $80,000.

However, two recently published books—Stephen Fox's *The Mirror Makers* and Michael Schudson's *Advertising, the Uneasy Persuasion*—suggest that even qualified optimism needs to be tempered. In his history of advertising in America, Mr. Fox contends that advertising is no longer the force in American life that it was in the 1920s when it spent much less than its current $54.6 billion a year. The paradox, he claims, is that "advertising has grown and prospered and yet has lost in-

"The Perils of Poetry" first appeared in *Salmagundi* (Spring 1987): 86–100. Reprinted with permission.

fluence." Not only does it have the trouble that most contemporary institutions have—"finding anybody to believe it"—but it may be a mistake to think that advertising manipulates society more than, or even as much as, society manipulates advertisers.

Most enemies of advertising, I suspect, are more likely to believe *Advertising Age* than Stephen Fox, even when the latter quotes that knowledgeable and literate ad-man, David Ogilvy: "The public is *bored* by most advertisements, and has acquired a genius for ignoring them." The obvious thing would seem to be that James Atlas has it right when he points out in an *Atlantic* essay (October 1984) that Madison Avenue uses increasingly sophisticated "psychographic" means to find out who we are and what we want, with the result that *Advertising Age* has more to cheer about all the time. Indeed, it is quite usual for the enemies of advertising to believe that it is both boring and irresistible: that is, boring to them and irresistible to the bourgeois masses.

One of the earliest post–World War II explanations of this combination of boredom and irresistibility came from S.I. Hayakawa, then a general semanticist but fated to become both a college president and United States senator. In August of 1945 he gave a paper, "Poetry and Advertising," at Columbia University (later published in *Poetry*) in which he distinguished between disinterested and venal poetry—the former being what we generally think of as poetry, or "true" poetry, the latter being the techniques and devices of the former as they are exploited for profit in the marketplace. "Almost all advertising" is thus "the poeticizing of consumer goods." The result is a degradation of language that makes disinterested poetry harder to write and in general increases public resources for disillusionment and cynicism.

Subsequent attacks on the world of venal poetry were well publicized and commercially successful. Frederic Wakeman's *The Hucksters* (1946) and Sloan Wilson's *The Man in the Gray Flannel Suit* (1955) did well as novels and movies, thanks in part to the venal poetry with which they were advertised. Vance Packards's *The Hidden Persuaders* (1957) carried the war into the spooky underworld of motivational research (territory now being re-explored in William Meyers's *The Image Makers*). When Wilson Bryan Key appeared on the scene with *Subliminal Seduction* (1973) and *Media Sexploitation* (1976)—books that found sexual motivation embedded or imprinted in the most unlikely places—he was cropping on well prepared ground. By 1983, when Steven M.L. Aronson's *Hype* arrived with its excoriation of the "abhorrent exorbitance and odious disproportion" employed in the merchandising of products and persons, it was as safe to use hype against the hype of the marketplace as it was to be in favor of Mother's Day. Who in broad daylight with everybody listening would like to contradict Aronson when he says that "hype routinely debases language"? Now it has become as easy to believe, as Key contends, that Ritz crackers have the word *sex* embedded in them as it was to believe that, as a tabloid recently reported, a baby girl was born pregnant. Certainly too it seems safe to say, as the literary critic Wayne C. Booth has said, that our society "finds itself offering immense rewards to a vast number of hired metaphorists, hired to make metaphors that will accomplish a predetermined end regardless of what they say about our character or do to it."

Now as always—and perhaps now more than ever—there is reason to be concerned about those abusers of the dialect of the tribe, the hired metaphorists. Who more than Professor Booth is qualified to detect the semantic shenanigans their venality prompts them to? But suppose the ongoing attacks on the venal poetry of advertising are at least in part, and sometimes entirely, a convenient form for a pervasive uneasiness with the entrancing powers not only of language but of all the media of communication?

This uneasiness expressed itself in reaction to rhetoric well before advertising became a favorite object of abuse. Henry Fairlie has complained in *The New Republic* (28 May 1984) about the political consequences in a democracy of the decline of oratory. Great oratory, which appeals in strenuous moral terms, is the means great leaders employ to persuade men and women to act or not act "with a joint will and purpose." To succeed, Fairlie believes, they need to assume a common body of allusions and a citizenry willing to be inspired, whereas all it has now "are reckless, self-interested, and pampered groups." But what great oratory also needs, and what Mr. Fairlie doesn't mention, is a leader class of respectable size that is not embarrassed by or suspicious of rhetoric, including the rhetoric of poetry.

Aristotle, who did not have to assume such an embarrassment in his audience, defined rhetoric "as the faculty of observing in any given case the available means of persuasion." The available means for him included not only the skills of the metaphorist (he would have agreed with Hayakawa that the rhetor and the poet arm themselves out of a common arsenal) but a knowledge of human personality types and human emotions. His great *Rhetoric* is therefore in its way an anticipation of motivational research: if you wish to motivate people for good causes you had better understand the psychological grounds of human action. He even knew about hype, which he called "heightening of effect." It is, therefore, not surprising that advertising consultants like John Witek (see his *Response Television*) sometimes advocate that creative admen go back to Aristotle and classical rhetoric.

Classical rhetoric as it comes to us through Plato, Isocrates, Aristotle, Cicero, Quintilian, and Longinus is the medium through which the foundations of Western civilization come to the Middle Ages and Renaissance and so to us. As Richard McKeon has pointed out in *Rhetoric in the Middle Ages*, the application of the arts of rhetoric was crucial to the formulation and communication of human effort in oratory, all kinds of public speaking, letter writing, theology, philosophy, and scientific speculation. In this tradition intelligent men always knew that sophists and demagogues were ever ready to exploit the arts of rhetoric, but they never doubted that the eloquent, even transporting, use of language in order to persuade others to do what, because of their ignorance, prejudice, selfishness, or sloth, they were inclined not to do was for the good person a moral imperative. Cicero might have been speaking for the whole tradition, and for Fairlie as well, when he said that the orator "teaches, delights, and moves the minds of his hearers; to teach them is his duty, to delight them is creditable to him, to move them is indispensable."

To us this sounds quite old-fashioned, if not dangerously naïve. We feel more at home when in *The New Organon* Francis Bacon says: "words plainly force and overrule the understanding, and throw all into confusion, and lead men away into numberless empty controversies and idle fancies." This was written at a time when there was still flesh on the bones of Isocrates, Cicero, and Quintilian but already the conflict between poet and scientist was beginning to take shape. In 1667 Thomas Sprat in his *History of the Royal Society*, and most likely with the rhetoric of the gone but hardly forgotten Puritan rebellion in mind, stated that the "ornaments of speaking" are "in open defiance against *Reason* and that eloquence ought to be banished out of all civil *Societies*, as a thing fatal to Peace and good Manners." A few years later in *An Essay Concerning Human Understanding* John Locke wrote that the art of rhetoric with its "artificial and figurative use of words" is "for nothing else but to insinuate wrong ideas, move the passions, and thereby mislead the judgment."

In the same passage Locke, who could on occasion be quite eloquent, goes on to compare eloquence to the "fair sex" and to observe how vain it is "to find fault with those arts of deceiving wherein men find pleasure to be deceived." It is not hard to imagine his reaction to a Revlon ad, but neither is it hard to imagine Hamlet's.

In *Hamlet* there is no more familiar example of beguilingly deceptive statement, whether in language or gesture, than that of the painted woman. "God hath given you one face," Hamlet says to Ophelia, "and you make yourselves another." In the graveyard scene, with Yorick's skull in his hands, he says, "Now get you to my lady's chamber, and tell her, let her paint an inch thick, to this favour she must come." Speaking with Rosencrantz and Guildenstern for the first time, he presents the universe itself in analogy with the painted woman so that its "majestical roof fretted with golden fire" is in ugly reality "a foul and pestilential congregation of vapours." The false Claudius himself in a memorable passage compares his "painted word" to "The harlot's cheek, beautied with plast'ring art."

By now, of course, the association of harlotry with the entrancing use of language, or with entrancing display generally, is commonplace in our literature. It seems inevitable to us that Melville should have made his Ishmael consider the frightful possibility that the whiteness of Moby Dick was a sign "that all deified nature absolutely paints like the harlot, whose allurements cover nothing but the charnel-house within." What better way to indicate that the ship which Coleridge's Ancient Mariner sees approaching the desperately becalmed crew has sinister designs than to have it captained by "The Night-mare Life-in-Death" whose "lips were red," whose "skin was white as leprosy"? How else can Frederic Henry sound authentic in Hemingway's *A Farewell to Arms* unless he is "always embarrassed by the words sacred, glorious, and sacrifice and the expression in vain"—unless for him the whole vocabulary of traditional eloquence is only a harlotry of proclamations "slapped up by billposters over other proclamations"? Indeed, modernism and postmodernism never sound more like themselves than when they assume a whorish disjunction between eloquence-making and truth-telling. Advertising, being both eloquent and venal, is on the side of the harlot's cheek and must take the consequences. In the meantime, we have gotten in the habit of overlooking the plain fact that for a long time now plain prose has been, as Hugh Kenner nicely puts it, "a perfect medium for hoaxes."

For many of the adversaries of advertising, the venal metaphorists of the marketplace are simply the agents capitalism uses to exercise the harlotry of its entrancing promises. To a Marxist, no doubt, the very hype of ads is a sign that the old whore is closer to a disastrous final disclosure than she realizes. Of course, not all attackers of advertising are Marxists. It is possible to believe that Madison Avenue is ruining the good system by exploiting the worst in us. William James's remark about advertising practices that seem rather primitive now is typical: "no acuter instance could be found of the way in which, in our country, private greed is suffered to override the public good."

Indeed, advertising offers a convenient point of attack for such a variety of dissatisfactions with America that in a negative way it is an important cultural unifier. Here it is in continuity with that hatred of the bourgeois that was a cultural unifier for the modernists, who could generally agree that any poetry preferred by the bourgeois was bound to be both vulgar and venal. This is why the late Lillian Hellman's appearance in a Blackglama ad was so shocking to some of her admirers: she had apparently sold out to the great whore of capitalism.

Conversely, of course, the adman is quite capable of co-opting the antibourgeois and antiestablishment values of modernism, so that any ad agency in action is a showcase for those who want to point out the cultural contradictions of capitalism. Thus the adman may congratulate himself on his Blackglama caper, but he only plays into the hands of his adversaries as he demonstrates once more his evil powers of entrancement. It is one thing to see people like Joe Namath and Orson Welles endorsing, respectively, panty hose and wine; we expect them, as public entertainers, to participate in an activity that if it is to be successful must come on like show business. But if such an intransigent and moralistic critic of American materialism as Miss Hellman, who would have scorned any attempt to classify her as a mere entertainer, could not keep her virtue intact, what chance have we lesser mortals?

The disgust that American intellectuals, especially literary intellectuals, so routinely express for the venal poetry of the marketplace helps to explain their attraction to the critical theories of European deconstructionism. What that heir to modernism has discovered is a way of protecting the reader-critic from the entrancing power of language as expressed not only in literature but in organized messages of any kind—including, of course, the messages of deconstruction. For the deconstructionist there is always a perspective from which any particular organization of information, especially if it is aesthetically effective, can be seen as a threat to or obscurer of other possible organizations. This is why "structure" became a dirty word in the liberated sixties, and why deconstruction can be seen now as a continuation of countercultural impulses. This is also why Jacques Derrida's *Glas* no less than the Virginia Slims ads promises enfranchisement not only from the straitjacket of the past but, even better, from the past that the present will soon become.

It is also why modernist, postmodernist, and deconstructionist writers have produced so much exposé writing. The aim of the exposé is to protect against what is seen as the dangerous entrancement of an established style and perspective. In the case of deconstructive criticism that aim is to expose the extent to which the apparently solid rocks of a work of literature are only papier-mâché after all. For those who tend to be overawed or inconvenienced by solid rocks this can be the same kind of morale-raising operation that Wilson Bryan Key's discovery of sexual titillation in Ritz crackers, or in the configuration of ice cubes in a highball, can be for those who need to believe that some benign force is countering the black magic of advertising.

Black magic to succeed must disguise from its victims that it is black magic. It must appear as a vision of reality to which any alternative is absolutely unthinkable. Victims of black magic lose their sense of point of view. Since a sense of point of view can be an isolating and intolerable moral burden that forces one to be constantly aware of mistaking metaphoric assertions for assertions of identity, the loss of it can be a great relief. Hence the liberating experience of the various cults that have proven to be so captivating, so morale-raising, to young and old. Fanaticism, which is a kind of hype, can be a way of survival under these circumstances: like terrorism and tabloid journalism, it is a flamboyant attempt to overwhelm other possible interpretations of information. One might say that fanaticism and all other forms of hype become possible in proportion as points of view multiply and crowd against one another. Hype is possible because point of view can be inexorable, which means that the aim of hype is to overwhelm all adversary points of view. In proportion as it is successful, then, hype as such ceases to be a problem. This is why totalitarian societies, even though they aspire to hyperbolic conditions of unity and order, can be called hype-reducing social mechanisms that provide a permanent cure for the fear of entrancement.

Faith commitments solve the problems of point of view, hype and morale. That faithful man, Maxim Gorky, in 1933 lectured Soviet writer-intellectuals as follows: "It is vitally essential for the creative work of our writers that they acquire the point of view from which—and from which alone—can be seen all the filthy crimes of capitalism, all the vileness of its bloody intentions, and all the grandeur of the heroic work of the proletarian dictatorship." We understand, and most likely his immediate audience did also, that it is the bloody capital-ists, who, taking their advertising as its own valuation, are imprisoned within a mere point of view as against the absolute truth of the proletarian dictatorship. Gorky was no more likely to waste his time with a mere point of view than Wilson Bryan Key is likely to waste his time with an asexual Ritz cracker.

In *The Invisible Writing* the late Arthur Koestler distinguishes between what once appeared to be beyond point of view and what in time turned out to be only point of view when he looks back over his life as a committed communist (1931–1938): "Never before nor after had life been so brimful of meaning as during those seven years. They had the superiority of a beautiful error over a shabby truth." Koestler's subsequent life indicates that he did not naïvely reduce the beautiful to the erroneous and the truthful to the shabby, a simplification that would have put him in a class with that prince of reductionists, Shakespeare's Iago. The latter is also the prince of deconstructionists who knows in his bones that all faith positions are epistemological nonsense, mere points of view, and that it is pointless to distinguish between true poetry and venal poetry because all poetry is venal and Quintilian is no more to be trusted than David Ogilvy. In this perspective advertising is a model of the attempt to reverse a painfully established ranking of shabby truth over beautiful error. The aim of this ranking has been to secure, Iago-fashion, an irreducible minimum of peace of mind on the faith position of a dogmatic skepticism.

Political rhetoric is of course political advertising. It is not surprising to find Alfred Kazin saying in *The New Republic* that presidential politics is now manipulation and indoctrination, a "shameless seduction of words used, authoritarian fashion, merely to rouse, to inflame, and so to set a patriotic mob to yelling, as they now regularly do at rallies." James Reston has complained in *The New York Times* that the two political

parties "somehow manage to distribute more mislead-
ing information at their nominating conventions than
all the other advertising hucksters combined." Even
John O'Toole, chairman of the board at Foote, Cone &
Belding Communications, Inc., has stated in *Newsweek*
that advertising spots used by political candidates are
giving advertising and politics a bad name.

There can be little doubt that the disgust literary
people have traditionally felt for the day-by-day work-
ings of democratic politics is inseparable from their disgust with the venal poetry of bourgeois political rhetoric. The mainly unsympathetic reaction to Secretary of
State George Shultz's address at the forty-eighth International Congress of PEN in New York was hardly unexpected. In fact, we are surprised when the writer re-
acting to the world of statecraft or politics does not
sound like Flaubert (the longer he lived the less faith he
had in any party), or Joyce (who, Richard Ellmann
writes, "did not wish *Finnegans Wake* to be banned
in any country because of its author's political bias"),
or Samuel Beckett (for him, his biographer Deirdre Bair
writes, "political activity," even discussion, "was a waste
of time").

In this context Beckett is especially interesting because of his current status as an intransigent rejector of
the world of venal poetry. The playwright Harold Pinter, for instance, has said that Beckett is "the most
courageous, remorseless writer going and the more he
grinds my nose in the shit the more I am grateful to
him . . . he's not taking me up any garden, he's not slip-
ping me any wink, he's not flogging me a remedy or a
path or a revelation or a basinful of breadcrumbs, he's
not selling me anything I don't want to buy . . . " It is
surprising to learn from Bair that in a bad time Beckett
considered enrolling in a London school to learn advertising copywriting, but it is not surprising to learn that
he admires Sade and Celine (though it should be noted
that they are hyperbolists of the first water) and has

been much influenced by Nietzsche and Schopenhauer. Such people are no more likely to give comfort to a champion of democratic oratory like Henry Fairlie than to the subscribers of *Advertising Age.*

There is a heroic purity in Beckett's suspicion— whether as a poet, playwright or novelist—of the entrancing powers of language. He is as certain as Hamlet and Ishmael sometimes are about the harlotry of the universe, or as Hemingway is most of the time about the evil of billposter words. His strategy against venal poetry is the way of those semantic minimalists charged in Orwell's *1984* with the perfection of Newspeak: less is beautiful. On the scale that runs from logorrhea to pregnant silence he occupies a place close to that of the traditional macho hero who communicates with his fists and gun and leaves words to the women, whose natural orality is itself a form of cosmetic. Convinced as Bacon is that "words throw all into confusion," Beckett is as suspicious of poetry with a capital *P* as Richard Rorty is of philosophy with a capital *P.*

Indeed, there is a puritanism in Beckett that suggests the asceticism so enthusiastically practiced in contemporary cults by the children of those bourgeois parents generally identified as the prime victims of venal poetry. Martin Esslin has understandably referred to him as a "rare, ascetic and saintly personality." There is something in him, in fact, of the stylites, those fifth-century anchorites who so dramatically advertised their low opinion of the world from the tops of the pillars on which they lived. In that airy solitude, of course, their rejection of the painted woman was as total as Beckett's. And one is reminded again of the ease with which in our culture the rejection of the painted woman becomes a rhetorical ploy for the rejection of women— that "fair sex" whose "arts of deceiving" are for Locke a model of eloquence. And one may be reminded too of Lionel Trilling's great essay "The Fate of Pleasure" in which the asceticism of the modernist writer is brilliantly linked up with his need to destroy the "specious good" of the bourgeois world, to rub its nose in the shabby truth.

If there is a transcendence in Beckett's saintliness it is the more to be admired because it hopes for nothing. Hoping for nothing, however, it is different from the saintliness of the historical Puritan or pillar dweller, who, entranced by heavenly advertisements, hoped for everything. It is nevertheless the expression of a genuinely liberating program of aesthetic renunciation. Perhaps the Beckett kind of Puritan can say with conviction that whatever agency is on the far side of the Big Bang ought to be ashamed of itself, but there is nothing to be done about it that does not court the risk of one more beautiful error, one more confining and entrancing point of view. *Endgame* is thus no more likely to encourage a riot or a revolution than *Madame Bovary*, and might even be called a conservative force in the world. In fact, Hamm in *Endgame* is what Emma Bovary might have become if, denied the comforts of arsenic, she had been forced to live into old age with only her disillusionment to keep her warm.

Perhaps something of this is what the Swedish Academy had in mind when in 1969 it awarded the Nobel Prize to Beckett for "a body of work that, in new forms of fiction and the theatre, has transmuted the destitution of modern man into his exaltation." Was the Academy, perhaps, pointing to the paradox of the brilliant *Krapp's Last Tape* in which the willed black magic of the aesthetic achievement undercuts the thematic assertion that nothing can be done and even suggests that much more might be done along the same lines, so that it is a comforting if somewhat disconcerting advertisement for the future after all? The British critic Harold Hobson has said of *Endgame* that those who know how to view it experience "a profound and sombre and paradoxical joy." In human terms, then, its enchanting staging of disenchantment may have the same utility for survival in the face of adversity that Bruno Bettelheim has claimed for fairy stories, so that Albert Camus may be right when he says that a literature of despair is a contradiction in terms. One wonders what creative breakthrough might have resulted had Beckett actually gone on to London to learn the advertising business. Might he not have fathered a school of metaphorists whose black if bleak magic would have made their work indeconstructible even by Wilson Bryan Key?

Beckett was not able to go to Stockholm to collect his prize and therefore did not make the traditional acceptance address. It is hard to imagine what he might have said. A brief homily expanding on Clov's question from *Endgame* might have been appropriate: "Why this farce, day after day?" Certainly he would have attempted nothing in the vein of Faulkner's 1955 address, which with its tricks and rhetoric (Hemingway's terms for it) affected many of his admirers the way Hellman's Blackglama ad did hers. "I believe that man will not merely endure; he will prevail," Faulkner said, and he also said that "The poet's voice need not merely be the record of man, it can be one of the props, the pillars to help him understand and prevail." Billposter language indeed.

Fairlie, I suspect, would have approved of Faulkner's address, seeing it, perhaps, as an example of the once-admired virtue of decorum, but it would have been unacceptable to Flaubert and Pinter. Since it is about the prevailing not only of man but the individual person, it is as contaminated by point of view as poetry, advertising, and political rhetoric generally are—however all three may on occasion exploit the entrancing powers of language in an effort to obscure or permanently change this fact.

The paradoxical, even embarrassing, thing is that advertising with its venal metaphorists, for its own selfish reasons, can end up on the side of individual freedom, just as political rhetoric, for all its oversimplifying hype, can end up on the side of democracy. We can as-

sume that the adman is not interested in developing the
individual's full potential, and certainly not concerned
to make the latter skeptical of the entrancing powers of
language, though the former may often enough have
that effect. Advertising addresses the selfish, insecure,
sensuous, and insatiable individual with the tantalizing
utopian promises of a campaigning politician. It is one
more of those agencies that, as Francis Bacon puts it,
incline the human understanding "to suppose the existence of more order and regularity in the world than it
finds." At the same time, however, it takes the individual's flesh-and-blood reality in the world seriously; it
assures him in its own interests that his epistemological
image of his environment is trustworthy, that he can resist deconstructive assaults on his pieties, and that he
will prevail in the pursuit of his specious good, if only
in order to continue to consume.

Taken by itself, of course, this may all appear egre-
giously venal, especially if one assumes that the first
concern of the user of any medium of communication
ought to be the integrity of that medium. But the advertiser exists in a pluralistic society with competing
points of view, some of which have quite other designs
on it as well as on the all too susceptible individual—
in particular, those designs for his transcendence in
self-abnegating harmonies that have proven over the
years to be the most potent black magic. Our democratic society's protective fear of such black magic may
be responsible for the shabby truth that Madison Avenue has had to recognize as a revision of the beautiful error of its salad days: that, as Stephen Fox reports,
it is itself being manipulated. The impulse-releasing
advertiser is thus maneuvered into being something
like the champion of the beleaguered individual that
the ascetic Beckett is. Society, to put it another way,
persuades advertising to reinforce society's own hard-
won late twentieth-century conviction that, given the
too often demonstrated insatiable lusts of the self-tran-

scending utopians, only selfish and pleasure-respecting utopias are safe to dream about.

Orwell, in fact, makes this point in *1984* by way of the painted woman, and in a context that suggests the perspective not of Hamlet but of a Revlon ad. When Winston Smith and Julia are in their hideaway love nest she displays herself to him with makeup on her face. The effect is to make her "not only much prettier," but, above all, "far more feminine." The cosmetics, especially in the light of the Party's own kind of transcendent person-denying and pleasure-abhorring puritanism, are not only a discovery of and an advertisement for the personhood of both of them but a means of indicating that any transcendent socio-political program that cannot accept and build on this fact is simply their enemy.

But even if one grants all this there is still the concern with the social value of truth and sincerity with which Roger Draper ends his essay on advertising, "The Faithless Shepherd," in the June 26, 1986 *New York Review of Books*. Society, he writes, "would collapse if we all thought of one another in the way most of us think of advertising." This sounds unexceptionable enough, especially to those of us who think of advertising as a thoroughly mendacious and profit-motivated activity and the good society as one characterized by absolute candor and an abhorrence of privacy. Maxim Gorky was not the first man to dream of such a society, nor the first to see that it demanded a new type of human being who would be the greatest, and perhaps the last, of human artifacts.

It may be useful, therefore, to put beside Draper's conclusion this from George Steiner's *After Babel*: "At every level, from brute camouflage to poetic vision, the linguistic capacity to conceal, misinform, leave ambiguous, hypothesize, invent is indispensable to the equilibrium of human consciousness and to the development of man in society." If Steiner is right the harlotries of advertising are as normal as those "arts of deceiving" thanks to which Locke's "fair sex" is able to give men so much pleasure, and only the most naïve utopian would dream of an utterly candid society. Certainly Gorky could accept Steiner's dark vision only if it could be seen as a depiction of the means that history in its cunning employs as it drives inexorably to its grand and sincere conclusion.

We can assume, however, that Steiner is no less convinced than Draper that the well-being of society depends on the continuing effort, coming from whatever quarter, to refine the language of the tribe, just as a physicist may believe that the welfare of the universe depends on its capacity to resist the entropy that cannot be separated from the processes that make the universe possible. Indeed, one senses behind both writers the fear, more common among literary intellectuals now than a decade ago, that civilization is threatened by a radical and wide-ranging skepticism about the possibility of using language to order human affairs. Nietzsche with his belief that there is a lie at the heart of poetry, Maurice Blanchot with his conviction that there is a correlation between clarity of communication and stonewalling against the truth, Derrida with his rejection of the New Critics' respect for the integrity of the text—all prepare for Key's deconstructive analysis of a Ritz cracker, indeed, make one wonder what subterranean perversities he or Roland Barthes might find lurking beneath the banalities of the fortune cookie. And this is to say nothing about the encouraging advertisements for the future the enemies of democracy see implied as the higher skepticism filters down into bourgeois politics.

Life in the quotidian world of buying and selling, loving, marriage and begetting, politicking and community-making—life in the public square, as Richard J. Neuhaus has called it—has always depended on the human determination to act as if language as conventionally given is a fundamentally reliable instrument, however its users must learn to live with Steiner's truth. No doubt there has always been some awareness among revisionists and avant-garde abusers of this determination that they are dependent on it as a hedge against their elitist extremism. How many poststructuralist critics, whether in France or at Yale, would be at ease in a society that attempted to act out the epistemological, social, moral, and political implications of their own rhetoric?

Certainly, literary intellectuals often enough act as if they believe that the real threat to our common survival comes from the venal metaphorists of the marketplace, attacking them with an acerbity they would hesitate to direct against attacks on bourgeois society coming from the higher revisionary metaphorists. Perhaps in their hearts they suspect that Orwell had a point when he said of those linguistically impoverished, sentimental, and cosmetic-using remnants of humanity, the proles, that hope lies in them. It is no easier to imagine Orwell than Beckett as an unqualified champion of venal poetry, but in the context of his satiric treatment of totalitarian minimalism the inference is clear. Not only must a man be willing to run the risk of the painted woman if he is to avoid lovelessness, but a democracy must be willing to run the risk of venality in its poetry and hype in its political oratory if it is not to become a tyranny of virtue. The apparently riskless alternative, particularly given the irascible perfectionism that is second nature to human nature, is all too likely to be an entrancing state of affairs in which, as in *1984*, reality and advertisement become indistinguishable and hype is simply the way it is. Or as Maxim Gorky seems to have wanted it, a single point of view is triumphant and the final great fairy story begins.

Chapter 13
Doctor Johnson Kicks a Stone

Readers of Boswell's *Life of Johnson* will remember the great Doctor's refutation of Bishop Berkeley's idealism. He and Boswell had just come out of a church in Harwich and were discussing the Bishop's "ingenious sophistry to prove the nonexistence of matter." Boswell observed "that though we are satisfied his doctrine is not true, it is impossible to refute it." To this Johnson responded, "striking his foot with mighty force against a large stone, till he rebounded from it, 'I refute it thus.'" For Boswell this was an argument from first principles that are as fundamental to metaphysics as axioms are to mathematics. To use Johnson's own phrase, it is an argument based on "the experience of mankind"—the ground upon which he confidently stood when he expressed his disapproval of such other philosophical contemporaries as Hume, Voltaire, and Rousseau (the latter "a rascal who ought to be hunted out of society"). Or as Walter Jackson Bate puts it in *The Achievement of Samuel Johnson*, the first principle of his thinking was "to go back to the living and concrete nature of experience."

Boswell thought Johnson a philosopher, though he admits in a famous passage that his table manners might have suggested otherwise. Apparently G.K. Ches-

"Doctor Johnson Kicks a Stone" first appeared in *Philosophy and Literature* (Spring 1986): 65–75. Reprinted with permission.

terton thought he had some claim to the term, for he called Johnson's novel *Rasselas* "a sort of philosophical satire on philosophy." Most likely Johnson thought of himself as among many other things a philosopher: the humanities had not yet settled snugly into their modern compartments. Now, of course, any undergraduate student of philosophy is willing to believe that Johnson's argument against Berkeley isn't worth much (he may be no less willing to believe that the Bishop's argument isn't worth much either). He may also know that in the perspective of the modern physicist Johnson's stone was not as solid as Johnson thought it was—though it is likely he would have thought this information no more relevant to the argument than Thales's belief that all things are made of water or Pythagoras's that all things are numbers. The important thing was whether a thinker violated the experience of mankind. When the Scotsman Lord Hunderland praised the ancient philosophers for the candor and good humor with which they disputed with one another Johnson would have none of it: "They disputed with good humour upon their fanciful theories," he said, "because they were not interested in the truth of them."

It is not hard to imagine the Doctor's reaction to our own fanciful theories in philosophy, linguistics, and literary criticism. Suppose him at the Mitre Tavern for an evening's defense of the experience of mankind against the ingenious sophistries of a company made up of Jacques Derrida, Geoffrey H. Hartman, Stanley Fish, Michel Foucault, Paul de Man, and Jacques Lacan—the lot of them variously committed to the belief that the proper job of philosophy is not the pursuit of the truth but the pursuit of the truth about the pursuit of the truth. Johnson eyes the group warily, expecting the worst. There are too many Frenchmen present, and as he made clear at supper one July evening in the Turk's Head coffeehouse, French writers are superficial "because they are not scholars, and so proceed upon the mere power of their own minds." Nevertheless, the assembled gentlemen present their positions: we are all prisoners of the total epistemological environment of our age, our *épistème*; locked linguistically into interpretive communities, we cannot know the text in itself; the proper function of the critic is creative free play, the text being merely a convenient occasion; language, being self-referential, cannot reveal a subject; human agency is a flattering but deceptive myth; transcendent systems of thought are impossible; if literature touches reality anywhere we cannot know it.

Meanwhile Johnson, than whom no man ever had "a more ardent love of literature, or a higher respect for it," is in high dudgeon, kicking figurative stones right and left, no real ones being available inside the Mitre. His adversaries observe him with indulgent good humor, amused but not impressed with this crude bourgeois display, having long ago learned how to treat inconvenient stones as if they were real in order to avoid stumbling over them while knowing very well that they are not. Besides, being well read in contemporary biographical theory they are prepared to believe that this antic figure in front of them is not the historical Sam Johnson, about whom no one can know much for certain, but a literary creation.

Placing Johnson in the company of such sophisticates is an easy way to disqualify him, or at least display him for better or worse as part of a world we have lost. "Johnson grew up in a world in which neoclassic culture was unquestioned and supreme, and lived on into a world in which it was undermined and soon to be toppled," John Wain observes in his good biography. Wain does not doubt that he has made significant contact with his subject, and having made it he helps us see why it is always a delight to return to Boswell's *Life*, not least because the idea of such a man—a distinguished, unalienated intellectual critically at ease with the experience of mankind—is good for one's morale. One is inclined to agree, at least provisionally, with Wain: Johnson "was a profound and wise man whose thinking

is fresh and original." Indeed, he can still come on brac-
ingly as an example of what Richard Rorty has called,
in his recent *New Republic* essay, "The Fate of Philosophy," "the modern Western 'culture critic' who feels free
to comment on anything at all" (see Oct. 18, 1982, p. 32).

Not that Johnson would take much comfort from
Rorty, whose theorizing about philosophy he would find
sufficiently fanciful to send him back to his kicking
stone. Rorty (whose essay appeared to be a distillation
of his book, *Consequences of Pragmatism*) anticipates a
"post-Philosophical culture" in which men and women
feel "themselves alone, merely finite, with no links to
something Beyond," making progress "toward, as Sartre put it, doing without God." The philosopher in this
sense (without a capital "P"), knowing that he dwells in
one of Foucault's *épistèmes*, is convinced "that there is
nothing deep down inside us except what we have put
there ourselves ... no rigorous argument that is not
obedience to our own conventions." He knows, that is,
that he has come to the end of Philosophy, and knows it
perhaps with the same exhilaration that a realist like
the French writer Jules Renard knew at the end of the
nineteenth century that he had come to the end of
Romance.

To us who live well into skeptical post-Johnsonian
times it is not odd that a professional philosopher
should take this position. Besides, we are familiar with
confident predictions about the end of things, whether
in optimistic or pessimistic contexts: the end of the
novel, the end of ideology, the end of the State, the end
of the family, the end of motherhood, the end of poverty,
the end of affluence, the end of print, the end of history,
the end of the bourgeoisie, the end of interpretation,
even the end of the earth. According to *Fortune*, it is
even possible now to imagine an end to the demand for
diamonds. Whether you are Nietzsche, Marx, Susan
Sontag, or Jonathan Schell, if you cannot frame your
subject in "end" terms you are not likely to get much of
an audience—which, according to some theorists, we

have also come to the end of, at least insofar as it is composed of relatively autonomous individuals capable of making rational choices. Often, no doubt, this preoccupation with "ends" is part of our hubris of the present, which Johnson would find as obnoxious now as when he wrote *Rasselas*—a novel that, beginning as it does by representing the Happy Valley in Abyssinia as a boring place, is also about the end of utopia.

That a philosopher should aspire to come to the end of Philosophy is understandable for another reason. Any philosopher who believes that he has arrived at the final Truth must at least be tempted to think that he has ended Philosophy. Rorty is no different than Plato, Berkeley, Kant, Nietzsche, and Ayn Rand on this score. Perhaps there is something in the very act of philosophizing that encourages the expectation of an exuberant reversal of the common experience of mankind that philosophy like everything else just keeps muddling along. Perhaps Nietzsche tried to end Philosophy for the same reason that Marx tried to end History: the last man is the best man who by subsuming all the others makes them irrelevant.

In any event, the layman may say of Rorty's pragmatism, with its categorical rejection of the absolutism of the Platonists and the positivists, what Boswell said of Berkeley: that he is satisfied about the falsity of the doctrine but still finds it hard to refute. In great part, I suspect, this is because philosophers—especially when they write as well as Rorty does—tend to come on like poets: tend, that is, to overwhelm us with the poetic absolutism of their vision. It is useful to remember how many philosophers have expressed their philosophies in poetic form: Hesiod, Anaximander, Parmenides, Empedocles, and Lucretius, for instance. Karl Popper seems to have had Plato's powers of poetic entrancement in mind when he entitled the first volume of *The Open Society and Its Enemies* "The Spell of Plato." Descartes's grand vision of a unitary universal science, coming to him, as he reports, in a dream, makes him sound like a poet overwhelmed by a Muse. Kant not only had a lifelong love for the philosopher-poet Lucretius but was once offered a professorship of poetry. Derrida has the same effect on many poetry-loving literary intellectuals, especially in America, that Ezra Pound had when his *Cantos* began to appear. It is hard to imagine anyone sounding more poetic than Nietzsche does in *Thus Spake Zarathustra*. These people overwhelm us with their vision of the way it is; they know something for sure, even if as with Isaiah Berlin's hedgehog it is only one big thing. Because their vision is customarily revisionary they are exciting, if often somewhat demoralizing at the same time, and taken on their own terms they are generally as hard to argue against as a well-made sonnet. When they drive us to kick the nearest stone it is sometimes a gesture of sheer frustration.

Rorty is in this company as he asserts the impossibility of doing Philosophy. The predecessors he values have shown that the sentences which are the central presuppositions of Philosophy "are 'true' only by courtesy and convention." Thanks to this rhetorical economy, we are left with a pragmatism grounded on "sentences that correspond to something." Rorty's is an optimistic program that has learned to dispense with those who are convinced that they have an access to Truth that transcends their particular *épistème*; it expects to do very well with people who are simply "good at being human." One may suspect that there is a moral imperative here just as there is in Plato or Descartes, or in any philosopher, for that matter: that philosophy which is better, if not best, ought to be followed. This, for the layman at least, seems to be implied in the fact that philosophers like poets tend not to bury their work in caves but publish it to the world. The layman might also infer this morale-raising prediction: if we go Rorty's way nothing of real value will be lost from the past and nothing of real value will be missed in the future. And at this point we may sense that we are close to an *épistème*-transcending Truth we can confidently live with, so that

Rorty's adversaries might say that he is after all doing Philosophy.

This may be, but Rorty still has a lot going for him, in particular the fact that he gives us a variation on one of the most engrossing of modern stories: the discovery of illusion in adequately adversative circumstances. The book-length publicity Marshall Berman has given to Marx's pronouncement in the *Communist Manifesto* that "all that is solid melts into air"[22] has probably helped Rorty's cause by reinforcing our tendency to expect that the serious thinker will identify himself by descending into the mighty past and at considerable hazard to himself reveal it to be a Cave of Error. Of course, all philosophers do this to some extent since the pursuit of the truth, however transcendent its aspirations, is a time-bound process; besides, insofar as philosophers are poets at heart they surely suffer a poet's anxiety of influence, which means that long before Ezra Pound and Yale professor Harold Bloom arrived on the scene they were motivated to some degree by the desire to make it new. Johnson obviously thought that many ancient and contemporary philosophers were exemplars of a fatuous absolutism and deserved to be melted into air, and in the pride he took in having helped to expose the Cock-Lane Ghost as a fraud he even anticipates the pleasures of the modern deconstructionist.

Nevertheless, Johnson would find Rorty's kind of antiabsolutism far too absolute in matters crucial to him. Rorty has no doubt that the Enlightenment was right in thinking "that what would succeed religion would be better," just as it is better now that the issue between religion and secularism has been decided in favor of the latter. Johnson as a truly pious man (his "Prayers and Meditations" was favorite reading for Wittgenstein) would not only find such ideas repellent in themselves, but as a sometime philosopher he might wonder what right a pragmatist—professing no links to "something Beyond," claiming access to no "extrahistorical Arche-

median point"—had to that word "better." He might
sense himself once more in the presence of that all too
human need, as characteristic of secularists as religion-
ists, to believe that one is part of a process moving inexorably toward a greater felicity, and might be reminded of the cautionary couplet in his poem "The
Vanity of Human Wishes":

> Nor deem, when learning her vast prize bestows,
> The glittering eminence exempt from foes.

For Johnson, of course, any rejection of religion was
a blow aimed at the human need of transcendence,
and he did not doubt that a rejector such as David
Hume suffered from a disturbance of his perceptions.
Nevertheless, he shares some of Rorty's suspicions about
the consequences of the appetite for transcendence. As
he makes clear in *Rasselas* and elsewhere, the cult of
the primitive as he found it in Rousseau and Lord
Monboddo was a misguided effort at a backward transcendence and deserved no more quarter than utopian
dreams of Happy Valleys, the hubris of scientific projectors, the attempts to escape the limits of one's time and
place by building pyramids, or the expectation of messages of enduring importance from Cock-Lane Ghosts.
"Perhaps if we speak with rigorous exactness," he has
his alter ego, Imlac, say in *Rasselas*, "no human mind is
in its right state"—from which it follows, as he later
points out, that visionary schemes not grounded in the
experience of mankind have a capacity to make us forget how absurd they first seemed to us.

Simply to be human, in other words, is to risk the intensely clarifying disturbance of the perceptions that
characterizes the fanatic—who, as he is defined in Johnson's *Dictionary*, is "an enthusiast, a man mad with
wild notions." If such a man has the gift of style he "is
better adapted to delight than convince the reason," as
Johnson observed in his brilliant attack on the reductive cosmic toryism of Soame Jenyn's "A Free Inquiry

into the Nature and Origin of Evil." Jenyn's brand of Leibnitzean optimism was a full-blown ideology; as an example of the higher fanaticism it was far more pernicious than the astronomer's harmless conviction in *Rasselas* that he could control the movements of the universe.

But Johnson's skepticism, even in the presence of the higher fanaticism, is a long way from that of Rorty, who stakes his claim "on the mortality of the vocabularies in which such supposedly immortal truths are expressed" and on the conviction that the criteria that support such truths are "no more than temporary resting places." Hard words, indeed, for the great organizer of our vocabulary. If he were among us now we would expect him to see that this is not a philosopher's distinction between useful and dangerous expressions of the need of transcendence, but an historical identification of that need with most of the troubles that have beset mankind. Such reductionism would be offensive to him not only because of its subject but because of the reductive process itself, for he was a champion (Wain and Bate are good at helping us see this) of what we now call holistic thinking. Certainly he was too aware of the ironies of the human condition and the interinvolvement of good and evil, too inclined to believe, as he puts it in "Reflections on the Present State of Literature," that "whatever may be the cause of happiness, may be likewise made the cause of misery," to believe that if we could eliminate the transcendental impulse we would be better at being human. Read, for instance, his sentiments on the pastoral life and the life lived according to nature in *Rasselas*.

Given the tendency of Johnson the thinker to go back to the living and concrete nature of experience, we might expect him to see that a bias against the transcendental as traditionally understood has become one of the commonplaces of our culture. He might encounter it, for instance, in George Steiner's novel, *The Portage to San Cristobal of A.H.* Here the aged A.H. (Adolph

Hitler), about to be brought out of his sanctuary in the Amazonian jungle, delivers a final defense speech in which he identifies the Judeo-Christian tradition of conscience and self-abnegating commitment as "the blackmail of transcendence" and sees it as the cause not only of his own acts but of previous atrocities without number. He is one of those crippled by his culture's inhuman demand that human beings push themselves too far. "I did not invent. . . . I was, in truth, only a man of my time," he says to his accusers, presenting himself as an Everyman-victim who, like Macbeth, was tricked by the higher fanaticism of evil powers into believing that he could put into practice his own higher fanaticism: could have it all, only to be left, also like Macbeth, appallingly empty-handed.

A.H.'s defense is the passionate reductionism of a demagogic scoundrel. The fact that some readers (those, that is, who do not entirely agree with it) find it at least temporarily unanswerable is the result not only of its capacity to make them take it on its own terms, as if it were a poem, but also of their realization that the speaker is so fanatically isolated within the structure of his defense that no counterargument can reach him. In the interest of the novel itself, of course, it has to be a defense hard to answer. It must not be too readily identifiable for what it is—the most available argument for any literate criminal intelligent enough to know how uncertain of their own values some of his listeners are—and Johnson, perhaps remembering his essay on fictions in *Rambler* No. 4, might complain as other critics have that A.H.'s charges are allowed to stand without adequate rebuttal, as if they had overwhelmed the author himself. He might have to kick a stone again, even though everything he knew about the living and concrete nature of human experience prompted him to say that the defense was eloquently beside the point. Indeed, he might see behind A.H.'s defense a Nazi version of the optimistic higher fanaticism that he had so soundly trounced in Soame Jenyns—and thus be led to

speculate how neatly the two fanatic visions comple-
ment one another in the ease with which they dispose of
the problem of evil.

At the opposite end of the cultural scale Johnson
might note with interest the success of Helen Gurley
Brown as editor and author, first of *Sex and the Single
Girl* and subsequently of *Having It All*. Certainly, Ms.
Brown and her *Cosmopolitan* magazine appear to have
demonstrated that life beyond A.H.'s blackmail of transcendence, as well as beyond the stranglehold of the
past that Rorty and Foucault complain about, can be
both attractive and profitable. In *Sex and the Single
Girl* she says that "not having slept with the man
you're going to marry I consider lunacy." She can be as
hard on cultural taboos as a French deconstructionist—almost as hard as Grace Lichtenstein, who says
in her *Machisma* that for the modern adultery-prone
woman "there are no cultural taboos, or at least no important cultural taboos, against doing whatever comes
naturally." Johnson, for all his strong sexual impulses
and delight in the company of women, might be less at
ease in such a liberated world than Boswell, but he
would be completely at home with its blithe assumptions about doing what comes naturally, having encountered them often enough in the fanciful theories of his
own contemporaries. Most likely, good reader of texts
that he was, he would have detected at work in the semantic underground of A.H.'s defense the plea that, all
things considered, he too had simply done what came
naturally.

But if Ms. Brown and her enterprises seem to be an
acting out on a bargain basement level of Rorty's doctrine "that there is nothing deep down inside us except
what we put there ourselves . . . and no rigorous argument that is not obedience to our own conventions," it
is only a seeming. She may not be easy to bring under
the umbrella of Plato or Comte, but with her there is
still a transcendent issue at stake: that of the passional
self as it strives to become a more passionately fulfilled

self, and the *épistème* in which this striving takes place
is not represented as simply better, as for Rorty secular
is better than religious, but as both cosmopolitan and
best. Here, in fact, we have something like the self-
transcendence of Nietzsche's Zarathustra watered down
for the bourgeois. Nor is it easy to miss the strong moral
imperative: those who win against the obligation to the
passional self will end up not in the Happy Valley of
vital living but in some kind of hell. So there is a blackmail of transcendence at work after all—just as there is
an old-fashioned kind of absolutism on the jacket of
Having It All. There the author is identified as a personal
advisor, "the kind who tells you the truth." The context
gives this "truth" the capitalization which the pub-
lisher, perhaps out of modesty, denied it.

We may suspect that Johnson, preoccupied with ethical issues as he was, would have detected Ms. Brown's
moral imperative, however he would have scorned its
assumptions, just as he would have detected it in Hugh
Hefner, though he probably would have thought Hefner's published philosophy not worth a kick at a small
stone. It would have amused him to find Hefner in-
stalled in a penthouse version of his Abyssinian Happy
Valley, as insouciantly at ease in his fabulous bed as Diogenes in his fabled wine jar, and apparently as immune
to A.H.'s blackmail of transcendence as Ms. Brown. Hefner is reported to spend most of his time in pajamas,
which might suggest the sartorial economy of Diogenes
were his pajamas not silk and his manner of life not
frankly hedonistic (Ms. Brown has described herself in
a *Playboy* interview as living "a sort of hedonistic life").
Nevertheless, like Diogenes he is a dramatic, even heroic, exemplar of his ethical system. He is proudest of
the fact that because of *Playboy* "things are a lot better
in the bedroom today than when I was growing up." The
system works.

If Johnson had lived another twenty years he might
have discovered not only one of Hefner's true progeni-
tors, but one of the presiding spirits behind A.H.'s de-

fense as well, in that ingenious sophist, the Marquis de Sade, a man made to order for Foucault's speculations since his society judged him to be both criminal and insane. Sade in his own *Philosophy of the Bedroom* is as certain as Sartre or Nietzsche that progress means "doing without God," as certain as A.H. and Nietzsche of the crippling effect of the injunction to love one's neighbor as oneself. He would like "a man to be free of ridicule and scoff at anything," for otherwise the stranglehold of the corrupting past cannot be broken. If it can be broken, if we can manage to make as few laws as possible and only those that are easy to obey, we will be able to live according to the laws of nature. Human beings will be honestly open to one another as brothers, not meanly hugging secrets to themselves, for modesty will have been exposed for the corrupter it is—this in anticipation of that transparency among people that Sartre in his later and somewhat utopian years saw as necessary for "true social harmony to be established." In Sade's Happy Valley women too will have their proper share: "Fair sex, you will be free; you will enjoy, as men do, all the pleasures that are your duty to nature; you will stop at nothing." They will have it all.

Johnson, who was all for accepting the duties of nature, would nevertheless probably agree with Rorty that in Sade no less than in Brown and Hefner we are offered not philosophy but Philosophy, not bits of truth but Truth beyond all possibility of falsification, and a full-scale attempt at another blackmail of transcendence—that, indeed, Sade like most utopians needs to generate a blackmail of transcendency to support his vision of utopia. For Johnson, utopians were deceptive models of human possibility, as they are for Karl Popper, whose belief that "there can be no human society without conflict" and "that values could not exist without problems" would have been much to Johnson's taste. Such a conviction would imply the corollary that in any problematic environment the continuing attempt to distinguish between benign and malign expressions of the human need of transcendence is crucial to survival—just as it is crucial to all efforts to avoid the poetic entrancements of the higher fanaticisms.

For Johnson, in fact, there could be no greater cause of misery than a culture's loss of its ability to make basic distinctions. That madmen or scoundrels are sometimes mistaken for poets or philosophers, that philosophers are sometimes called mad when they are only inconveniently wise, he knew as well as anyone. But as a pragmatic moralist and defender of civilization he would surely wonder about the filter-down consequences of an epistemological relativism that found the distinction between philosophers and scoundrels less interesting than the deconstructive analysis of the distinction-making process itself. Perhaps he would wonder too why our philosophers, subtle as they are, do not see that no matter what shape their fanciful theories take they can easily increase the sum of human misery by underlining the distinction between themselves and the rest of us. For even when philosophers try scrupulously to avoid Philosophy, as Rorty does, do they not in the very act of philosophizing hold the rest of us to impossible standards of critical attention, in effect blackmailing us, as philosophers and poets always have, with their implication that unless we submit our disheveled lives to their kind of transcending close scrutiny our lives will not be worth living?

Perhaps this is why, after the philosophers have with their fanciful theories put in doubt the experience of mankind, we take such comfort from those moments in their biographies when they seem close kin to us after all: Derrida, for instance, being mistaken for a drug smuggler by Czechoslovakian authorities; Wittgenstein enjoying Betty Hutton and Carmen Miranda movies; Nietzsche persuading a friend to duel with him so that he could be honorably scarred; Kant on his daily walk insisting that a servant follow with an umbrella even on clear days; Sartre in old age reading detective stories and drinking too much; Bishop Berkeley believing that tar water would cure practically anything. With such intimations of untranscended mortality in mind we can even believe that the philosophers sometimes find us as hard to refute as we find them. How often, knowing in their hearts what jerry-built structures our epistemologies are, must they, like Dr. Johnson, be content to counterargue with a frustrated kick at the nearest stone?

Part Three
Chaos and Character
The Ironies of Belief

Chapter 14
What Is Literature Good For?

In an essay-review on domestic architecture in *The New York Review of Books* (4 December 1986), the novelist Diane Johnson wonders whether good art makes people better or happier than kitsch, and goes on to remark: "Every teacher of literature knows that good literature has no improving effect whatever—at least to judge from our own character and those of our colleagues." Those who spend their time, whether as teachers, critics, or producers of art in any form, are familiar with this complaint about the lack of correspondence between aesthetics and ethics, and most of them, I suspect, would be reluctant to take a strong stand against Ms. Johnson, having themselves seen plenty of evidence that her thesis is right at least as often as it is wrong. But most of them, I also suspect, would take little comfort from this fact and never cease to be upset when they encounter real-life repetitions of Browning's Duke in his dramatic monologue "My Last Duchess": persons whose good taste in literature and the arts does not keep them from being moral monsters. Perhaps the literary humanist Richard Poirier is right (see *The New York Times Book Review* for 8 February 1987) when he opposes the notion "that the writing and reading of literature have a culturally redemptive power."

"What Is Literature Good For?" first appeared in *The Georgia Review* (Summer 1988): 238–49. Reprinted with permission.

Indeed, what makes a historical figure more memorable than a combination of great power, evil deeds, and an attraction to or competence in literature or the other arts? Nero, one of the evilest rulers who ever lived, wrote poetry, played musical instruments, and sang dramatically in public. The Roman historian Suetonius tells us that when his enemies had finally driven him to bay Nero "wept and said again and again: 'What an artist the world is losing!'" Hitler aspired to be a painter, playwright, and architect during his bohemian youth in Vienna. Albert Speer, to whom Hitler gave one of his youthful watercolors, thought him a frustrated artist. And Hitler's biographer John Toland quotes an early letter in which he expresses the conviction that "the world has lost a great deal in that I could not attend the Academy and learn the technical end of the art of painting." According to the Russian composer Shostakovich, Mozart's *Piano Concerto no. 23* was on the record player as Stalin lay dying and might have been the last thing he heard. Readers of the American edition of Anthony Burgess's *A Clockwork Orange* may be reminded that at the end of the novel the young social menace Alex is "redeemed" by Beethoven's *Ninth Symphony* from society's attempt to neutralize him. And this is to say nothing of those ambiguous figures who, in the tradition of the Medicis and the Borgias, have served the cause of art well enough as patrons or collectors whether or not they knew the difference between schlock and Botticelli.

In his poem "The Choice" William Butler Yeats writes: "The intellect of man is forced to choose / Perfection of the life or of the work." The extent to which human beings are "forced" to make this choice is a matter of endless debate. Are we to imagine the judgment coming from a privileged position outside the apparently irresistible lines of force, so that there is some possibility of free choice after all? Does Yeats anticipate a reader who knows at what rate his hyperbole must be discounted so that it is still possible to blame the artist (to say nothing of the businessman, athlete, or statesman) if he makes the wrong choice? In any event, it is apparent that artists routinely act as if they had no choice in the matter, the consequence being that combination of artistic accomplishment and conspicuous failure, if not downright delinquency, in the life that characterizes the biographies of so many romantic, modernist, and postmodernist artists. Not only do we expect our artists to be unfaithful to their spouses (if they bother to marry), neglectful of their children, careless if not disdainful of civic obligations, improvident, and immoderate in appetites, but we tend to suspect their authenticity in proportion as they are reliable and contract-honoring members of the human community, naïvely convinced that what they create will stand firm for all time against deconstructive onslaughts. Poets ought to live like Byron or Baudelaire; novelists like Genet, George Sand, Céline, or Hemingway; painters like Klimt or Gauguin; composers like Berlioz or Wagner. Such a list not only supports those who agree with Johnson and Poirier but plays into the hands of those who agree with Oscar Wilde (see his preface to *The Picture of Dorian Gray*) that "all art is quite useless."

For some of us, of course, a universe in which aesthetics and ethics are utterly incompatible (and kitsch a matter of little concern to either) is not fit to live in. We need to believe that somehow or other, however immeasurably, literature and the arts make us better human beings, and that such figures as Nero, Hitler, and Stalin (along with Browning's Duke and Burgess's Alex) are monstrous exceptions. Indeed, we may wonder, who is to say that even they wouldn't have been worse if their experience of particular arts hadn't had the effect of reducing their potential for evil? We might have to concede that it is all too easy to find evidence supporting the Johnson-Poirier line, especially when the evidence is so often biographically attractive, but we might still wonder about the advisability of rely-

ing upon an all-or-nothing perfectionism to prove the
utility of the arts against the human record of folly, corruption, sentimentality, and confusion.

It is not easy to concede this possibility in these skeptical times, the skepticism being, as usual, an attempt
to live with failed perfectionist expectations. The subject of the relation between the beautiful and the good,
between art and life, was once a much simpler one.
Some of us can still remember when schoolchildren
were told that if birds disappeared from the face of the
earth human beings would soon disappear also. The argument was less ecological than aesthetic; it was not so
much that birds help to maintain a balance in nature,
the way predatory animals do, but that human beings
are absolutely dependent on the image of uninhibited
movement and spontaneous song that makes birds so
valuable to the Romantic poets. This image gives the
same kind of moral, aesthetic, metaphysical, and epistemological comfort that Renaissance Neo-Platonism
did with respect to the relations between the good, the
beautiful, and the true. In "An Hymne in Honour of
Beautie," for instance, Edmund Spenser (having the advantage of being able to poetize before Jacques Derrida
came on the scene) says this:

> Therefore where euer that thou doest behold
> A comely corpse, with beautie faire endewed
> Know this for certaine, that the same doth hold
> A beauteous soule, with faire conditions thewed . . .
> For all that faire is, is by nature good;
> That is a signe to know the gentle blood.

The ethical corollary (native no less to fairy stories
than to propaganda and advertising) is that there will
be a match between physical and moral ugliness—as
there is, for instance, in the picture of Richard III we
get from Tudor historians and (through them) from
Shakespeare. Spenser knows that it is not quite this
simple ("Yet oft it falles that many a gently mynd /

Dwels in deformed tabernacle drownd"), but he did not lose faith in the congeniality of beauty, goodness, and truth. There is good reason to believe that Shakespeare on the whole agreed with Spenser and kept the faith, however disillusioned characters like Thersites, Timon, and Hamlet make him sound to some readers or playgoers. Writers begin to sound modern to us in proportion as they lose the faith. Among the bird-loving romantics no one sounds more modern than Byron does in the first canto of *Don Juan* when he mocks the false expectations of Platonism: Plato with his "confounded fantasies" is responsible for more immoral conduct "than all the long array / Of poets and romancers." But it isn't so much that Byron was absolutely faithless (he couldn't have written much if he had been); it was more that he had learned to appropriate for satiric purposes the energy that was locked up in traditional faith structures.

Oscar Wilde's statement that all art is quite useless would have been as incomprehensible to Spenser as to Nero, Byron, and Hitler. Of course, when we apply to Wilde's words the rate of discount that the context demands, the meaning is reversed: nothing is as useful as art. As he tells us in "The Soul of Man Under Socialism," art is what we would spend our time doing in the ideal society, which would be a social culmination of the aesthetic principle. (His friend John Ruskin, disturbed with the amount of second-rate art this principle was already responsible for, might have contemplated such a possibility with some apprehension.) For Wilde, one of the highest uses of art is to protect the elite that values it from kitschy bourgeois demands that it be useful. For Wilde this is a highly moral matter; indeed, his preface is as moralistic as that earlier deconstructive anti-bourgeois document, Marx's *The Communist Manifesto*, which, theoretically speaking, has no business sounding moralistic. When Wilde also says that "no artist has ethical sympathies," he means that the artist's own moral imperatives oppose any moral system that puts the imperatives of the life ahead of those of the work. Wilde's is an aesthetic ethics that is as non-negotiable as the ascetic ethics of a troglodyte—and is just as concerned with despising the world lest one perish with it. This is why the famous conclusion to Pater's *The Renaissance* (appropriately included as an appendix to the Oxford University Press's 1974 edition of Wilde's novel) still reads like an encyclical issued by the Holy Office of Art. To put it another way, the questions "What is art good for?" and "What is asceticism good for?" can be answered the same way. Both help to keep burning, if to different ends, that "hard gemlike flame" that for Pater is "success in life." But as some of the great ascetics knew, the high moral imperative of such an effort could disguise its world-hating egoism.

The ascetic can reject the bourgeois as an anti-life force just as categorically as Flaubert did, but it is not ascetic rejection in *Madame Bovary* that interests the distinguished Peruvian novelist Mario Vargas Llosa in his recently translated *The Perpetual Orgy: Flaubert and Madame Bovary*. For Vargas Llosa, Emma Bovary is less to be remembered as "a woman of false poetry and false sentiment" (Flaubert's description of her) than as a true heroine whose stubborn commitment to the pleasures of the body drives her to defy all the pleasure-rejecting interdictions of family, class, and society, and of course all the creeds, moralities, and ideologies that culture enlists to the end of that rejection. As the creation of "the first modern novelist," Vargas Llosa's Emma dramatizes the conviction that the invidious function of culture is to deny the individual the full passional life he or she yearns for—and to which, one might recall, the Marquis de Sade had already decreed that he or she was by nature entitled.

Here there is no question that literature is good for us, provided that it is (as Vargas Llosa apparently believes it must be) authentically transgressive of an establishment morality that is antipassional and cliché-ridden. For the true artist, then, there is no painful choice between the perfection of the work and perfection of the life: the former cannot help but serve the latter. For Vargas Llosa, one may suspect, this would be true of Burgess's Alex as well—provided that he is not the Alex of the original English edition, who in a final chapter becomes bored with his violent antiestablishment life and turns in a more hopeful direction. For Llosa this would be equivalent to a repentant Emma returning home to serve husband and child and would suggest a Burgess who had lost his nerve.

Vargas Llosa's reading of *Bovary* suggests, too, that all authentic art is an attempt to correct the disinformation about human possibility that is propagated in Genesis. There the Devil is represented as a con artist who tricks Eve, and through her Adam, into believing that all that stands between their present condition and the experience of godhood is God's interdiction. Vargas Llosa might seem to imply that our creaturely enslavement by culture is a consequence of the bad press the Devil has gotten in the Judeo-Christian tradition, so that we fail to see not only that he is the transgressor-liberator that Prometheus was for Byron and Shelley but also that, as the poet William Blake said, all true poets are of the Devil's party, whether they know it or not. In this moralistic and didactic view, true literature is good for what ails us now and at any time because it is a salvation story, just as *Madame Bovary* was for Vargas Llosa at a time when, as he tells us, he was in despair and tempted by suicide. He was saved by a great novel just as Emma is saved by the romantic kitsch that inspires her to a life-affirming transgressiveness.

The problem for many readers is that of deriving a vicarious salvation experience from a heroine whose sensibility belongs not with what they regard as truly great and salvational art but with kitsch. Burgess's Alex at least knows good music when he hears it, a fact that no doubt lends some credibility to the original last chapter. Vargas Llosa is too easily co-opted by those sons of Sade who believe that the traditional distinction between good literature and kitsch, like the distinction between good literature and pornography, is simply culture's way of protecting itself from pleasure-oriented transgressions. Those who are still impressed with these distinctions are probably more inclined to see *Madame Bovary* as so imbued with Flaubert's famous disgust with the bourgeois and the kitschy that it anticipates what Lionel Trilling a quarter of a century ago called "the perverse and morbid idealism of modern literature." This ascetic idealism rejects the pleasure principle. In its perspective, what Vargas Llosa sees as a novel that endorses Emma's heroic and incurable materialism becomes a brilliant, and potentially even didactic, depiction of a vulgar pursuit of illusion. Such a reading warns us against a lust for life that begins with the kind of daydreams that have death by arsenic programmed into them, and is in effect a deconstructive attack on the trashy romances that made Emma's life so disastrously bovaristic. Nor should we forget the utilitarian claim Wilde made for his own "useless" novel when he wrote to his editor friend Arthur Fish that *The Picture of Dorian Gray* had a "strong ethical lesson inherent in it." It was, in fact, no more useless than the highly moral tales in *A House of Pomegranates*, which it resembles.

Thanks to the tradition of courtly love, many—perhaps even the most memorable—of our love stories are stories about transgressors. Tristan and Isolde, Abelard and Eloise, Launcelot and Guinevere, Romeo and Juliet (to say nothing of Nabokov's Humbert Humbert and Lolita) all rebel against the social interdictions opposing the erotic symbiosis that Paolo and Francesca yearn for and are last seen enjoying in Dante's hell. Their romances are just the sort of literature that a naïve, impressionable, and discontented young wife like Emma ought not to be reading. Yet the culture has tended to see them as useful rather than subversive because they are so intimately involved with indispensable virtues. Thus many have worried about the consequences of loss of faith in romantic love. As Diana Trilling put it (in "Whatever Became of Romantic Love?"): "With the disappearance of romantic love other ideals—courage, self-sacrifice, personal and social expansiveness, even great friendship—are also vanishing." But if you want to argue that the Candlelight and Harlequin romances are compensating for this disappearance and therefore ought to be looked at more seriously, you risk ending up in the Johnson-Poirier camp: kitsch is just as likely to improve people as good literature.

In any event, Emma Bovary is no Francesca, even though Flaubert consigns her to his own kind of secular hell. Like Burgess's Alex, she is too egoistic for an unconditional and self-abnegating love of another person. What she wants is the life-enhancing erotic experience inherent in the traditional love story, which means that she is a sentimentalist. In the erotic supermarket she is a freeloader; if she were less an innocent she might have become a female Casanova who in her few leisure moments would have preferred something like *Playgirl* and *Cosmopolitan* rather than Candlelight romances. She may think of herself as the heroine of romance, which is not the way true heroines of romance think of themselves. If she were an unself-conscious heroine, she would have no time left over for the heroic and incurable materialism that makes her so attractive and useful to Vargas Llosa. He needs a heroine whose life is authentic in proportion as she makes it for herself—who if she ends up in some bourgeois hell would not be surprised to find herself alone.

Emma's appropriation of the erotic energy operating within the traditional romance anticipates the discovery by twentieth-century literary critics that literature may be useful in a way unimaginable to earlier critics. Now it is possible to believe that literature serves no culture-conserving or redemptive function, that it is too self-referential to have any significant connection with life outside it, but is yet a structured repository of

energy and excitement that can be appropriated in a
critical counterliterature that is often as incurably materialistic as Vargas Llosa's Emma. In *Criticism in the
Wilderness*, for instance, Geoffrey Hartman expresses his
discontent with a kind of criticism that subordinates itself to the text in a traditional effort to make it more
available "to industrious hordes of students" in a mass
culture. Now the enlightened teacher-critic will use the
text (as conventionally respected and interpreted) the
way Emma uses her boring bourgeois condition: as
the takeoff point for an exciting act of transgressive creation. Now literature is both useful and redemptive: the
teacher-critic is saved from not only the sterile repetitions of his discipline but also the longueurs of the mass
mind, just as surely as Emma is saved from her domestic hell. He also participates in that rage against society
which, according to Vargas Llosa, saved Flaubert from
a hermetic aestheticism. And it is that rage, along with
his conviction that "genuine literature would always be
dangerous," that makes Flaubert a proper model for the
modern writer, whether novelist or teacher-critic.

The conspicuous strain of bovarism in poststructuralist criticism indicates how interrelated are the loss of
faith in literature (as traditionally understood) and the
discovery of endless possibilities for a new life of courageous transgression. In this new life, literature is re-
cycled like garbage so that nothing of real value is lost,
all that is valueless is exposed and discarded, and in the
transmuting magic of the process the critic-artist is
born and flourishes. As for the social, moral, and political usefulness of *his* highly didactic literature, it is
nothing less than the discovery of the illusions under
which Western civilization—misled, like Emma and
Don Quixote, by its reading—has labored so long. Since
the artist-critic-teacher must also make the Yeatsian
choice between the perfection of the work and perfection of his life, it is not surprising that his students
sometimes feel that they are being asked to serve ends
not entirely their own.

No doubt, behind the argument that literature and the arts have no improving or redemptive effect there is often a genuine love of literature coupled with a fear that it will suffer as a valued subject if it is asked to do what it cannot possibly do—as some sports lovers fear that sport will be disvalued in the effort to justify it as a form of character building. But when the argument comes from a poststructuralist position, it is quite possible that it expresses a fear that literature, having created the false consciousness it needs to survive, is all too likely to influence conduct adversely. In that case, it becomes a dangerous idol the worship of which is involved with social, political, ethical, and aesthetic values that, because they are grounded on illusions, are in effect dehumanizing means the past uses to clutch stiflingly to its bosom the authentic self always struggling to be born. And in this view nothing opposes that struggle more than the failure to realize the truth of what Flaubert once wrote in the preface of a friend's book: " . . . style, art in itself, always appears insurrectional to governments and immoral to bourgeois."

Traditionally, literature and all the arts have modeled and propagandized the various forms of self-transcendence. Arthur Koestler once argued that, perhaps because our neocortex evolved too fast, we suffer not from "an overdose of self-asserting aggression, but an excess of self-transcending devotion," so that we can do the most terrible things for the most noble reasons. This post-Enlightenment paradox has become a commonplace of our cultural criticism, and was recently at the heart of things in *The Portage to San Cristobal of A.H.*, the novel in which George Steiner worked out his theory of the blackmail of transcendence. Both Vargas Llosa's Emma and Burgess's second Alex model escapes from such dependence on person-crippling transcendence. But so does the transcendence-fearing deconstructive critic, who is quite capable, in fact, of deconstructing Vargas Llosa's or anyone else's Emma. The danger to the critic, of course, is that he will be widely accepted as an epistemological hero—someone like the late Paul de Man, perhaps—who models one more vision of transcendence: his transmuting magic creates a new redemptive literature, a necessary ground-clearing for an unillusioned and truly human life.

This has always been the expectation of those for whom pornography is the same transgressive means to an intenser passional life that Flaubert's novel is for Vargas Llosa. Pornography may appear to be incurably materialistic and incurably against transcendence. In the act of desecrating romance, pornography appropriates romance's energies just as the literature of antiheroism degrades epic in order to appropriate *its* energies. But in doing so pornography resolves the conflict between the perfection of the work and perfection of the life in a transcending and utopian vision of life as pure passion. The most serious of its champions (see Peter Michelson's *The Aesthetics of Pornography*, for instance) have none of the doubts that so often torment traditional humanists concerning the redemptive value of their subject. When the latter begin to lose their faith, the prospect of an all-out censorious attack on pornography—with its threat of foreclosing not simply one possible new faith but others as well—can make them uneasy. It is then all too easy for them to give up the hope that literature will turn out to be on the side of humanism for fear that even the hope will put them on the side of the censor. An apostate humanist with no place to go, with no kitsch to enrage him and no hard cold flame to burn in, can be a pitiable person.

Censorship tries to make sure that literature is good for people by minimizing its capacity to give attractive form to the temptation to transgress established limitations. The censor wants character-building, society-supporting literature, and he wants to reduce all signs of conflict between the urge to perfect the work and the urge to perfect the life, since the troubled artist is too obvious a sign that all may not be well in the society. One consequence, as we see in the Iron Curtain countries, is that some writers are driven underground to produce a counterliterature, as if in defense of the principle that, while transgression by itself will not result in literature, where transgression is impossible there can be no literature. Censor and rebellious writer thus interrelate in a cultural melodrama in which the writer attempts to appropriate the moral capital of the censor. If he appropriates enough of it, his readers, given their natural reluctance to disjoin beauty and truth, will probably find him aesthetically admirable as well. In the meantime, their inclination will be to believe that any literature the censor opposes must be the product of a morally admirable, even heroic effort that cannot help but be useful.

Our relation with the censor becomes more complicated in proportion as we see the extent to which the evaluative structuring itself has the effect of censorship by discriminating among options. Life in a liberal society, even after the censor has gotten a thoroughly bad reputation, remains a highly censored affair. We have been well lectured on the theme that the very language we speak is a tissue of interdictions so that we live in it the way birds live in cages, beating vainly against the bars. Under these circumstances it is not surprising that our literature is so ambivalent about the transgressor—when, that is, it cannot imagine the interesting, good, or heroic person in any other form. The problem with Vargas Llosa's Emma, then, is not that she is strange to us; she is familiar to the point of being a stereotype. The problem is that she must go against the moral grain of the novel. The latter required five years of unremitting effort, forcing Flaubert, as he wrote to his "Muse" and sometime mistress, Louise Colet, to live "an austere life, stripped of all external pleasure." His arduously achieved novel cannot help but be a celebration of the bourgeois virtues without which its author would have been able to do nothing with his own bovarism except wallow in it—or, as he suggested to Colet, make of it the kind of art that is "a drain-pipe for pas-

sion, a kind of chamberpot." There is even reason to say
that as author he was what the eponymous writer Tonio
Kroger finally admits about himself in Thomas Mann's
novelette—a bourgeois manqué.

But this is also true of Vargas Llosa's book about the
true meaning of Flaubert's novel: insofar as it is any
good it demonstrates the quite familiar virtues necessary to any worthwhile accomplishment but conspicuously lacking in Emma. This is true of all literature and
all art. So far as it is authentic it reeks of the moral effort to resist sloth. Flaubert knew this when he wrote to
Madame Schlesinger that his novel was "moral, ultra
moral." It is sloth, that spiritual sluggishness in the exercise of human capacities, that so often tempts the
writer into settling for the kitschy drainpipe of passion—an agreeable enough settlement for those readers
who are anxious to have sloth redefined as the virtue of
doing what comes naturally.

The image of sloth overcome in the aesthetic ordering
of a great work of literature is morally exhilarating and
morale-raising: it argues that this having been done, so
much more is possible. It is no doubt why many people
will continue to believe what many people have always
believed, Nero and his kind notwithstanding: that literature, no matter how insistingly and disturbingly it
may urge new perspectives on us, is indispensable to the
effort to humanize our lives. The common recognition
of the need for this image, which always demonstrates
the interdependence of disciplined restriction and creative release, is no doubt why we are so inclined to let
the writer off lightly when, having chosen the perfection
of the work, he messes up his life. Flaubert knew as well
as Yeats that his life could not measure up to his work;
perhaps that is why he was so fascinated with that heroic sloth-resister, the ascetic. Indeed, if he had ever
managed to write his book about nothing—one, as he
told Colet, "with almost no subject" which would be
held together only by the strength of its style—it would
still have depended as much on heroic sloth-resistance

as *Madame Bovary*. Certainly it would not prove out the popular belief that the truest and most useful works of art are in their spontaneity as independent of moral effort as bird song.

Vargas Llosa's valuation of Emma has a great deal to do with the fact that she is not a sloth-resister. If she were, she would be on the side of that tradition-bound life-inhibitor, the censor. Like any narcissist, she is inclined to take the course of least resistance as she attempts, unaided by the writer's bourgeois discipline, to be the most that she can be. If she had committed herself energetically to the given conditions of her life as wife and mother, she might have realized in that life the same creative interdependence between disciplined restriction of egotistic impulse and release of human potential that characterizes the novel. It is, of course, hard to imagine Flaubert spending five years of his life with such an Emma, inclined as he was to think of normal family life as an appalling state of affairs. She is nevertheless present, perhaps even tragically present, as a might-have-been person whose greatest mistake as she attempts to find meaning in her life is not imitating the highly disciplined novel in which she is condemned to being only a possibility. The reader's awareness of such a fate enriches the novel, which can no more do without this absent Emma than Cervantes can do without a Don Quixote who might have stayed home and tended to the business of his estate like any other responsible gentleman of La Mancha.

But Vargas Llosa needs a heroine for our time, useful only if she commits herself in a blind act of faith to the belief that the interdictions that have structured her life are dehumanizing. The novel is useful to her only as a means of transcending her limitations, the implication being a rather old-fashioned view of fiction in which story (the chrysalis) is subordinate to character (the butterfly). Such an Emma represents the transgressive spirit that lusts against the order that gives it life— a spirit implying that a truly useful literature is self-subverting, just as culture itself must be if it is to release its prisoners. Unlike Tolstoy's Anna Karenina, Dostoevski's Raskolnikov, or Shakespeare's Iago, she has not been set courageously, even riskily, against an established order and then controlled by her creator for critical purposes far beyond her comprehension. On the contrary, she needs to take over the novel in order to put it behind her, and if she fails in the valiant and life-enhancing effort there is more glory for her. In the meantime, she demonstrates the "negative participation in life" that for Vargas Llosa characterizes the modern spirit.

Here we have a highly utilitarian view of literature. With its insistence that fundamental questions about the relations between literature and life be answered categorically once and for all, this view has all the passionate simplification of a bovarism. Like any bovarism, it censors out all hostile and faith-threatening possibilities. Thus it is protected from the dangerous thought that a culture-endorsing, even redeeming, literature may turn out to be like those microscopic but life-supporting trace elements (potassium and iodine, for instance) whose biological indispensability can be proven only when they are in dangerously short supply or totally absent.

Chapter 15
How Fast Should We Go?

The world is getting faster. In Batavia, Illinois, the Fermi National Laboratory has spent $130 million on a four-mile circular tunnel in which it has pushed protons close to the speed of light. The new Cray X-MP computer with its pack of 240,000 silicon chips will run at 400 million operations per second. Revolutionary techniques in genetic engineering manipulations are making Darwinian evolution look like a parade of arthritic turtles. Aviation people are beginning to think of transporting three hundred to five hundred passengers at Mach 5 speed from Los Angeles to Tokyo in two hours. Blanchard and Johnson's *The One-Minute Manager*, with its promise to increase productivity and profits in just sixty seconds, stayed on the *New York Times* best-seller list for fifty-five weeks. Meanwhile, video dating clubs are combining speed with detailed information in a way that makes singles bars and personals columns look like a waste of time. In New York now if a man wants to be talked to by a sexy lady he can have instant satisfaction by erotic telephone, all major credit cards accepted. According to Craig Stanton's *Bio-Imagery Method of Breast Enlargement and Waist Reduction*, it is possible for a woman to go from a 32A

to 34C in a mere sixteen weeks without surgery, gim-
micky exercises, or diets—an acceleration of mammary
time that, all things considered, makes the Concorde
look slow.

Nevertheless, there have been remarkably few com-
plaints since the 1974 reduction of the speed limit on
American highways to fifty-five miles per hour. No
doubt the well-publicized connection between speed,
the wasting of gas, and the killing of people has been a
factor, but our modern ambivalence about speed has
been a factor too. Even if the government had acted on
Ivan Illich's earlier recommendation of a strictly en-
forced twenty-five-mile-per-hour speed limit, reduced
to fifteen in country areas, quite a few people would
have applauded the restriction. Most of us are still
willing to believe that we go too fast, just as we are willing to believe that we eat too much junk food—which
doesn't keep us from continuing to do both, often at
once.

Illich's thirteen-year-old recommendation in *Deschooling Society* was specific for developing countries,
but it was apparent then as now that he takes a dim
view of the modern world's willingness to subordinate
the welfare of the person to the institutional need to go
places and do things in a hurry. No doubt, he is as much
a hyperbolist on this subject as he has been on schooling
and medicine, or (to judge from his more recently published *Gender*) on relations between the sexes. Nevertheless, his hyperbole can as usual be taken heuristically as
a device that forces us to ask once more that most unsettling modern question: how fast should we go?

Our dreams, which are supposed to be important
sources of information about our real attitude toward
such basic questions, give an ambiguous answer, one
familiar nightmare in which we are speeding dangerously out of control being countered by another in
which we are agonizingly unable to move fast enough.
With literary intellectuals it is no different. They are

often believed as a class to favor the speediest possible changes in all categories of human activity, especially politics. Among them are those radicals of the Left to whom Winston Churchill once referred as "bloody-minded professors," and bloody-mindedness makes any established political process look too slow. But at least as abundant are the spiritual descendants of those literary intellectuals about whom C. P. Snow was saying over a generation ago that their ignorance and distrust of science made them dreamers of impossible dreams so that they could not keep pace with modern realities. Since then, according to many of the contributors in the spring 1983 "Scientific Literacy" issue of *Daedalus*, the situation has not improved. Despite the comforts and conveniences science has made available, far too many humanists continue to identify it as a dangerously accelerating force in the world.

No one expresses our fear of going too fast more effectively than Shakespeare. His world is speeded up by the specialist's immoderate and dangerously restricted view of reality, whether expressed as passion, ambition, or fanaticism. When Macbeth admits killing the grooms after Macduff has discovered the murdered Duncan, he explains, "The expedition of my violent love/Outrun the pauser reason." This is no less true of Romeo. When he tells Friar Lawrence of his sudden passion for Juliet, having lately professed the same passion for Rosaline, the Friar warns: "Wisely and slow. They stumble that run fast." But all Romeos are by definition speed merchants; they hear counsels to decelerate as rationalizing clichés for the faint of heart. This Romeo outruns the pauser reason as disastrously as do Macbeth, Tybalt, Hotspur, Troilus, Othello, Coriolanus, and Lear. Such figures have bequeathed to us compelling monitory images of life in the fast lane and have the effect of a cultural bias against the expeditiousness of all our violent loves, including our utopian political expectations. In fact, if we wanted to increase the tempo of our culture, and at the same time reduce C. P. Snow's two-culture gap, we might begin by trying to censor the Shakespeare canon out of existence and out of memory.

Americans are the least likely of candidates for such a censoring, their notorious love affair with Shakespeare being perhaps one kind of cybernetic response to their sense of being committed to a political and cultural experiment that in its very beginnings had a high potential for speeding out of control. Certainly the authors of the *Federalist Papers* were aware of this potential; hence the frequency with which they address themselves to what Madison and Hamilton call the disease of faction. If representative government proceeds according to plan, the political tempo will permit the constitution to do its beneficent work. But this cannot happen if, as Madison warns, a number of citizens "activated by some common impulse of passion, or of interest, adverse to the rights of other citizens, or to the permanent and aggregate interests of the community" demand quick satisfaction. Either we go wisely and slow, proceeding by due process, or the "cabals of a few" will intemperately destroy the enterprise. Indeed, Americans can learn from the frequent failures to establish democracies in Third World countries the extent to which a democratic constitution must be accepted by those under it as a decelerating political mechanism, lest the cabalists with their violent loves exploit its permissions to achieve as quickly as possible totalitarian slowdowns.

But the braking power that is crucial to democracy has helped, especially in America, to produce conditions in which speed and wealth easily translate into one another. To go from rags to riches is to go a long way in a hurry, but perhaps to arrive breathless and exhausted and so specialized in the process that wealth is meaningless. Hence the ambition "to get rich quick" so that one can enjoy being rich, a state that can be defined as the sense of being able to close quickly the gap between desire and fulfillment. Such an ambition is more compatible with the privately owned jet plane than the three-wheeled, fifteen-mile-an-hour donkey cart that Dr. Illich has proposed. It anticipates the test pilot Chuck Yeager (Tom Wolfe's hero in *The Right Stuff*) and his refusal to accept the sound-barrier limits of Mach 1. But the ideal of quick wealth, appealing as it does to avaricious predators of all sorts, can dangerously speed up the environment. Thus we have the counter-ideal of wealth by means of the Protestant work ethic, in which character oriented to public service is a decelerator. Andrew Carnegie in his famous "The Road to Business Success: A Talk to Young Men" counsels a determination "to live pure, respectable lives" (liquor and fast women are out) and assumes that "you save and long for wealth only as a means of enabling you the better to do some good in your day and generation." Similarly, Russell H. Conwell's "Acres of Diamonds" lecture (delivered very profitably over six thousand times) champions the desire for honestly acquired wealth "because you can do more good with it than without it." There is ample maneuvering room for hypocrisy here, which is regrettable; nevertheless, hypocrisy, by respecting the moral structure of society, keeps it from changing with unmanageable speed. The speedsters are those who, like John Brown and teetotaler-absolutionist William Lloyd Garrison, insist too passionately on a congruity between prescription and practice. In their own way they want to get rich quick so that they can have everything.

In "The Impossible Culture" (*Salmagundi*, Fall 1982– Winter 1983) Philip Rieff tells us that the irreducible function of culture is to prevent the expression and experiencing of everything. Carnegie and Conwell could assume a puritan work ethic that would keep this Faustian desire on a tight rein. When they counseled honesty it was the virtue as Shakespeare understood it: the habit of honoring commitments to others. If people around us are honest in this sense, if we can expect them to keep their pledged faith, then life seems properly paced and we are able to anticipate a manageable future. This is "slow" honesty. But we have had to learn to live with the "fast" honesty of individual impulse, which can involve a principled rejection or avoidance of commitments to others and a violation of contracts. If the self is seen as an immense, even infinite, reservoir of possibility, then Shakespearean honesty can appear as an immoral decelerating force, hypocrisy-generating and authenticity-preventing, and therefore to be put behind one as quickly as possible—perhaps with the help of a get-rich-quick drug like cocaine that affords short-term relief from the anxieties of life in the fast lane of the affluent.

In Jean Stein's and George Plimpton's *Edie* we get a fascinating look at a world in which fast honesty is as important a term as slow honesty is in *Othello*. In a world in which everyone is trying to harvest his or her acres of diamonds as quickly as possible, in which all speeds short of Mach 1 are a snail's pace, no one goes faster than Edie Sedgwick, and no one is more honest. Robert Rauchenberg says of her: "In any situation her physicality was so refreshing that she exposed all the dishonesty in the room." Her inevitably early death places her in a pantheon with such exemplars of fast honesty as Jimi Hendrix, Sid Vicious, Janis Joplin, and Jim Morrison. In this pantheon there is no place for those who go wisely and slow for fear of stumbling: it exists, in fact, to rebuke the donkey-cart tempo of the pusillanimous laity. Far different are those heroes of *Star Trek*, Captain Kirk and Mr. Spock, who, as they go boldly and at unimaginable speeds where no man has ever gone before, nevertheless display the slow honesty and work-ethic character structure that Carnegie advocates.

Neal Cassady, who has starring roles in Tom Wolfe's earlier *The Electric Kool-Aid Acid Test* and Jack Kerouac's *On the Road*, has an honored place in the speedster's pantheon. He was, as Wolfe writes, "the Denver kid, a kid who was always racing back and forth across the U.S. by car, chasing, or outrunning, 'life.'" Ken Kesey says of him: "He is going as fast as a human can go," and when at the end of the book he is found dead beside a Mexican railroad track, others say of him that "he had been going at top speed for two weeks." Yet even Cassady can't overcome the one-thirtieth of a second sensory lag "between the time your senses receive something and you are able to react" that preoccupies Kesey. Thus he is condemned to spend his days watching a mere movie of his life. But he knows that the true way is to keep trying for a total, gap-closing breakthrough into Now, which gives him some affinity with that earlier advocate of gap closing, C. P. Snow—a man otherwise far too slow to keep up with Cassady and with Chuck Yeager, whose assault on the sound barrier in Wolfe's later book includes "those traditional essentials for the hot young pilot: Flying & Drinking and Drinking & Driving."

In their own context figures like Edie Sedgwick and Cassady are identified as being exciting and memorable personalities. Their reputations as magical persons benefit from the more or less spectacular confusion they generate as they attempt to experience everything. An outsider, however, is likely to see them as blank checks available to be filled out in terms of the inchoate needs of other speedsters. The latter are forever reporting on the great insights they have achieved, yet the insights we get from them are generally on a level with what Joe Klein, referring to *Playboy*'s interview with John Lennon and Yoko Ono, called cosmic gumdrops. Such personalities are usually moving too fast and are too dependent on the terrain through which they move to wear well. Going with the flow, they are gone with the flow. Personalities that stick in the mind tend to be both structured and slowed down by the old slow honesty. In effect, they have renounced the desire to experience everything in the interest of conserving energy to·experience something memorably. They must, of course, be willing to run the risk of hypocrisy, just as Madison's representative form of government must be willing to run the risk of faction.

One of the most compelling features of the computer is its lack of hypocrisy. If you put garbage into it, it does not mask the garbage as a gourmet dish before giving it back—and if, as some expect, it comes in time to recognize garbage in all its subtle variations as garbage, it will no doubt quite frankly, and perhaps even obscenely, say so. With its binary confinement to 1 (yes) and 0 (no) it would appear to conform to Saint Matthew's injunction: "All you need say is 'Yes' if you mean yes, 'No' if you mean no; anything more than this comes from the evil one."

Of course, all machines are honest, even when, like rigged gambling devices, they are used for dishonest purposes. The thing is that the computer is honest in circumstances of extreme speed, when humans, for fear of stumbling, are most inclined to depart from or dispense themselves from the prescriptions of strict honesty. Greatly assisted by the stimulus of two world wars, the computer has progressed from electromagnetic relays through tubes and transistors to silicon chips, in the process ever becoming faster and smaller but always with a clear conscience. In a hyped-up age, which it has helped to hype up, it has always resisted the temptation to hyperbole, which no doubt helps to explain the hyperbolic expectations it has aroused in its creators of being able to use it, or be used by it, to go safely, missing nothing of value, at breakneck speed.

This expectation takes its most utopian form in the anticipation of the truly intelligent machine. Thirty years ago in *The Human Use of Human Beings* Norbert Wiener, to whom we owe the term *cybernetics*, was saying, "The dominance of the machine presupposes a society in the last stages of increasing entropy, where probability is negligible and where the statistical differences among individuals are nil. Fortunately, we have not yet reached such a state." Ten years later in *God and Golem* he hadn't changed his mind: "Now the future offers little hope for those who expect that our new mechanical slaves will offer us a world in which we may rest from thinking."

Arthur C. Clarke, collaborator with Stanley Kubrick in *2001: A Space Odyssey*, is not so pessimistic. In his influential essay "Are We Thinking Machines?" he states that "the merely intelligent machine will swiftly give way to the *ultra*intelligent machine," that the latter will end what little is left of Carnegie's puritan work ethic, make possible new art forms, conquer boredom and conflict among nations, and end history as we have known it. Robert Jastrow, former director of NASA's Goddard Institute for Space Studies and author of *The Enchanted Loom*, believes that computers will ultimately beat us at everything. In the meantime, enough people have seen the Disneyland humanoids, played video games, taken computer courses, become addicted to science fiction, read books like Alvin Toffler's *The Third Wave* with its optimistic prediction of "the electronic cottage," or seen movies like *Star Wars* and *Star Trek III*, to give widespread credence to the belief that with the computer anything is possible, that if because of it we are tempted to go too fast, it will itself be the reason that we slow down.

Crucial to the controversy is the definition of intelligence and creativity and the question whether the gap between neural system and mind is an illusion. On these terms Joseph Weizenbaum, professor of computer science at M.I.T., gives little comfort to true believers like Clarke. In *Computer Powers and Human Reason* Weizenbaum points out that truly creative thought "to the extent that it is based on analogical and metaphorical reasoning ... gains its power from the combination of hitherto disparate contexts." The creative human intelligence selects "from among the infinite of similarities shared by every pair of concepts precisely those two

244 CHAOS AND CHARACTER

frameworks that shed the maximum illumination on one or both of them." The computer, however, is *given* the relevant criteria it needs to fuse frameworks.

This is a congenial approach for those humanists who are willing to believe that the metaphor is the supreme human organizer of information and that computer speed assumes and is subordinate to human metaphoric speed. When Friar Lawrence sees Juliet hurrying to keep her appointment with him and Romeo he says, "O, so light a foot/Will ne'er wear out the everlasting flint." To analyze this seemingly offhand remark in terms of the information it organizes (the act of organization is inconceivably faster than the intemperate speed that is its subject) would require far more words than the play itself has used to this point, since all related imagery in the play that is in any way involved with its theme of intemperate speed would have to be analyzed. Confronted with this accomplishment one might say (and Weizenbaum seems to imply it) that when human beings define the mind as a machine, thereby closing the gap between brain and mind in order to predict the ultraintelligent machine, they are actually using their metaphoric powers in an effort to slow themselves down. For if the metaphor is fast it is also risky, prone not only to the petrifications of cliché but to those abuses of analogy of which the mind-machine metaphor is a prime example.

What Friar Lawrence knows is that two passionate young people in the situation of Romeo and Juliet can easily get caught up in a system far too fast for them to control—a fact that they might themselves learn from the system, but only after the system has worked its way with them. The play assumes that the question, How fast should we go? cannot be answered unless one recognizes that human existence demands the capacity to live with a variety of tempos, some of which are vastly incommensurate with those we are most at ease with. Wiener has this in mind when in "Some Moral and Technical Consequences of Automation" (*Mind*, 6 May

1960) he states that "man and machine operate on two distinct time scales" so that "even when machines do not in any way transcend man's intelligence, they very well may, and often do, transcend man in the performance of tasks." Therefore, we may understand their performance only "long after the task which they have been set has been completed." Thus "by the very slowness of our human actions, our effective control of our machines may be nullified." It follows that we can "by no means justify the naïve assumption that the faster we rush ahead to employ the new powers for action the better we will be." The danger then is not simply that we will stumble if we go too fast, having naïvely taken the pace of the Big Bang as a safe model, but that we may discover too late that what we took at the time to be an admirable and safely imitable caper must be redefined as stumbling.

Shakespeare expects us to see that Romeo is too young and too Romeo-ish to know all this. Isaiah Berlin might, in fact, be speaking for the play when he says in an interview (*Partisan Review*, no. 1, 1983): "Young men are not deeply inspired by the ideal of a perpetually uneasy equilibrium, which is the only thing that can keep things going without grave suffering and injustice." The repeated and often painful rediscovery of this truth has made the individual who is capable of graceful changes of pace a compelling cultural model.

Meanwhile, the recurring painful consequences of not being able to change pace gracefully also make us easy prey to the hasty factionists to whom anything short of perpetual equilibrium is intolerable. They suggest the extent to which the dream of the ultraintelligent machine is the expression of a fanatic impulse. Indeed, our long love affair with machines has made it all too apparent that, like LSD, their initial promise to expand consciousness tends to be countered by their capacity to restrict consciousness by fanaticizing it. This unsettling possibility was long ago made brilliantly clear by Jonathan Swift when in the third part of *Gulliver's Travels* he

sent his hero to Laputa where he could observe the fanatic speedsters of the Academy of Projectors happily at
work. Swift helps us see why for some people California's Silicon Valley can turn out to be the Slough of
Despond.

Total immobility when one's mind and body are set
on speed can be as disturbing as the sense of excessive
speed. Thus shortly after having been stalled for ten
minutes between stations in a London underground
train it was with mixed feelings that I sat in the University of London library and read in *The Listener*
(12 January 1978) George Steiner's first annual Bronowski Memorial Lecture—delivered at Cambridge as
Snow's two-culture lectures had been twenty years before. Steiner, however, was much less optimistic than
Snow about the forward thrust of science. His thesis
was that our culturally induced addiction to the drug
of absolute thought, our predatory tendency to pursue
truth regardless of its social consequences, may be
speeding us toward disaster. Science has arrived at the
point where "there are doors immediately in front of
current research which are marked 'too dangerous to
open,' which would, if we were to force them, open on
chaos and inhumanity." Steiner saw some hope in a
scientist-humanist-socialist like Jacob Bronowski, who
would "have made a distinction between suppressing
truth and pursuing new truth at any cost."

Certainly there is no indication in Bronowski's widely
read *Science and Human Values* that he would have
been an irresponsible opener of doors, and certainly
he was too impressed with the metaphoric powers of
the human mind, and too out of sympathy with positivism, to celebrate the possibility of Clarke's ultraintelligent machine. One may wonder, nevertheless, how
sympathetic he would have been to Steiner's notion of
the "blackmail of transcendence," implicit in his Cambridge lecture but explicit in his earlier *In Bluebeard's
Castle* as well as in his later novel *The Portage to San*

Cristobal of A.H. There is a troubling extremism in the idea that much that we value most in Western civilization, and especially in our Judeo-Christian heritage, can, in its capacity to urge us to transcend ourselves, be reduced to blackmail. Steiner drives one back to Wiener's question whether the scientist's archenemy is Manichean or Augustinian—a contrary force opposed to order or the very absence of order itself. Wiener, of course, is Augustinian, so he quotes with approval Einstein's "The Lord is subtle, but he isn't simply mean." Steiner's implied Lord seems a bit mean. He may also seem to leave too little maneuvering room between the stalled background train and Illich's fifteen-mile-an-hour donkey cart.

Steiner, nevertheless, expressed fears that are widespread among literary and scientific intellectuals, and for obvious reasons these fears like to center on issues raised by the computer—that symbol of our worship of high technology, as Weizenbaum puts it. Weizenbaum himself wonders whether instead of expanding computerized and automated information systems the better course might not be "to attempt to contain the information explosion." He presents us with a series of disturbing questions, one of which is: "What is the impact of the computer, not only on the economies of the world or on the war potential of nations and so on, but on the self-image of human beings and on human integrity?"

It is of course unlikely that a significant number of scientists have seen themselves as irresponsible accelerators of the human condition. But the advancement of science depends on specialization, and specialization, as a half-century ago Ortega y Gasset emphasized in *The Revolt of the Masses*, tends to result in the barbarism of the dangerously limited perspective. What we pay too little attention to, in science or in human affairs generally, is the morale-raising function of specialization. To concentrate all one's energies on doing well a very limited thing is to induce the sense that it is not only worth doing but will sooner or later have good consequences.

The scientists who so intrepidly open the doors that may result in Nobel prizes are caught up in an optimistic enterprise, and the exponentially increasing speed with which it races away from its primitive beginnings is probably just as exhilarating to them as breaking through the sound barrier was to Chuck Yeager. They are no more likely to feel uneasy as they strain against established barriers than Ken Kesey did when he contemplated the possibility of "some kind of total breakthrough" that would get us beyond the one-thirtieth of a second sensory lag.

That old factory manager, Andy Warhol, of whom Edie Sedgwick was a part-time protégée, has been quoted as saying: "The things I like to show are mechanical. Machines have less problems. I'd like to be a machine, wouldn't you?" It is unlikely that this remark will end up in some future edition of *Bartlett's Familiar Quotations*; nevertheless, it expresses not only what many of us believe about the machine but what we expect of an ideal commonwealth. A computer may be honest in its special sense but it does not depend on voluntary assertions of virtue for efficient operation. Its honesty is automatic and predictable, uncomplicated by attempts at subterfuge that would only give it problems and slow it down. Human systems, on the other hand, have been understood traditionally as dependent on voluntary assertions of virtue, complicated by passion and environment and directed by a metaphoric intelligence quite capable of misconstruing the data of the senses and mistaking cosmic gumdrops for profound insights. The result has been the wild fluctuations of tempo and the stumbling that have marked human history—and maddened utopians.

One of Marxism's most compelling features is its vision of a social system so unproblematic that it does not depend on voluntary cultivation of virtue in its members. The necessary virtues are the property of the dialectical system that will induce them as necessary to achieve its ends. If Marx was a great humanist—as many, including the late Eric Fromm, have believed—it may be necessary to redefine the humanist as the sensitive reed through whom the irresistible and benevolent humanistic system moves. Because the system does not depend on individual assertions of virtue, the dangerous fluctuations of tempo that result from Steiner's blackmail of transcendence cannot ultimately do it any harm. The faster bourgeois capitalist society goes the sooner it will run its appointed course and the sooner its very stumblings will be revealed to have been necessary. As Ernst Topitsch has pointed out in *Encounter* (May 1982), thanks to the wonders of dialectical reasoning, even apparent disconfirmations of the system in particular times and places can be seen as part of the plan: for the system, like the Judeo-Christian God, has the capacity to arrive at its destination by labyrinthine ways. Dialectical materialism is thus history seen as Clarke's ultraintelligent machine, able not only to debug itself as it operates but to transmute the garbage of human muddling and stumbling into the caviar of the classless society.

The crucial question, of course, is: *will* this come to pass, or *might* it come to pass? Marx the social scientist could no more tolerate the subjunctive *might*, with its implied dependence on voluntary assertions of virtue and an all-too-erratic human management of tempo, than he could tolerate the philosopher Karl R. Popper's maxim, "A theory which is not refutable by any conceivable event is non-scientific." Marxist prediction, like that of such tabloid psychics as Jeanne Dixon and David Guardino, is out of necessity in the indicative mode, the mode of categorical assertion in which, in the interest of keeping up morale, most of us spend most of our time. Those comforters, our heroes, are expected above all to be indicative: they *will*, not *might*, head the rustlers off at the pass, break through the sound barrier, or land on the moon. Like Saint Matthew or the computer, they must confine themselves to the *yes* and the *no* of it and leave *maybe* to the faint of heart.

On the other hand, the question, How fast should we go? is subjunctively involved with all the demoralizing uncertainties, the imponderables, and the moral imperatives of the human condition. To live comfortably with the subjunctive requires the ability to live with Isaiah Berlin's perpetually uneasy equilibrium, and thus assumes a faith reinforced with irony. Indeed, irony can be defined as the awareness that the subjunctive never ceases to be the alternative that haunts the indicative, just as the human predicament itself can be defined as the gap between the indicative and the subjunctive.

Marx and the ultraintelligent machine, no less than Neal Cassady's LSD, promises relief from the burden of this gap. Both look forward to a society untroubled by irony and hypocrisy. In such a society the factions that bothered James Madison would not be possible because there would be no options, and by the same token it would not occur to anyone that what he is experiencing is somewhat less than everything. And the question, How fast should we go? with its unsettling implication that we *might* be wise to go faster or slower, would be unaskable.

Notes

(Full citations for books appear in the Selected Bibliography of Secondary Sources.)

Introduction

1. This quotation is from "Fanaticism and Survival" (see John P. Sisk: Selected Chronological Bibliography).
2. Also from "Fanaticism and Survival."

Chapter 1. On Intoxication

3. A reference to Cohn's *The Pursuit of the Millennium*.
4. Antonin Artaud is an influential French actor, director, and dramatic theorist, whose *The Theatre and Its Double* proposes what has been called a primitivist and ritualistic "Theatre of Cruelty."
5. Sisk's summary of O'Brien's position is in "The Gentle Nietzscheans," *The New York Review of Books*, 5 Nov. 1970.

Chapter 2. Salvation Unlimited

6. The Club of Rome is a nonpolitical multinational group of scientists and humanists that promotes research and reflection on global problems and how to approach them.
7. John Passmore is an Australian philosopher best known at the time of this essay for "Paradise Now," *Encounter*, Nov. 1970, which eventually became the final chapter of his *The Perfectibility of Man*.
8. R. D. Laing is a British psychiatrist best remembered for *The Politics of Experience*. Laing emphasizes the family as the prison of the individual, the collective madness of society, and the binding of the individual by education.

Chapter 4. The Promise of Dirty Words

9. Shulamith Firestone is the author of *The Dialectic of Sex: The Case for Feminist Revolution*. Firestone proposes a radical solution to

our social problems: the dismantling of the family and a political breaking down of traditional sex-roles in the interest of a truly humane future. William Reich is the author of the famous *The Greening of America*.

10. Pierre-Joseph Proudhon (French) and Peter Kropotkin (Russian) were nineteenth-century anarchists. See George Woodcock, *Anarchism: A History of Libertarian Ideas and Movements*.

11. Geoffrey Barraclough is a British historian who publishes frequently in this country, especially in *The New York Review of Books*.

Chapter 5. Honesty as a Policy

12. A reference to Lifton's "Protean Man," *Partisan Review* 35 (1968). In "Protean Man" the emphasis is on adapation to change and flux, not on stability of character and personality. The subject is open to all possibilities. "In attention, as in being, nothing is 'off limits.'"

Chapter 7. Cowboy

13. See note 12.

Chapter 8. Untested Innovations

14. For Sale's notion of "technofix," see "The Miracle of Technofix," *Newsweek*, 23 June 1980.

15. Gregory Bateson is an anthropologist best known for his study of New Guinea tribal culture, *Naven*.

16. Arthur Koestler is an ex-communist devoted to the anti-authoritarian cause, best known for his novel, *Darkness at Noon*. Sisk is here contrasting Koestler's relative pessimism about human progress with Bateson's more optimistic notion, mentioned earlier, of "stochastic" processes that "make it possible for events to evolve by leaps and bounds."

Chapter 9. The Devil and American Epic

17. See Hofstadter's *Anti-Intellectualism in American Life*.

18. For Mike Gold's criticism of Hemingway see Carlos Baker, *Ernest Hemingway: A Life Story*. Writing in *The Daily Worker* on *For Whom the Bell Tolls*, Gold found Hemingway narrow and limited by class egotism and poverty of mind.

19. See William Van O'Connor, "Why *Huckleberry Finn* is Not the Great American Novel," *College English* 17 (1955).

20. See Geismar's *Mark Twain: An American Prophet*. Geismar, a critic who wrote from the radical left, is now pretty much forgotten.

21. See David Riesman with Nathan Glazer and Reuel Denney, *The Lonely Crowd*. The "inside dopester" is the individual who in a message-crammed and complex society gets attention and power

by claiming to have information available only to an elite of knowing ones.

Chapter 13. Dr. Johnson Kicks a Stone

22. See Berman's *All That Is Solid Melts into Air.*

Selected Bibliography of Secondary Sources

Aaron, Daniel. *Writers on the Left: Episodes in American Literary Communism.* New York: Avon, 1965.

Alvarez, A. *The Savage God: A Study of Suicide.* New York: Random House, 1970.

Anderson, Quentin. *The Imperial Self: An Essay in American Literary and Cultural History.* New York: Knopf, 1971.

Aronson, Steven M. L. *Hype.* New York: Morrow, 1983.

Artaud, Antonin. *The Theatre and Its Double.* Trans. Mary Caroline Richards. New York: Grove Press, 1958.

Barnes, Hazel Estella. *Sartre and Flaubert.* Chicago: University of Chicago Press, 1981.

Barthes, Roland. *Mythologies.* Trans. Annette Lavers. New York: Hill and Wang, 1972.

Bateson, Gregory. *Naven: A Survey of the Problems Suggested by a Composite Picture of the Culture of a New Guinea Tribe Drawn from Three Points of View.* 2d edition. Stanford: Stanford University Press, 1959.

Berman, Marshal. *All That Is Solid Melts into Air.* New York: Simon and Schuster, 1982.

Bernheimer, Richard. *Wild Men in the Middle Ages.* Cambridge: Harvard University Press, 1952.

Bettelheim, Bruno. *The Uses of Enchantment: The Meaning and Importance of Fairy Tales.* New York: Random House, 1976.

Blanchard, Kenneth H., and Spencer Johnson. *The One-Minute Manager.* New York: Morrow, 1982.

Bronowski, Jacob. *Science and Human Values.* New York: Messner, 1956.

Brothers, Joyce. *How to Get Whatever You Want Out of Life.* New York: Simon and Schuster, 1978.

Brown, Norman. *Love's Body.* New York: Random House, 1966.

Bugliosi, Vincent. *Helter Skelter: The True Story of the Manson Murders.* New York: Norton, 1974.

Cohn, Norman. *The Pursuit of the Millennium.* New York: Essential Books, 1955.

Commoner, Barry. *The Closing Circle: Man, Nature, and Technology.* New York: Knopf, 1971.

Cooper, David. *The Death of the Family.* New York: Pantheon Books, 1970.

Copperman, Paul. *The Literacy Hoax: The Decline of Reading, Writing, and Learning in Public Schools and What We Can Do About It.* New York: Morrow, 1978.

de Rougemont, Denis. *The Devil's Share: An Essay on the Diabolic in Modern Society.* Trans. Haa Kon Chevalier. New York: Pantheon Books, 1944.

Ehrenpreis, Irvin. *The Personality of Jonathan Swift.* New York: Barnes and Noble, 1969.

Erickson, John R. *Modern Cowboy.* Lincoln: University of Nebraska Press, 1981.

Fieve, Ronald R. *Moodswing: The Third Revolution in Psychiatry.* New York: Bantam, 1975.

Firestone, Shulamith. *The Dialectic of Sex: The Case for Feminist Revolution.* New York: Morrow, 1970.

FitzGerald, Frances. *Cities on a Hill: A Journey Through Contemporary American Cultures.* New York: Simon and Schuster, 1986.

Fox, Stephen R. *The Mirror Makers: A History of American Advertising and Its Creators.* New York: Morrow, 1984.

Furnas, J. G. *The Life and Times of the Late Demon Rum.* New York: Putnam's, 1965.

Gaines, Steven. *Heroes and Villains: The True Story of the Beach Boys.* New York: New American Library, 1986.

Gass, William H. *The Habitation of the Word.* New York: Simon and Schuster, 1985.

Geismar, Maxwell. *Mark Twain: An American Prophet.* Boston: Houghton Mifflin, 1970.

Gunn, Giles. *The Culture of Criticism and the Criticism of Culture.* New York: Oxford University Press, 1987.

Harris, Frank. *My Life and Loves.* New York: Grove Press, 1963.

Hartman, Geoffrey. *Criticism in the Wilderness: The Study of Literature Today.* New Haven: Yale University Press, 1980.

———. *Saving the Text: Literature, Derrida, and Philosophy.* Baltimore: Johns Hopkins University Press, 1981.

Havelock, Eric A. *Preface to Plato.* Cambridge: Harvard University Press, 1982.

Heilbroner, Robert Louis. *An Inquiry into the Human Project.* New York: Norton, 1974.

Hofstadter, Richard. *Anti-Intellectualism in American Life*. New York: Knopf, 1963.

Hollander, Paul. *Political Pilgrims: Travels of Western Intellectuals to the Soviet Union, China, Cuba, 1928–1978*. New York: Oxford University Press, 1981.

Huizinga, Johan. *The Waning of the Middle Ages*. Garden City, New York: Doubleday, 1954.

Illich, Ivan. *Deschooling Society*. New York: Harper and Row, 1971.

Jastrow, Robert. *The Enchanted Loom: The Mind in the Universe*. New York: Simon and Schuster, 1981.

Johnson, Paul. *Modern Times: The World from the Twenties to the Eighties*. New York: Harper and Row, 1983.

Johnston, Jill. *Lesbian Nation: The Feminist Solution*. New York: Simon and Schuster, 1974.

Jonas, Hans. *The Gnostic Religions*. Boston: Beacon Press, 1958.

Kaplan, Justin. *Mr. Clemens and Mark Twain: A Biography*. New York: Simon and Schuster, 1966.

Key, Wilson Brian. *Media Sexploitation*. Englewood Cliffs, New Jersey: Prentice-Hall, 1976.

Koestler, Arthur. *The Invisible Writing: Being the Second Volume of Arrow in the Blue, an Autobiography*. New York: Macmillan, 1954.

Laing, R. D. *The Politics of Experience*. New York: Pantheon Books, 1967.

Linton, Ralph. *The Study of Man*. New York: Appleton-Century, 1963.

Marcuse, Herbert. *An Essay on Liberation*. Boston: Beacon Press, 1969.

Michelson, Peter. *The Aesthetics of Pornography*. New York: Herder and Herder, 1971.

Morgan, Marabel. *Total Woman*. New York: Pocket Books, 1983.

Olschki, Leonardo. *Marco Polo's Asia*. Trans. John A. Scott. Berkeley: University of California Press, 1960.

Ortega y Gasset, Jose. *The Revolt of the Masses*. New York: Norton, 1957.

Packard, Vance. *The Hidden Persuaders*. New York: McKay, 1957.

Passmore, John. *The Perfectibility of Man*. New York: Scribner's, 1971.

Popper, Karl. *The Open Society and Its Enemies*. 4th edition. Princeton: Princeton University Press, 1963. 2 volumes.

Reage, Pauline. *The Story of O*. New York: Ballantine, 1981.

Regan, Tom. *The Case for Animal Rights*. Berkeley: University of California Press, 1983.

Reich, Charles. *The Greening of America*. New York: Random House, 1970.

Revel, Jean-François. *Without Marx or Jesus: The New American Revolution Has Begun*. Garden City, New York: Doubleday, 1971.

Rieff, Philip. *The Triumph of the Therapeutic: Uses of Faith After Freud*. New York: Harper and Row, 1966.

———. *Fellow Teachers: Of Culture and Its Second Death*. Chicago: University of Chicago Press, 1985.

Riesman, David, Nathan Glazer, and Reuel Denney. *The Lonely Crowd*. New Haven: Yale University Press, 1970.

Roszak, Theodore. *Where the Wasteland Ends: Politics and Transcendence in Postindustrial Society*. Garden City, New York: Doubleday, 1973.

Sanders, Ed. *The Family: The Story of Charles Manson's Dune Buggy Attack Battalion*. New York: Dutton, 1971.

Sanford, Charles L. *The Quest for Paradise: Europe and the American Moral Imagination*. Urbana: University of Illinois Press, 1961.

Schudson, Michael. *Advertising, The Uneasy Persuasion*. New York: Basic Books, 1984.

Singer, Peter. *Animal Liberation*. New York: Avon, 1977.

Skinner, B. F. *Beyond Freedom and Dignity*. New York: Knopf, 1971.

Smith, Henry Nash. *Virgin Land: The American West as Symbol and Myth*. Cambridge: Harvard University Press, 1970.

Stein, Jean, and George Plimpton. *Edie, an American Biography*. New York: Knopf, 1982.

Steiner, George. *After Babel: Aspects of Language in Translation*. New York: Oxford University Press, 1975.

Sturrock, John. *Structuralism and Since: From Levi Strauss to Derrida*. New York: Oxford University Press, 1980.

Thomas, Keith Vivian. *Man and the Natural World: A History of the Modern Sensibility*. New York: Pantheon Books, 1983.

Toffler, Alvin. *The Third Wave*. New York: Bantam, 1981.

Trilling, Lionel. *The Liberal Imagination*. New York: Viking, 1950.

Turnbull, Colin M. *The Forest People*. New York: Simon and Schuster, 1962.

Tuveson, Ernest Lee. *Redeemer Nation: The Idea of America's Millennial Role*. Chicago: University of Chicago Press, 1968.

Unwin, J. D. *Sex and Culture*. London: Oxford University Press, 1934.

Vargas Llosa, Mario. *The Perpetual Orgy: Flaubert and Madame Bovary*. Trans. Helen Giroux. New York: Farrar, Straus and Giroux, 1986.

Voegelin, Eric. *The New Science of Politics*. Chicago: University of Chicago Press, 1952.

Wakeman, Frederic. *The Hucksters*. New York: Rinehart, 1946.

Weizenbaum, Joseph. *Computer Power and Human Reason: From Judgment to Calculation*. San Francisco: Freeman, 1976.

Wiener, Norbert. *The Human Uses of Human Beings: Cybernetics and Society*. Boston: Houghton Mifflin, 1950.

———. *God and Golem, Inc.: A Comment on Certain Points Where Cybernetics Impinges on Religion*. Cambridge: MIT Press, 1964.

Witek, John. *Response Television: Combat Advertising of the 1980s.* Chicago: Crain, 1987.

Wolfe, Tom. *The Electric Kool-Aid Acid Test.* New York: Farrar, Straus and Giroux, 1968.

Woodcock, George. *Anarchism: A History of Libertarian Ideas and Movements.* New York: World, 1962.

John P. Sisk: Selected Chronological Bibliography

"The Myth of the Successful Boob." *Prairie Schooner* 23 (Spring 1949): 140.

"American Pastoral." *Thought* 27 (Autumn 1952): 365–80.

"Crime and Criticism." *Commonweal* 64 (April 1956): 72–74.

"The Executive as Hero." *Commonweal* 65 (November 1956): 127–28.

"Western Hero." *Commonweal* 66 (July 1957): 367–69.

"Rags to Riches." *Commonweal* 67 (January 1958): 352–54.

"The Complex Moral World of J. F. Power." *Critique* 2 (Fall 1958): 28–40.

"Beatniks and Tradition." *Commonweal* 70 (April 1959): 75–77.

"Keats' American Dream." *America* 102 (March 1960): 706–08.

"The Confessional Hero." *Commonweal* 72 (May 1960): 167–70.

"Conservatism on Campus." *Commonweal* 73 (January 1961): 451–54.

"Disease in Our Flesh." *Commonweal* 74 (May 1961): 143–46.

A Trial of Strength. (Carl Foreman Award for novel.) New York: Harcourt Brace Jovanovich, 1961.

"Writer in America." *Commonweal* 75 (December 1961): 271–74.

"America and the Dream." *Commonweal* 76 (July 1962): 397–400.

"Writers and Scientists: The Two Cultures." *Ramparts* 1 (September 1962): 17–22.

"The Mirrors of Advertising." *Commonweal* 79 (March 1964): 707–10.

"The Fear of Immortality." *Commonweal* 81 (December 1964): 415–18.

"The Dream Girl as Queen of Utopia." *Sex in America*. Henry A. Grunwald, ed. New York: Bantam, 1964.

"The Late Demon Rum." *Commonweal* 82 (April 1965): 113–16.

"The Specter of the Poor." *Commonweal* 82 (June 1965): 437–40.

"The Human Management of the News." *Ramparts* 4 (October 1965): 59–63.

"F. Scott Fitzgerald's Discovery of Illusion." *The Gordon Review* 10 (Fall 1966): 12–23.

"Bondage and Release in *The Merchant of Venice*." *The Shakespeare Quarterly* 20 (Spring 1969): 217–23.
"The Intolerable Allegories of Dissent." *The Catholic World* 210 (November 1969): 55–58.
"Making It in America." *The Atlantic* 224 (December 1969): 63–68.
"The Future of Prediction." *Commentary* 49 (March 1970): 65–68.
Person and Institution. Notre Dame: Fides Press, 1970.
"The Cybernetics of *Othello*." *The New Orleans Review* 2 (Fall 1970): 74–77.
"Hamlet y el detectivo privado." *Folia Humanistica* (October 1970): 819–29.
"Sex and Armageddon." *Commentary* 50 (December 1970): 83–92.
"Crisis on the Left." *The Critic* 29 (July–August 1971): 18–26.
"On Intoxication." *Commentary* 53 (February 1972): 56–61.
"Honesty as a Policy." *The American Scholar* 24 (Spring 1972): 251–64.
"Strictly Personal." *The Atlantic* 229 (June 1972): 42–44.
"The Hatch and Brood of Time." *Worldview* 15 (November 1972).
"Roszak's Pagan Gospel." *Worldview* 12 (December 1972).
"That First Postwar Season." *The New York Times* Travel Section (December 1972).
"Hot Sporting Blood." *Commonweal* 97 (March 1973): 495–98.
"The Curious Analyzer." *Commentary* 55 (May 1973): 62–68.
"War Fiction." *Commentary* 56 (August 1973): 58–66.
"On Being an Object." *Harper's* 247 (November 1973).
"Chomsky, the State and the True Believer." *Worldview* 17 (February 1974).
"The Fear of Affluence." *Commentary* 57 (August 1974): 61–68.
"The Uses and Abuses of the Past." *Worldview* 17 (August 1974): 45–50.
"In Praise of Privacy." *Harper's* (February 1975): 100–07.
"The Necessary Utopia." *Worldview* (February 1975): 58–61.
"The Promise of Dirty Words." *The American Scholar* 44 (1975): 385–404.
"Losing Big." *Harper's* 251 (November 1975): 79–85.
"Variations on an American Dream." *Scholia Satyrica* 1 (Summer 1975): 9–15.
"Salvation Unlimited." *Commentary* 61 (April 1976): 52–56.
"Fanaticism and Survival." *Worldview* 19 (November 1976): 12–18.
"The Tyranny of Harmony." *The American Scholar* 46 (Spring 1977): 193–205.
"At War with General Forrest." *The Virginia Quarterly Review* 53 (Spring 1977): 288–310.
"Getting Rid of the Pains of Sin." *Worldview* 20 (June 1977): 4–8.
"Sexual Stereotypes." *Commentary* 64 (October 1977): 58–64.

"Prince Hal and the Specialists." *Shakespeare Quarterly* 28 (Autumn 1977): 520–24.

"Pornography, Censorship, and the Cult of the Wild West." *The American Spectator* 11 (January 1978): 5–7.

"When Love Is Soon Hot, Soon Cold." *The American Spectator* 11 (March 1978): 11–15.

"Human Sexuality." *Worldview* 21 (June 1978): 54–57.

"Ceremony and Civilization in Shakespeare." *The Sewanee Review* 86 (Summer 1978): 396–405.

"The Bitter Truth of Gossip." *The American Spectator* 11 (October 1978): 10–14.

"The Quality of Life." *Commentary* 65 (October 1978): 51–57.

"All the News That Fits the Story." *Worldview* 21 (November 1978): 49–52.

"The View From the Edge." *Harper's* 258 (March 1979): 127–29.

"The Unceremonious American." *The American Spectator* 12 (September 1979): 12–17.

"The American Experience as Tall Tale." *Worldview* 22 (October 1979): 28–29.

"Correspondences." *Harper's* 260 (June 1980): 72–79.

"Important Horses." *Harper's* 260 (July 1980): 73–75.

"Beings of Good Cheer." *The American Spectator* 13 (September 1980): 16–20.

"The Man Who Counted." *The Atlantic* 246 (December 1980): 45–55.

"Untested Innovations." *Harper's* 262 (May 1981): 69–74.

"Ah, Wilderness." *Pacific Northwest* 18 (November 1981): 28–31.

"The Playboy and the Czar: Images of Insatiability." *The American Spectator* 14 (December 1981): 19–24.

"'Tis Not an Easy Thing." Review of *The Letters of John Wilmot, Earl of Rochester*, edited by Jeremy Treglown. *The American Scholar* 51 (Winter 1981–82): 116–20.

"All for Love: Europe in the Springtime." *The American Spectator* 15 (June 1982): 22–26.

"Nuclear Culture: Living in Bluebeard's Castle." *Pacific Northwest* 16 (June 1982): 57.

Review of *Take Five* by D. Keith Mano. *The American Spectator* 15 (October 1982): 31–32.

"Mass for the Dead." (Review of *The Truants* by William Barrett). *The American Scholar* 51 (Autumn 1982): 279–82.

"The Worm in the Big Apple." *Commentary* 74 (November 1982): 49–53.

Review of *Monsignor Quixote* by Graham Greene. *The American Spectator* 16 (January 1983): 33–34.

"The Critical Moment." (Evaluation of the Literary Essays of Phillip Rhav). *Contemporary Literary Criticism* 24 (1983): 354–55.

"A Fear of Imitation." *The Georgia Review* 38 (Spring 1984): 9–20.

"For Man Made." (Review of *Man and the Natural World: A History of Modern Sensibility* by Keith Thomas). *The American Scholar* 53 (Summer 1984): 416–18.

"Call of the Wild." *Commentary* 78 (July 1984): 52–56.

"Seeing Afresh." (Review of *Signs of Life* by Alfred Appel). *The American Scholar* 53 (Autumn 1984): 568–69.

"Cultural Contradictions." *Commonweal* 111 (2–16 November 1984): 622–23.

"The End of Boredom." *The Georgia Review* 39 (Spring 1985): 25–34.

"Our Savage Spectacles." *Harper's* 271 (July 1985): 64–68.

"Trouble and Travel." *The American Spectator* 18 (July 1985): 20–21.

"Hitting Below the Limen." *The Northwest Review of Books* 1 (Summer 1985): 4, 20.

"Poetry and the Forgetting of History." *Salmagundi* 68–69 (Fall 1985–Winter 1986): 66–77.

"Reading Text to Text." (Review of *Flawed Texts and Verbal Icons: Literary Authority in American Fiction* by Hershel Parker). *The American Scholar* 55 (Spring 1986): 262–64.

"Dr. Johnson Kicks a Stone." *Philosophy and Literature* 10 (April 1986): 65–75.

"How Fast Should We Go?" *The Antioch Review* 44 (Spring 1986): 137–48.

"The Doors of Deception." *Chronicles* 10 (October 1986): 17–21.

"The Powerful Simplifiers." *Commentary* 82 (November 1986): 70–73.

"What Is Necessary." *Salmagundi* 72 (Fall 1986): 144–47.

"The Dialectics of Nudity." *The Georgia Review* 40 (Winter 1986): 897–906.

"The Devil and American Epic." *The Hudson Review* 40 (Spring 1987): 31–47.

"The Order of Virtue." *Chronicles* 11 (June 1987): 16–20.

"In the Shadow of Iago." *The Quarterly* 2 (Summer 1987): 226–37.

"Cowboy." *The American Scholar* 56 (Summer 1987): 400–06.

"The Perils of Poetry." *Salmagundi* 74–75 (Spring–Summer 1987): 86–100.

"The Politics of Transfiguration." *Stanford Literature Review* 3 (Fall 1987): 184–94.

"All for Love: Europe in the Springtime." In *Orthodoxy: The American Spectator's Twentieth Anniversary Anthology*, R. Emmett Tyrrell, Jr., ed. New York: Harper and Row, 1987.

"The Fear of Crisis." *Chronicles* 12 (March 1988): 16–19.

"Art, Kitsch and Politics." *Commentary* 85 (May 1988): 50–53.

"What Is Literature Good For?" *The Georgia Review* 42 (Summer 1988): 238–49.

"Traveling in Style." *The Quarterly* 10 (Summer 1989): 211–26.

"The Bias Against Specialization." *This World* 26 (Summer 1989): 92–101.

"Taking History Personally." *The Antioch Review* 46 (Fall 1988): 428–37.

"The Doubtful Pleasures of the Higher Agape." *The Southern Review* 24 (Winter 1988): 134–44.